SEVEN TIMES,
Stand Up
EIGHT

Mental Toughness *for Everyone*

Second Edition

Cindy + Nicole,
I hope that
you enjoy the read!
Be Well!
Brent

Brent Macdonald, PhD

Kendall Hunt
publishing company

Cover image: Traveler's Rest, Lighthouse/Back cover images:
Stacked Rocks and Author Headshot © Emma Guy-Macdonald/Emma
Macdonald Photography

www.kendallhunt.com
Send all inquiries to:
4050 Westmark Drive
Dubuque, IA 52004-1840

Copyright © 2021, 2022 by Kendall Hunt Publishing Company

ISBN: 978-1-7924-9528-1

Published in the United States of America

Contents

Preamble

Throughout this book, I will be using a number of personal and professional experiences to highlight certain concepts. In all cases, names have been changed and in some cases, details have also been changed to protect the privacy of my clients. Additionally, some client experiences that I present will be composites of more than one client to best clarify the point. Every effort has been taken to ensure that all information presented is done so in a way that is respectful of the experiences of the individuals involved.

Additionally, the bibliography at the end of the book provides the sources for much of the research cited throughout the text, but this work is not intended as an academic treatise; rather, it is a book for everyone and to enhance its readability and functionality, references are provided but not directly cited throughout the text.

Preface and Acknowledgements

The world of mental toughness is not one I expected to find myself in. I am not an athlete—far from it! Nor am I elite in any sense of the word. I am an average person with average abilities overall. I believe that in general, I am below average in athletic abilities but perhaps higher than average in knowledge of trivia. Books about mental toughness do not exist for those who are relatively good at trivia. Thus, I decided to write a book for the rest of us, those of us who live happily in the normal curve, but who believe that we have some exceptionalities that make us special and unique. I have been humbled by my mistakes, just like you. You have learned from failed relationships, just like me. We have all experienced challenges and we have all struggled. So, this book is for all of us "normies."

I have learned a lot from writing this book, but far less than I have learned from my clients and the students with whom I have had the opportunity to work over the past number of years. I can truly say that the genesis of my interest in mental toughness arose from my learning experiences with clients who, in a strange twist, came in to see me for support, only for me to learn more from them than perhaps they did from me. I have learned to have the utmost respect for my clients and the students with whom I work—the value of the experiences they have brought forward is immeasurable and I hope that I have encapsulated at least some of their experiences accurately.

Writing a book (he said, as if he's written many) is a solitary affair that requires a lifetime of interactions with others. I have been truly privileged to have worked with a great number of talented and truly gifted educators, therapists, psychologists, academics, and other professionals, and since there are simply too many to mention, I will take the cowardly route (for fear of missing someone) and just say to those of you whose paths I have been honoured to cross: thanks!

By way of special thanks, I would like to thank Doug Strycharczyk and the team at AQR International for all of their support over the past few years as they have encouraged me on my journey to better understand mental toughness. I would also like to thank Elizabeth Palmer and Chris Canejo at

Kendall Hunt Publishing, who helped me as a neophyte author to get the work published.

Special special thanks to my wife, Emma, and my stepson, Dylan. Their support, not only through writing this book over lot of weekend afternoons and evenings, but also in the formation of our own unique clan (as a blended family, we dubbed ourselves the "Clan Macguybert," an amalgamation of each of our last names: Macdonald, Guy, Lambert) has been an ongoing source of strength for me. Left to my own devices, this book would never have been written, so I am grateful for their support.

Finally, to you, the reader. I hope that somewhere in here, you find a passage, a story, a piece of research, something that resonates with you and encourage you. Something that helps you to see your own mental toughness. Something that you can take along with you in your own journey to become *You 2.0.*

About the Author

Dr. Brent MacDonald is a registered psychologist and educator who has worked with individuals with complex learning needs for over 25 years. He maintains an active psychological services practice with a focus on counselling and assessment. He is also a sessional instructor, adjunct associate professor, and sought-after public speaker who has appeared on CBC TV and Radio, CTV, Global Television, and CITY TV, among other media platforms. Additionally, Brent has also presented and been an invited keynote speaker at local, national, and international conferences. Brent has served as a leader in public education and advocacy with the Psychologist's Association of Alberta, the Canadian Psychological Association, and the American Psychological Association, among others.

Brent has worked extensively with children, adolescents, young adults, their parents, educators, administrators, coaches, athletes, and executives in a wide range of contexts including public, private, and charter schools, universities and other post-secondary institutions, along with corporate teams, and community parent groups. He is a passionate believer in human psychological wellness and the need for public awareness to enhance communities and reduce stigma associated with psychological challenges.

Brent lives in Calgary, Alberta with his wife, Emma, and his stepson, Dylan. In his spare time, Brent enjoys travelling, cooking, listening to good progressive rock music, pretending that he can play the bass, and looking for the nearest pet to hang out with at unstructured social engagements.

Brent can be reached through his website, where you can also learn more about his practice and check out his blog at www.complexlearners.com

Introduction

What I Hate About Mental Toughness

Mental toughness is a ridiculous idea.

Straight up, when I first heard about the idea of mental toughness, my first thought was "Great, another corporate buzzword that will make people think that unless they are prepared to bulldoze over others, that they are weak and doomed to failure—and those who bully and plow their way forward regardless of the impact on others will 'win' at life." The entire concept, based on my limited understanding at the time, was that mental toughness was the worst of all things—a pop-psychology approach to serious issues that minimized genuine struggles, magnified power and control, emphasized strength over vulnerability, and—perhaps most worrisome of all—would be a concept that would appeal to those already with a great deal of power. It seemed like a perfect combination of all of the things that concerned me about pop psychology, easy answers, poor science, and enhancement of power at the expense of the vulnerable.

I know better now.

Perhaps you have some of the same concerns—which makes me wonder why you picked up this book in the first place. In learning more about mental toughness, I have discovered that my own biases and intellectual arrogance prevented me from seeing what was, in fact, perhaps one of the most important psychological principles that had been active in my most challenging clients, a principle that drew on intrinsic strength and resilience and, on occasion, was associated with a sense of helplessness and hopelessness. Mental toughness underlies a wide range of human thinking, behaviour, and emotion; I have learned that, properly understood and used, mental toughness is a powerful tool for understanding not only my clients, but also my colleagues, my social and intimate relationships, my function as a husband and step-parent, and ultimately, myself. Even without my conscious understanding, a significant part of my work as a psychologist and educator over the past 25 years or so has been discovering, along with my clients, colleagues, friends, and family, how mental toughness enhances performance, encourages growth, and helps people work through challenging situations, while also helping to explain why some people struggle repeatedly with the same challenges and issues over and over, despite knowing what they should do to improve their situation.

I have agonized over the phrase "mental toughness." Tough, per a quick check of a Merriam-Webster's online dictionary, is defined as being "strong enough to withstand adverse conditions; the ability to endure hardship or pain; not easily broken." To that extent, perhaps it is possible that the idea of toughness has been inaccurately portrayed in public discourse. Being tough is something we all do—we have all withstood pain, we all have strength, we have all faced situations that could have broken us, but we survived. So where did tough become essentially synonymous with "Suck it up, Buttercup"? Toughness is embedded in us all, as is vulnerability. We need both. It seems, though, that toughness has been associated with competitive aggression and power when in fact, toughness is simply resilience redefined. But, in an effort to avoid the negative connotations of "toughness" and being particularly aware of my position in the world as a white, English-speaking heterosexual Christian male with no visible disabilities or anything else that would impinge upon my success in contemporary North American culture, I sought another way of describing the principles of mental toughness without using the "T" word (which, in turn, is often also viewed as being macho, power-oriented, controlling, conflict-seeking, arrogant, and brazen—almost narcissistic).

I have, as a result, spent hours trying to arrive at synonyms and alternative phrases that better encapsulated what mental toughness was describing. I arrived at a number of alternatives, but ultimately, the research kept leading me back to the original phrase. The phrasing challenge is similar to other unfortunate terminologies in psychology and education. For instance, I work extensively with students with Learning Disabilities, another phrase I detest. It is widely open to misinterpretation, it leads to misconceptions, it carries with it a stigma of limitation, and in no way does the phrase "Learning Disabilities" encapsulate the reality of any individual who has one. But, as a psychologist, I am tied into the phrase as it is the one that psychologists and educators have been using for decades when studying those who meet the criteria for those particular learning challenges. A student with a Learning Disability is no more universally disabled than a person who has characteristics of mental toughness is universally tough. Additionally, "toughness" has tonal implications that are not particularly positive. Surely there has to be a better phrase!

Having gone through any number of alternatives, the research again kept pulling me back to the original phrase. So, I understand if you are uncomfortable with the phrase "mental toughness," but I do ask that you understand why that phrase is used. The negative and limiting connotations are noted, but in order to keep ourselves grounded in appropriate research and clinically based evidence, we will use mental toughness phrasing through this book. And to be clear, while there is a lot of contemporary research on mental toughness, not all of it will be cited directly in this book, as my goal is to facilitate understanding with an ease of communication. Endnotes, footnotes, and ongoing references to various studies have a very significant place in academic literature, but can detract from the reading experience. This book is more of a handbook than an academic treatise, a guide that the layperson can use easily and practically. But to use this book at all, we need to clarify our language, bringing us back to what mental toughness is.

Defining Mental Toughness

Perhaps the most comprehensive and contemporary definition of mental toughness, and the one we will be using through this book, has been provided by Peter Clough and Doug Strycharczyk, two of the leaders in research and the development of mental toughness. They define mental toughness as:

> *The personality trait which determines in large part how people deal effectively with challenge, stressors, and pressure, irrespective of circumstances.*

More on this definition later, but for now, and in summary, mental toughness is not about being rigid, overpowering, invulnerable, or controlling. Rather, it is about self-awareness and how we approach the challenges of daily life.

I'm Neither a Navy SEAL nor an Elite Athlete

Many books on mental toughness have been written by people with exceptional life stories—people who have overcome significant challenges to become elite athletes, corporate giants, and a distressingly high number of books about mental toughness have been written by former Navy SEALS, those highly respected military members who are often described as being the "toughest of the tough." With all due respect to those writers (and in the case of the Navy SEALS, I *really* mean that! Please don't hurt me!), their experiences may not mirror those of the vast majority of us more "average" folks. Outside of a few publications and websites, there is not much out for the rest of us. You know, us "Normies." I am in no way a superstar in my field, nor am I a person who has undergone a life-changing experience that is even close to the SEAL's well-documented "Hell Week." I'm just—me. And you are just you. Nothing wrong with that, in fact, good for you for being you! However, can you be a better version of you? Can you learn to become more resilient when faced with challenges to the point that you actively seek out challenges? Can you learn to soften your edges so that others do not perceive you as being rigid, controlling, angry, demanding? Can you learn to set your course through a storm in a planful way that makes the risk of the voyage tolerable but not so risky that you fear or avoid setting sail? Mental toughness may well be the missing component that can facilitate positive change for you and, ultimately, for those around you.

I decided to write this book for one main reason—having seen thousands of struggling students over the years, I often found myself wondering "Why do some of these people do so well, despite their challenges, while others seem to experience such damaging failure?" I wanted an answer that was not always "It depends on the individual." That is a truism, and while clinically helpful, it is not an effective explanation for the larger trends I was seeing over and over in practice. Mental toughness put a name on something I had long suspected: that people, particularly children and adolescents, have traits of toughness that are not necessarily stable over time/situation, and these traits can be intrinsic to the individual, but are not concrete and, as such, are changeable with appropriate guidance.

There is a Latin phrase (well, there's a Latin phrase for pretty much *everything*, but I digress) that reads *Cui Bono* ("Who benefits?"). My hope in writing is that readers will benefit not only as individuals who are wanting to enhance their performance and relationships, but also enhance their capacities as students, teachers, administrators, employees, leaders, supervisors, athletes, artists, parents, siblings, friends, and, ultimately, as members of society.

Not only does mental toughness have positive implications for *anyone* wishing to learn about it, it also can lead to development in a wide variety of areas. Mental toughness has been shown to help us deal effectively with stressful situations. As of this writing, we are undergoing the COVID-19 global crisis and a recent study has shown that while almost everyone in the sample reported increased depression, stress, and anxiety, those who were identified through the MTQ Plus psychometric instrument as being more mentally tough reported *comparatively* lower rates of depression, stress, and anxiety. Mental toughness enhances performance (at work and school), enhances our sense of control, helps us set positive and realistic goals, promotes tenacity, encourages assertiveness, increases self-efficacy (the belief that we have the wherewithal to actually do something well) and encourages us to set higher goals in our path to improvement. So, lots of positives. But are there downside to being mentally tough? You bet! Too much of pretty much anything can cause problems, so, the best advice is often the oldest advice: "All things in moderation."

One of the most critical aspects of mental toughness is that it is an active process, not a static concept. Like pretty much anything we want to improve at—playing guitar, painting, photography, public speaking, baking the perfect cookie—it takes practice. To make mental toughness an applied process that you can actually practice, you will be asked at numerous times through this book to answer some questions. Some of you will choose to write out your answers and I strongly encourage journalling or writing your responses down somewhere—but I also know that as a reader, I prefer to read and then reflect quietly or while listening to music. Your call. Make it work for you. Write notes, talk with someone, reflect quietly, whatever works. The first one question is this: **What are *your* beliefs about what mental toughness is, both positive and negative?**

My Journey with Mental Toughness

I've read and watched a *lot* of biographies of rock musicians, and most of them follow the same rough trajectory (brilliantly satirized in *Walk Hard: The Dewy Cox Story*, which is a not-so-subtle stab at Oscar-bait films such as 2005's *Walk the Line*, a well-done but somewhat formulaic biopic on the life of Johnny Cash). The trajectory goes something like this:

- Opening: Moments Before the Life-Changing Gig
- Flashback to childhood/adolescence; introduction of parent figure (either domineering and abusive or angelic and supportive)
- Emergence of talent
- First steps toward fame
- Fame
- Introduction to debauchery
- Continued and accelerated debauchery
- Collapse

- Moment of truth
- Recovery
- Redemption at gig alluded to at the start of story

Invariably, the least interesting parts are typically those involving the encouraging parent figure and emerging talent. We want to get to the good stuff! Bring on the drug-fueled backstage bacchanal!

I'm no rock star, so those searching for debauchery will be sorely disappointed in this book (but on the other hand, if you are interested in debauchery, why did you get this book in the first place!?). In the coming chapters, the "good stuff" is the information and learning you will engage in as we describe and discuss mental toughness. So let's get the boring stuff out of the way (and if you wish to scooch ahead to the good stuff feel free, I'll not be hurt much).

My journey to explore mental toughness was based in no small part upon my upbringing and experiences as a child and eventually as a young adult and emerging professional. Coming from Prince Edward Island on the East Coast of Canada, I was a small-town kid who learned from my family to treat others with respect. In a small town, if you don't treat others with respect, word get round—fast! PEI is a place where most everyone knows everyone, and if you don't know someone, that is typically resolved with a simple couplet of questions (the accent is best if you read it out loud without moving your jaw, and deep from your chest—that's the trick to a proper Island accent):

"Who's yer faather?" "What's he do, then?"

I was also raised in a church-going family. The church and small-town nature of my community made it almost impossible to do anything privately. So, I learned—as so many small-town dwellers do—to hide in plain sight and keep my privacy private. We would now call this "boundary-setting." Back in the day, to not be 100% honest was to be 100% dishonest, and judgement would be fast (if subtle).

Don't get me wrong, I loved growing up on the Island and my family was loving and supportive. But certain characteristics of being raised in a small town can be frustrating. To me, like many others, an escape was necessary and I saw university as a means to do so. While I stayed on the Island for my undergraduate degree, my eye was being drawn to other places and new leaning opportunities. In the meantime, though, I had quite accidentally fallen into a long-term love affair with psychology.

Though high school, even as far back as junior high, I had wanted to be a marine biologist—I love the water and being on an Island made the pursuit of marine biology a no-brainer to me. In particular, seals drew my interest—the great big, noisy harbour seals common on the east coast. Once, while kayaking in Charlottetown harbour, a harbour seal (which is a huge beast full of blubber and anger!) surfaced 3 ft away from my kayak, startling me and almost causing me to do my first, probably catastrophic, kayak roll. I was simultaneously terrified and fascinated. I wanted to learn more about these beasts.

And—and please forgive me for this, I was young and kind of stupid—my other contact with seals involved hunting them for bounty. Yes, I was a seal bounty hunter. Sounds pretty cool! But I don't blame you if you want to return this book now. Sorry. I will say this—we hunted big grey harbour seals, not harp seals, the ridiculously cute baby-fluffballs of white fur often associated with the infamous seal hunts of the 1970s and 1980s. Not that makes it okay. Just, not quite as horrible, maybe. Fortunately, I was not a particularly *good* bounty hunter and my entire short-lived career resulted in exactly zero seals hurt.

What happened was this—my father had a small 16-ft motorboat and my friend, Chris, had a shotgun. We'd gotten the idea somewhere that there was a $50 bounty on harbour seals (which, in all fairness, are a nuisance and are hard on the fishing industry). We just had to take in a seal jawbone into the Conservation Office and we'd be given a cheque for $50. Easy money!

So, we went out in the boat, with me piloting and Chris taking up the stern with the shotgun, loaded with 0.12-gauge lead slugs. We set out to the seal colonies around the far side of the harbour, crashing through the cold surf, excited about the hunt. Once we sighted some seals, I laid in a pursuit course and Chris started blasting away.

Did I mention how windy it was? How high the surf was? No? Probably should have. It was really windy and we had a 16-ft motorboat in waves that were almost 4 ft in height. This combination does not make for easy navigation or accurate marksmanship. We hit nothing that day, or any other day, since that day ended with Chris falling backward into the cabin and discharging the gun almost directly into the boat, narrowly missing both my leg and the fuel tank. Our seal hunting days were over, but my desire to continue pursuit of a career as a marine biologist continued unabated.

Until approximately 7:25 p.m. ADT on September 29th, 1988, which was on a Thursday evening. Some friends and I signed up for an Introductory Psychology course at the University of Prince Edward Island simply because it fit our schedules and it was pub night on campus—though a non-drinker at the time, I was very interested in the girls who went to the campus bar! I was sitting in the back row and our professor started class by mentioning the recent scandal in Canadian sport—Canadian sprinter Ben Johnson had just been found to have tested positive for steroid use following his record setting 100-m sprint at the Seoul Summer Olympic Games. It was all the conversation and we spent some class time talking about Johnson, his performance in the race, his use of performance-enhancing substances, and our national identity crisis. Canadians didn't *cheat*! But on this day, a switch went off in my mind and all thoughts of marine biology left me.

THIS was interesting stuff! Why did Johnson cheat? Why did his trainer and team physician allow this to happen, even encourage the use of illegal drugs, despite the high probability, almost certainty, of getting caught? What motivated a highly respected icon to do something so foolishly risky? Why do people make life-altering mistakes? What made him such a competitor in the first place, and at what point was he persuaded to use anabolic steroids to enhance his performance, and by whom was he so persuaded? I became immediately and irrevocably fascinated with human performance, the concept of being "best" at all costs, and psychology in general, and have not since turned back.

My specific interests have changed somewhat over the years, but I have pursued with passion the psychology of the human being. Specifically, what were the factors necessary for success in human endeavors, what were the limiting factors, and how could we help people overcome those limits?

My own academic experience provided some guidance in terms of human behaviour and the desire to excel, as I had always been told (and I felt) that I was reasonably curious and bright enough to get by. Good for me! But—my handwriting was (and remains) atrocious. So, from grades 3 to 7, I was placed in resource support to work on my handwriting which often necessitated my missing PE and other fun classes. I did not respond positively to these interventions and in grade 7, I found a co-conspirator in Gordon, another poor-penmanship guy (mainly because he was a lefty and couldn't navigate the coiled binding in most notebooks) who had also been relegated to resource help. We staged a tidy little *coup d'état* and simply hid from the resource teacher. This strategy worked (certainly, she had better things to do than chase after two wayward boys who didn't appreciate her efforts).

Because of my challenges, I became interested in working with students who had similar, but much more profound, challenges. So I entered into teaching and ultimately pursued my master's degree in school psychology and, eventually, my PhD in counselling psychology. I was determined to find out more about success factors for folks who struggled not only with learning, but with living successful lives in general.

I found that my best work was immersed in the positive 1:1 relationships that I could build with students, so I took my passion for psychology and thought about how best to use psychology with kids, and becoming a school psychologist seemed like the best approach. So, I did my master's degree in school psychology and really valued the assessment and collaboration/consultation models to which I was exposed. I enjoyed assessment work—it had *corners*, unlike therapy which, at that point in my career, was simply too vague for me to really get a handle on. As I progressed in my school psychology work, I became more comfortable with the counselling required of such work. So, I travelled west to do my doctoral work in counselling psychology. My research was on developing an understanding of identity issues faced by young men with testicular cancer, which was initially quite interesting and professionally gratifying, but I did not enjoy the research process. I enjoyed consuming research, not conducting it. So, my focus shifted away from academia into clinical practice.

Through this whole process, I was always mindful of trends among my clients and, having now worked with thousands of children, adolescents, young adults, and their families, along with educators, executives, and other professionals, the idea of mental toughness began to resonate more clearly and in a more crystalized fashion. My clinical experience as a private practitioner, as a consultant in schools (ranging from programs for students with highly complex needs to elite-level private schools—kids are kids and even kids at elite private schools have their challenges, many associated with "affluenza," the pressure to maintain a high degree of performance in all areas), and as a post-secondary instructor and professor, has provided me with a wide range of clinical experiences, success, failures, and some really interesting stories. But at the heart of all of this work has been the common, underlying thread: "Why do some succeed where others do not?"

This question would lead me to mental toughness. I was, and continue to be, fascinated by trends in human thought. Specific therapeutic "manualized" programs do not appeal to me as a psychologist. I have never been a fan of prepackaged approaches to psychological wellness. I have studied cognitive-behavioural therapy (CBT) in no small part because it is considered in most graduate training programs to be perhaps one of the "best" approaches to therapy, largely because it can be measured and evaluated. But I tend to see CBT as being akin to a set of tools. In themselves, invaluable, but without a blueprint, without a plan, they are not particularly helpful "Give a person a hammer," the saying goes, "and everything becomes a nail." So, I leaned heavily toward existential, narrative, and positive psychology, each of which encouraged depth of relationship between the therapist and client. Relationships will not let you down when your favourite CBT strategy fails. Again, as we will discuss, mental toughness is a component of both of these areas of our own psychological work.

Mental toughness is, at its core, an intuitively sensible approach that incorporates the very best of high-quality psychological work—it is evidence-based, accessible, inexpensive to administer, and results-oriented. Through the following chapters, we will journey together to gain an understanding of what mental toughness is and how it works. I'll warn you straight-away—I am a geek. I'll reference *Star Wars*, *Star Trek*, Harry Potter, comic superheroes, oddball films, and the occasional Yes or King Crimson album. But don't worry—I'll also use examples from sports, business, marketing, music, and, perhaps most importantly, academia (but in a user-friendly manner, so no talk of multivariate analysis of variance or factor analysis, or other detailed statistical descriptions will be found herein!). My goal is to ensure that you, the reader, develop an understanding of mental toughness and how it has an effect on your own psychological health and on your social relationships. We will discuss how mental toughness plays a role in your academic and occupational success. And ultimately, we will learn about our own mental toughness profile and how to best use this knowledge to lead us to a joyful and content life.

Why Mental Toughness?

As she slumped down in her chair, eyes downcast, I found myself at a loss. What do I say? I had been working with this 17-year-old client since she was 12. Initially, her parents brought her in to see me because she was struggling with school in almost every way possible. She seemed bright enough, but her reading was way below what it should have been, especially compared to her peers; her math skills seem to come and go like tides— sometimes she was full of understanding, other times it was like she had never seen even basic calculations before. Her written work was abysmal, both in terms of fluency and content. Her printing was indecipherable and her keyboarding skills were rudimentary at best. She struggled with her peers—she was likeable enough, but would burn through friendships like a prairie grassfire—intense, but fleeting, leaving behind the ash of disintegrated relationships. She was a living contradiction, but one I felt I could help—after all, my practice focused on supporting complex learners, and this girl certainly fit the bill.

We conducted a comprehensive psychoeducational assessment and, despite some of the challenges inherent in such assessments, we found that

Megan[1] had a Learning Disability—well, a cluster of Learning Disabilities, actually, along with difficulties associated with Attention Deficit/Hyperactivity Disorder (ADHD) and anxiety. On the upside, she was very bright indeed, capable of considerable depth of thought and complex reasoning. We developed a plan, focusing on her strengths and working toward enhancing some of her academic skills and executive functioning capacities. Her parents were working-class folks, but we found private school that specialized in providing support for students with Megan's profile and she was accepted into the program. Things were looking up, her anxiety diminished and her confidence started to creep timidly from the corners of her psyche into her public persona.

Upon starting at her new school, her academic performance started to grow exponentially, but not without a lot of work on her part. She made friends, she enjoyed her classes, and her teachers grew fond of her enthusiasm. My work with her started to become less frequent and intense, and became more broadly supportive in nature. She was becoming stronger by the semester.

Then—old problems started to creep up. Some friendships started to deteriorate, as they often do in a junior high setting. While she knew that such things happen, she personalized these losses. She blamed herself. She began to put up walls to block potential friendships and as a result, became isolated in the small school. Academically, she seemed to hit a wall—her efforts remained strong, but she was not seeing the gains she had previously been making. Not surprising, since she had started at such a low point that any initial gains seemed huge; now, success was being measured in ounces as opposed to pounds, by perhaps single decimal points as opposed to the double-digit grade improvements she had initially been earning. She started to shut down academically, socially, emotionally.

Before long, though, she discovered wrestling. An individual sport for which she was uniquely equipped—she had a strong core, a great deal of flexibility, and a fiery competitive streak. She tried out for the school team reluctantly, and then only to put an end to the incessant pestering of the wrestling coach, who was ultimately looking to basically fill a roster with a female in her weight class. However, once on the mat, Megan was a force. She outclassed her female teammates, even those above her weight class

---

[1] As noted in the preamble, client names and any other potentially identifying information has been changed throughout this book; additionally, in some cases, client details have been altered to present a more cohesive presentation of an individual or a case, which may incorporate features of more than one individual.

and those with more experience; she easily beat boys in and above her weight class. By grade 9, the only competition she had within the school was a bruising grade 12 boy who topped out at 190 lbs. to Meagan's 130. Everyone else had been beaten soundly. She performed against other schools, handily humbling her competitors at tournaments across her district. Her confidence returned, and she took her successes from the mat to the social and academic arenas, doing well in both.

By grade 11, she was again experiencing a high degree of confidence and my work with her again focused on maintenance of a positive attitude and planning for bringing her attitude of positivity to her post-secondary life. She still had challenges, but they were minor and day-to-day issues common to high school students. She didn't drink or use drugs, but she still attended school parties, where her abstinence was admired, not mocked.

In the summer between grades 11 and 12, Megan took a couple of summer courses at an on-line based program so that she could free her grade 12 year up for more competitive wrestling—she was in the market for an athletic scholarship and did not want to lose out on the opportunity by missing tournaments or having an excessive academic load. She did better than expected in her on-line work, and she was excited to share her results with the school, anticipating a positive and enthusiastic response to her achievements. Instead, the response deflated her. School administrators were disbelieving of her marks and suggested, without a hint of subtlety, that either the program was "slack" or that she had cheated. For a student who valued honesty and who had never had her integrity challenged, these accusations burned like acid on an open wound.

Megan was crushed, but not defeated. Her competitive spirit was her reserve tank, and her manifesto for grade 12 was "I'll show them!" And so she did. To the point that at the end of the year, the school administrators, apparently having forgotten having accused Megan of cheating, asked her to act as an ambassador for the school in their marketing. This request was a bitter validation for Megan—no matter how hard she worked, someone else was trying to claim credit for her success. She turned them down without a moment's consideration.

Through all of this, Megan maintained occasional therapy sessions, working primarily on her confidence and anxiety, along with her social relationships. We had developed a trusting relationship, and she would openly share that she trusted me, her mother, her father, and, sometimes, her brother. And that was basically it. I felt highly honored—her trust did not come easily and we had worked hard to get there.

She contacted my office to arrange a time to come in early in her grade 12 year. When she came in, it had been a few months since I'd seen her. When she came into my office, she looked drawn out, pale, tired, and generally miserable. She took her seat and sat quietly for a few minutes. A few minutes of silence is a LONG time and even as an experienced therapist, I felt an urge to break the uncomfortable tension. She drew in a deep breath and said, "You can't tell my parents this—I know about confidentiality and safety, and if you have to, I get it . . . but listen first and then we can talk about if and how we can share this with my mom." I agreed to listen, but not before reiterating the limits of confidentiality in therapy and what my requirements as a psychologist were.

"I was at a party 2 weeks ago." My stomach turned. I immediately and instinctively knew where this line of conversation was going. It is an unfortunate and honestly sickening reality that in doing therapy with adolescent and young adult females, at most points when they say, "I was at a party," what follows is almost always a recounting of a horrible invasion of some sort. I hate to say this, but it is not a concern I have when working with males, at least not to the same extent. I can count on my fingers how many boys I have worked with over 20+ years as a psychologist who have disclosed a sexual assault. To be able to say the same for girls, I'd need a calculator.

And sure enough, she went on to recount a situation in which she was at a party with some friends, including some guy friends, one of whom separated her from her friends and found a way to assault her in the spare bedroom. In my office, she slumped down in her chair and I struggled to find the words to say. She appeared to be devastated by this violation at the party, this breach of trust and of personhood. But at the same time, there was a subtle, yet powerful strength in her tone. She had learned over time how to be tough—at school, with friends, with adults, on the wrestling mat, and this latest injury was not going to pull her under.

After some discussion, she agreed to let me share her story with her mother. She wanted to be in the room when I told her mom, so we scheduled a follow-up session. It's amazing how often teen clients will not want to share things with their parents, but they are very much okay with having the psychologist do so. In an unrelated situation, one of my clients disclosed that she was pregnant, but that she couldn't tell her parents as she was afraid they would respond in anger. But, she was more than comfortable to have *me* share her situation, which I did with her present—it was actually one of the most positive experiences I've had as a therapist to see her visibly relax when her parents, upon hearing the news, simply said "Okay, we are happy to know—and we are here to help you 100%."

Megan shared some more details with her mom and after I informed her mom of the assault and we worked through the situation in collaboration with her mother, who was also shattered for her daughter but simultaneously empowered to provide support to her child. Through the following months, Megan worked through the complexities of her young life—the sexual assault, while a violation, was also a turning point for her. She was no longer willing to allow life to happen to her. She wanted to become stronger, to become more tough in the face of challenges. She drew on her successes and her challenges. Her confidence in her own abilities grew, her commitment to herself and those for whom she cared increased; she truly began to value *herself*, not just her skills.

As of this writing, Megan has successfully gone on to her post-secondary studies (with her wrestling scholarship intact, along with an academic scholarship, putting rest to any questions as to her "cheating" in the on-line program). She is a strong advocate for herself and others who have faced similar challenges. She is a mentor to her younger teammates. And she is a client for whom I have little fear as she continues her journey into adulthood, because she is tough.

Specifically, she is *mentally tough*. She has guts.

This book is designed to provide readers with the tools necessary to understand the principles of mental toughness and, perhaps more importantly, how to enhance it—ideally, without having to go through the traumas many people have to in order to develop their own mental toughness. **Mental toughness can be learned.** Unfortunately, we often think that the only way we can develop mental toughness is through trauma or pain and to be sure, there is some truth in that thinking—there is a difference between reading about something and going through something! But between these two approaches lies coaching—some of the best athletic coaches, particularly at the elite level, are not the best players themselves. They tend to be the ones who struggle, who work hard with moderate success. But they know failure. They understand defeat. And if they have mental toughness as part of their profile, they know how to use defeat to their advantage.

A good example is Major League Baseball's manager with the most wins (in the modern era—the all-time, and probably untouchable leader, Connie Mack, leads the pack by a solid 1,000 wins. . . so good luck topping that!) is Tony LaRussa, an underwhelming player who spent 5 years in the big leagues (on four different teams), before spending the rest of his playing for minor league teams in small markets across the States. But as an MLB manager with the Chicago White Sox, Oakland Athletics, and St. Louis Cardinals, he was a master—a shrewd leader who could manipulate a lineup the same way Da Vinci manipulated oil paint. No one would say that LaRussa was a great player—he had the skill to play in the Bigs, but was at best a carpetbagger who didn't embarrass himself. But in his time in the minors, he learned about the sport from a different angle—how players work together, or not, and how their characteristics could create a winning chemistry, or not. He may have been a mediocre player, but he is the most winning manager in modern MLB history. He exhibited mental toughness though losing seasons and overcame his own challenges as a player, finding his leadership strengths and using them to piece together championship teams over decades as a manager.

In the following chapters, we will learn together about mental toughness and how it can be expressed in individuals and, ultimately, in teams. We will learn how leaders can understand their own mental toughness profiles and how they can help their team members become as effective as possible, both as individuals and in groups. There will be a focus on different areas in which mental toughness has particular relevance, such as education, athletics, business, relationships, and so on. But it is very true to say that mental toughness can, when properly understood, infiltrate all aspects of our daily lives. It is within our ability to capitalize on these areas, while also acknowledging areas that perhaps we have to work on. Of course, as a psychologist, I am a believer in self-reflection and understanding as being necessary conditions for change. Let the change start now!

Self-Awareness

As we learn about mental toughness, it will be important to *truly* engage in learning. Decades of educational research has been clear on only a few things consistently, but one of the things researchers have come as close to consensus on is that active, engaged learning yields the best, longest-lasting effects. Simple passive learning (i.e., reading a book alone with no discussion, no reflection, no *action*) is neither efficient nor valuable learning. As such, as we learn about mental toughness, I will be engaging in my own learning by actively engaging in some of my own history, my own experiences, and my own beliefs, hopefully challenging some of these latter on a fairly consistent basis. In doing so, I will be asking you, the reader, to interact in a similar active engagement with the content of this book.

I will be also using some examples from pop media, literature, film, sports, history, and other areas of interest. But the most interesting learning often comes from within us, so as we proceed through the coming chapters, I will be asking you to reflect on how the concepts of mental toughness apply to you through your personal experiences. You bring a unique and valued perspective that only you have access to, and in using your personal experiences, you will invariably find that mental toughness has always been a part of your life.

One experiment we can start with is as follows: **Think about the first time you recall failing at something.** I mean, like absolutely, no-question-about-it failing; not just failing to do your best. I mean a time when you absolutely blew it. For many, this recollection may be painful to think about and I certainly do not encourage you though think about something that may have been traumatizing. A mistake is simply a mistake; a trauma, on the other hand, is typically something that happens to us that is beyond our control. A mistake is simply a failure to act in a way that leads to success or, sometimes, is an absence of success even when you feel like you did everything correctly.

Have an example in mind? Here's mine: When I was about 8 years old, some friends and I were out playing and one of the neighborhood kids who we did not like came along and started playing with us. You know that expression that kids can be cruel? Yeah, that was us. This kid did nothing wrong and, in the intervening years, I became aware that he was actually quite kind and was desperate for friendships. But in my drive to be accepted by the other boys, I went along with the frequent teasing and more frequent ostracizing we engaged in toward this particular boy. This specific day was a beautiful summer day—we were free-range kids in my neighborhood, basically outside from breakfast to dusk. This boy was usually at home, watching TV by himself. Today, he approached us to play.

We sniggered at his pale white skin—we were all tanned from hours in the sun while he was pasty-white and Gollum-esque due to long hours in front of his TV. We didn't say "go away," but we were certainly not welcoming either. So we asked if he wouldn't be happier at home (i.e., away from us). "I'm locked out—I left the key in the house, and my mom and dad aren't home, so I have to stay outside. Can I play with you guys?"

I can't recall who specifically came up with the idea, but one of us suggested that perhaps we swing by his place, see if there was an open window he could use to get inside and get back to his TV (and away from us). We went to his house and the lower-level windows were all closed. There was a small window in the bathroom that was open, but it was on the second floor. We scouted a ladder from under his patio and decided that I should be the one to go inside since I was smallest and the window was pretty tiny. So, up the ladder I go, squeezing through the window, dropping into the house, and went around to the back door and opened it up. He slowly walked up the landing stairs, head down, muttered "thanks," and closed the door quietly behind him.

I didn't feel good about it, but at the same time, I was quickly busy with play. Later that evening, his parents showed up on our doorstep, furious. We had left the ladder leading into the bathroom window propped against the house and they confronted their son about what happened. In their (justifiable) anger, they accused 8-year-old me and my friends of break-and-enter and threated to involve the police. I felt horrible, not because *I* was in trouble, but because *he'd* gotten into trouble and we had truly acted in a hurtful and reprehensible manner.

This failure to care for another human being's emotional well-being remains vivid to me because it was one of the first times that I became aware of my own misconception of myself as a good person. How could a good person do such a miserable thing to someone else, especially someone so lonely and vulnerable? While I was years away from understanding the idea of mental toughness, I became vividly aware of a number of aspects of the principles of mental toughness all at once. Ideas such as Emotional Control (including empathy), Life Control (I had an active choice in this situation, and I'd made a poor one), Risk Orientation (I'd taken a risk and it did not work out in my—or anyone's—favour), and Interpersonal Confidence (this one most of all: in my insecure desire to be liked by the more popular kids, I'd acted in a reprehensible manner—I had lacked the Interpersonal Confidence to act in a way that was consistent with my actual beliefs).

But here's the thing: I learned. My Learning Orientation (more on that later) is and remains an area for growth. I need to repeat mistakes sometimes in order to truly learn. I have the multiple speeding tickets, often from the exact same location where speed traps are frequently set up. I have broken, misassembled IKEA furniture that proves that I have some odd need to *not* read instructions first. My wife could cite many examples of "Brent being Brent" that are basically a list of things I have had to do numerous times incorrectly in order to actually, truly learn. In the B&E situation, the extreme discomfort I'd felt afterward led me to swear to myself that I would not make that kind of mistake again. While I have not always been consistent in practice, I have done my best not to hurt others and tried to lead with empathy. I make mistakes (as we all do) and have hurt people close to me, but I do my level best to learn.

Now, think of your example of a mistake you have made—specifically, the first, most significant mistake you can think of. My short-lived career as a B&E specialist was not the first mistake I'd made, but it was certainly one of the most meaningful to me in terms of growth. Your mistake, whatever it was, is first and foremost, well in the past. Nothing you can do about it now. Self-forgiveness is hard, but I would argue that it is a prerequisite for actual learning. From a biological perspective, it is difficult to engage in higher-level learning when coming from a place of high emotionality. Our amygdala, the bit of our hindbrain that evaluates and alerts us to threat, can become over-active and once that part is activated, the higher-order thinking associated with our forebrain, or frontal cortex, largely shuts down. After all, who needs reason when we are deep in our evolutionary responses?

If we get stuck at the purely emotional level as a result of our recollec-tions of past mistakes, we can find ourselves immersed in guilt. It is very hard indeed to recover from guilt. Note that I say "immersed" in guilt as opposed to "feeling" guilt. Feelings of guilt and shame are normal, natural, and arguably helpful emotions which, when managed in moderation and with a slight sense of detachment, can lead to positive change. Immersion is, unfortunately, where we find ourselves when dealing ineffectively with deeply uncomfortable emotions, especially guilt and shame.

So, if you are thinking of an early mistake and you feel immersed or even paralyzed with feelings of guilt, please try to remember that this mis-take you made was long ago and that you are allowed to, and are expected to, feel some degree of unpleasantness. But imagine the mistake as through a rear-view mirror in a car. The thing is still there, receding as you move forward. And from a logical perspective, a rear-view mirror is a very small portion of a car windshield—the MUCH larger windshield allows you a clear view of the future, what lies ahead. The rear-view mirror serves to show you what is past and receding. It's still there, no mistake, but hope-fully it's in its proper perspective.

The development of mental toughness can go a long way to helping us put past mistakes into perspective, making them into learning opportunities as opposed to reservoirs of shame and guilt. Mental toughness is largely embedded in enhancing self-knowledge, which is a cornerstone of moving past self-blame. It does not, however, mean that we are free from account-ability; quite the opposite. **As we learn about our own mental toughness profiles, we actually become *more* accountable.** For some, this may feel uncomfortable, as accountability entails responsibility, and don't we all have more than enough responsibilities in our lives? Fair, but isn't the hope of truly feeling in control of these responsibilities (and the possibility of acquiescing things for which we cannot be responsible) a freeing idea?

Mental Toughness and the Normal Curve

For each area of mental toughness, I will occasionally use the phasing "high in . . ." or "low in . . ." when referring to different components of mental toughness. High in Goal Orientation, low in Confidence in Abilities, for instance. I use these phrases to ease the overall readability of the text, but perhaps a better way to think about the degree of mental toughness one might exhibit would be using phrases such as "mentally tough, "mentally flexible," and "mentally sensitive." I will clarify later, but essentially, mentally tough refers to being "high" in a specific area related to mental toughness functioning, while mentally sensitive refers to capacities in which one may experience less overt confidence and more, well, sensitivity. Mental flexibility speaks to the majority of folks. Those areas in which one is mentally flexible are those in which they can be more responsive to different situations.

The best way to think about mental toughness is not along a continuum or even a spectrum, but as being along a normal curve. One of my earlier statistics professors explained the concept of the normal or "bell" curve as follows:

> An ancient monastery has a long flight of stone stairs leading up to the monks' living quarters from their chapel. Over decades and even centuries, thousands of trips up and down these stairs were made. Over time, one of the monks noticed a pattern in the stone. The centre-most section of each stair had developed a small crescent-shaped indent, while the edges of each stair closer to the wall on either side, were less worn. The monk realized that the highest number of steps had been taken toward the middle, with fewer taken along the sides. This was a normal curve—the highest number of events are in the middle, with fewer along the sides.

While the normal curve has been used as a statistical standard for centuries, it has also been misused for any number of reasons. Malcolm Gladwell's *Outliers* and Richard Herrnstein and Charles Murray's *The Bell Curve* are among many others that present different perspectives on the use and misuse of the normal curve from historical, anthropological, and sociocultural perspectives. The normal curve underlies the most frequently used psychometric measures of intelligence, academic achievement, behavioural and emotional functioning, among other areas. For our purposes, we will rely largely on the work of Peter Clough (University of Hull), Doug Strycharczyk (AQR International), and their respective teams that focus on the assessment and development of mental toughness. Their work presupposes mental toughness as falling with a normal curve, so only about 16% of the population would be considered, at any given time, at the "high" level of mental toughness, and the same percentage for those in the mentally sensitive classification, leaving most of us (approximately 68%), most of the time and in most areas, falling in the mentally flexible range. It is a bit more complex than this, but for the sake of keeping this from turning into a statistics textbook, to quote Forrest Gump, "that's all I've got to say about that."

Just Do It and Other Bad Advice

It's often been said that we all have the same number of hours in a day. We all get 24 hours/day, whether we are the president of the United States, and Instagram influencer, a dentist, a dog walker, or a grade 6 student. 24 hours/day. Yet many of us exclaim over and over "there's not enough hours in a day!" There ARE enough hours in a day—and most of us do our very best to take full advantage of that time, yet we fall short. Something is always pushed off for tomorrow. That's fine. We all do it. Personal enhancement gurus often suggest that we simply (and how the word "simply" fails to inspire hope! If it were simple, it'd be done!) maximize our time, a feat we are often told can be achieved through multitasking. Actually (*nerdily pushes glasses up bridge of nose*), multitasking is the path to mediocrity in that our brains, while highly complex, are simply not good at multitasking. Try this out—try brushing your teeth with your nondominant hand while standing on one foot, without leaning on anything. Easy? With practice, perhaps, but the challenge of engaging in even basic tasks become comically complex when combined with one another. So *simply* maximizing our time by multitasking is somewhat of a fool's errand for most of us.

Another way of maximizing our time (remember, this is *simple*) is by taking advantage of all of our time. Again, leaning upon Latin, we are encouraged to *Carpe Diem* (Seize the Day)—the ancient Roman version of *YOLO!*. But, that's not enough—we probably should *Carpe Noctem* (Seize the Night) as well! To quote David Spade's fast-food manager to a slacking employee in *Reality Bites*, "You got time to lean, you got time to clean, buddy!" I recall earlier in my career, I subscribed to this sort of thinking, that the best way to improve was to work harder. I remember saying to colleagues and students "Sleep is for the weak." What a jerk—glad I grew out of *that* particularly obnoxious phase! But again, working all the time was a solution—it's *simple*!

The mentally tough recognize that there is some degree of lunacy behind Nike's well-intended, ubiquitous *Just Do It* campaign. The ethos of *Just Do It* lies in a mostly false concept that hard things are really quite simple, they just require a positive mindset. The campaign, I will remind you, was popularized around NBA legend Michael Jordan, he of "got cut from high school team only to become arguably the best basketball player of all time" fame. It's safe to say it's somewhat easier for someone of Jordan's physical prowess to *Just Do It*. What of unskilled, 5'6" skinny guys— can we also *Just Do It*? Rather depends on what *It* is, does it not? The mythology of "you can be anything you want" is admirable in its aspirations, but on the court, in the field, in real life, it is not always easy of advisable to *Just Do It* when *It* is not realistic. That said, I do admit that "Try your best to do reasonable things that push your limits, but are ultimately achievable" doesn't look nearly as good in a magazine ad.

What Lies Ahead

In the following chapters, we will learn about the history of mental toughness—it's been around far longer than we think, simply disguised as other constructs. We will also become familiar with the 4C model and will discuss how we—you and I—can enhance our mental toughness. This is an exciting journey, one many of us have been engaged in for much of our lives without knowing it—we have simply been travelling along a path that is sometimes clear, sometimes steep, sometimes crowded, sometimes lonely, but mostly full of twists and turns with no real sense of direction. Mental toughness can be a compass that can help us navigate our way along this path, helping us to both avoid getting lost in the weeds while also giving us a sense of direction and a means to clear a path when the path itself becomes treacherous.

Let's take a walk!

Chapter 1

Mental Toughness, Mental Sensitivity, and Mental Flexibility

Pretty much everyone knows who Wayne Gretzky is. Even people who have never watched more than a minute of hockey are familiar with his name. Even if you don't know his records or his history, his central role in the establishment of modern hockey is well-known. While there may be arguments about his dominance in the more contemporary game today, there is no argument whatsoever that he was the dominant player of his era. There is a well-known quote attributed to Gretzky, and occasionally to Michael Jordan, and even, infamously and hilariously to both Gretzky and Jordan as mis-sub-quoted by *The Office*'s Michael Scott, that says "you miss 100% of the shots you don't take." This expression has become well-embedded in meme culture and images of extreme athletes or mountain vistas or racing cheetahs accompanied by this or similar quotes hang on thousands of classroom and office walls and for good reason. It is a truism that resonates with many people who, for lack of drive/motivation/ initiative/desire/initiative/whatever reason, may never take a risk.

But here's the thing about Gretzky. He was almost never the biggest, fastest, toughest, or the most accurate player on the ice. He was a combination of physical and psychological excellence that is built on a unique chemistry of characteristics, none of which in and of themselves would have been identified as being the dominant single component contributing toward his success. His unique combination of strength, skill, perception, and game sense were all contributing factors to success. However, when looking at his minor hockey career, it becomes clear that this combination by itself was not enough to create the franchise player he eventually became. When he was in minor hockey, Gretzky was a target. Everyone wanted to take him down. He learned to use his speed and agility, rather than body size or sheer strength, to evade, to outskate, and to outshoot his competition.

In numerous interviews, Gretzky has cited the experiences he had as a minor hockey player to be formative to his game play style as a pro. He learned to set up shop behind the opposition goaltender's net so that he could have space to scan the surface of the ice to find his wingers; so he could make laser accurate passes, allowing his teammates to score. By setting up behind the net, he created space for himself, while limiting the attack range of his opponents. His explosive speed, especially in a confined space, made it almost impossible for opposition skaters to touch him, much less get close to the puck. The inability for the opposition players to catch him was a source of great frustration, putting the opposition off their own game, forcing them to play the Great One's game.

It is entirely possible that Gretzky's skill set, based on athletic prowess alone, would have still led him to an exceptional hockey career. However, it could be argued that his complete dominance of the game through the 1980s could be attributed in no small part to the challenges he faced as a minor player. Opposing teams would send in their fastest skaters, but they were no match for Gretzky's intensely accurate passes. They would send out their strongest players to try to hold him back, and he learned how to not just evade, but also trip up these aggressors. They would send out their most fearsome enforcers, only for him to skate away from them and rarely, if ever, getting into fights that would see him in the penalty box rather than on the ice. He was a team player above all, despite his ridiculously impressive individual skill set.

However, as noted, he was almost never the biggest, fastest, or strongest player on the ice at any given time. He was a combination of all of these things, but it was his mental game that made him dominant.

In my work as a psychologist, I often have the opportunity to work with people who are outstanding in many ways. While the majority of my client base is composed of people who have complex learning profiles, I also work with individuals who have successful careers; they are often top academics, or are exceptional athletes; they have substantial social skills, along with any number of other positive attributes. Yet they struggle. They struggle with finding happiness, finding joy, and finding contentment in their lives. They have goals that they do not reach, despite trying and trying and trying. Or, alternatively, they lack direction and cannot find the wherewithal to set goals independently. They find themselves living, as a British put it, "lives of quiet desperation." Others set reasonable goals, but find it difficult to take the risks necessary to achieve those goals. Others yet may believe that they do not have any active control over their own lives, but instead, life "happens" to them.

These characteristics are not unique to clinical populations. We all know people who fall short of their goals, or set no goals at all, others who struggle with taking risks, and yet others who seem to constantly be in a position of reactive panic due to high risk-taking behaviors. These are otherwise intelligent, rational, and reasonable human beings. What is it that underlies these seemingly self-sabotaging behaviours? And why is it that some others who seem to have very little going for them can find a great deal of success through perseverance, moderate risk-taking, and interpersonal confidence?

There does seem to be an overarching construct that goes a long way to explaining these variations. Mental toughness is a field of study and practice that has been around for a long time. In fact, it could be argued that the study of mental toughness, under different names, has been in practice since the days of the earliest philosophers. The concept of virtues has been a long-standing and well-respected idea that is guided cultures in relation to ethics, morality, social equity, and personal development.

Mental Toughness: The 4C Model

"Fall seven times, stand up eight"

—**Chinese proverb**

This book's title is based on a well-known Chinese proverb. It's overt meaning, if you fail, keep trying, is simple, practical, and direct. However, as with many proverbs, there are layers. The thing that strikes me most about this expression is the specificity of the numbers. Why seven? Why not two? Or four? The number seems oddly specific. Stumbling seven times suggests that making mistakes and experiencing failure is something we are *supposed* to do. It normalizes risk-taking and perceived failure, but also acknowledges the need to keep trying. Standing up to have another go after seven failures suggests resilience, grit, determination, and commitment to a goal. The encouragement to stand up and try again, even after multiple challenges, is at the essential core of mental toughness.

So ultimately, what is mental toughness? As described by Clough and Earle (2002), mental toughness is *how one appraises and evaluates challenge, the degree to which they are willing to take risks to achieve their goals, and their confidence in finding success.* An alternative definition describes mental toughness as being a personality trait which determines, in large part, how individuals deal with stressors, pressures, and challenge, irrespective of the situation. These definitions will be discussed in detail later, but for now, and for our purposes, the latter definition will be used.

Using this definition, mental toughness can essentially best be described as falling within the 4C model, which includes the following areas of focus:

- **Control**
- **Challenge**
- **Commitment**
- **Confidence**

As indicated in Figure 1, each of the 4Cs can be further subcategorized into different orientations. Each of these will be discussed in later chapters. For now, it is important to know that mental toughness can be a valuable tool that that could help us develop confidence in how we approach difficult situations, how we appraise those situations in the first place, the degree to which we feel we have power to make a difference, and our commitment to see things through to their final completion. This all sounds very well and good, but it is probably best explained by using examples that we see on a day-to-day basis, and I will also include some examples from my clinical

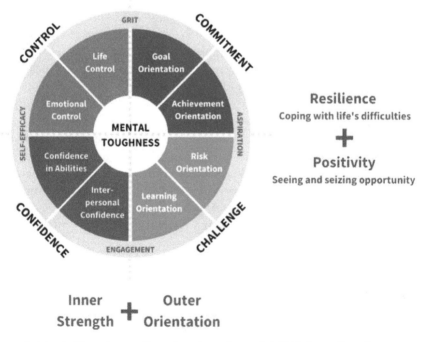

Figure 1 Mental Toughness Overview (courtesy of AQR International)

practice that exemplify how mental toughness can have an impact upon individual development, and, indeed, team development as well.

The Evolution of Mental Toughness

Like many psychological principles, mental toughness has an extensive history of evidence that precedes its emergence into contemporary psychological nomenclature. We can look through historical lenses at various accounts of individuals who exhibited what we could now call mental toughness. From a Biblical perspective, the paragon of mental toughness would most likely be Job, the man upon who God and Satan wagered to test his faith. Job was subject to various miseries, yet refused to blame God, or anyone else for that matter, for his pain. He had challenges beyond reason thrust upon him, yet he maintained a positive and consistent belief that he could persevere. Granted, the story of Job is not a perfect example—not all of those who struggle will be rewarded in abundance as Job was. But the analogy holds—Job's confidence helped sustain him through extreme pain. He was mentally tough.

Sun Tzu's *The Art of War*, certainly a book containing a significant number of ideas consistent (although some very inconsistent) with mental toughness, has been quoted extensively in the many centuries that have passed since its publication in the 5th century BCE. Shakespeare's heroic characters, such as they were, could be analyzed from a mental toughness perspective. Hamlet, for instance, might be considered a paragon of a character who lacks a sense of life control, feeling that life happened to him as opposed to actively engaging in his own existence. Greek, Norse, Native American, African, Asian cultures all have narratives in which their hero's struggle in the face of challenging opposition. They may not always defeat these challenges, but that is not the point—the point lies in the struggle. Mental toughness addresses how it is that individuals and groups overcome more contemporary challenges.

Mental toughness is strongly allied historically and philosophically with the 3rd century BCE Greek philosopher Zeno of Citium, a student of Plato's philosophy, and the roots of Stoicism. To paraphrase from Greek (not Latin for a change!), stoicism is rooted in the phrase *stoa poikile*, which is translated to "painted porch." History has it that Zeno had conversations with his fellow philosophers and other members of his community on a porch decorated with various images that relayed some of the stories they told. It became well-known as a place to gather and tell stories. The modern use of the word stoic is often a misinterpretation of what Zeno and his colleagues intended. When we think of someone being stoic, we think of someone unemotional and remote, a human machine bereft of feelings of any sort. Yet stoicism is rooted in self-examination, learning about one's own personhood and engaging in enhancing our self-awareness. Stoics believed in evaluating our own judgements and behaviours, which may require some degree of emotional detachment, but such detachment is not required to truly engage in self-examination. Mental toughness is, at its fundamental core, a means to engage in a truly stoic search for self-awareness and then using that self-awareness to guide judgement and behaviour in our future interactions.

Underlying stoicism, to continue with a philosophical understanding of the mental toughness concept, are the Platonic cardinal virtues, characteristics that are critical to our self-awareness. The cardinal virtues—wisdom, courage/fortitude, justice, and temperance—are all easy to relate to mental toughness concepts. Wisdom, the ability to discern a specific course of action following reflection on options, relates to both goal and achievement orientations under the mental toughness 4C model, while courage/fortitude (the ability to take risk and endure challenge) are correlates of risk and achievement orientations. Justice ties into emotional and life control, while Temperance, which refers to restraint and self-control, allies nicely with emotional control as well. These cardinal virtues also align with mental toughness in that they all focus on prevention of unnecessary harm and pain. The more we are aware of our virtues, the more aware we are of our mental toughness, the less harm we cause and the less unnecessary pain we feel. As such, mental toughness is not simply an isolated psychological construct; rather, it is a means of developing a philosophy of living.

One of the factors that perhaps is missing from the mental toughness model is what could be referred to as a moral orientation. However, while such an orientation has not been empirically linked with the 4C model, it could be argued that a strong sense of morality is an umbrella under which all of the 4C model resides. A moral orientation suggests that even armed with self-awareness, we do not use our mental toughness to take advantage of others or use such awareness to harm others. Morality is a means of engaging empathy both on a micro- and macrocosmic level. Those who are mentally tough ideally have a strong moral orientation embedded in their identity. If not, mental toughness risks becoming what Nietzsche referred to as the Will to Power, an innate drive to control self and others, essentially regardless of consequence. Morality is a check against using our mental toughness in unhealthy, even abusive ways, and prevents those who have mental toughness in different capacities from being enamored with the idea of taking advantage of others who may not share their "toughness." I would go so far to argue that people who are "mentally tough" and take advantage or harm others are, in fact, not mentally tough at all; rather, they are immature and exhibit proto-mental toughness in the same was a playground bully can temporarily become quite intimidating, but essentially at their core, they exhibit limited real power.

Beyond philosophy, mental toughness has a significant place in the sciences as well. Charles Darwin would likely find the concept of mental toughness to be largely consistent with some of his core beliefs related to adaptation in adversity. It is worth noting that Darwin himself was not terribly comfortable with the ease to which many powerful people adopted his idea of the Survival of the Fittest. Survival of the Fittest suggests that successful species (and individuals within that species) are those that are the most successful in competitive environments. So, the common thinking is that strong competitors are those most likely to be successful, not only in terms of biological superiority, but also in society. Yet Darwin believed that equally, if not more, important was the concept of compassion and empathy. He wrote: "Those communities which included the greatest number of the most *sympathetic* members would flourish best and rear the greatest number of offspring" (italics added). In mental toughness terms, those with higher degrees of interpersonal orientation and emotional control would be more likely to be biologically and socially successful than those with the overvalued drive to be the best.

Contemporary Psychology Theory and Mental Toughness

William James, the Harvard lecturer known as the father of American psychology, was perhaps among the first in the germinal stages of psychology as a science to describe, in essence, what mental toughness is. In his famous 1896 lecture *The Will to Believe*, James said that "faith in one's own ability to accomplish tasks" and "adopting a believing attitude" were fundamental principles underlying human success. These statements are not dissimilar at all from the 4C model of mental toughness. Decades later, in 1948, Abraham Maslow visited with members of the Blackfoot Nation in Alberta, Canada, where his interactions with the Blackfoot people further enhanced the ideas related to his theory of a Hierarchy of Needs, which essentially stated that we move from basic needs such as food and water to higher successive stages leading to self-actualization, which is a true sense of self-awareness, a core principle underlying mental toughness in general and the 4C model in particular. Julian Rotter wrote in 1954 about the Locus of Control, which again underlies principles related to mental toughness by describing how we attribute our successes and failures. If we succeed, perhaps it is because we were mentally tough. If we fail, perhaps we lacked a sense of confidence, or did not set appropriate goals, both explanations falling well within our understanding of mental toughness.

Mental toughness is, to an extent, also consistent with the well-known Big 5 Personality Traits, developed in the 1980s and still widely seen as a valuable means of understanding and, to some extent, compartmentalizing personality traits in a meaningful manner that is neither too simplistic nor too complex. The Big 5 traits are openness to experience, conscientiousness, extraversion, agreeableness, and neuroticism/negative affect; the OCEAN acronym is a helpful reminder of these traits. **O**penness to experience speaks to curiosity and willingness to explore a variety of experiences; **c**onscientiousness refers to self-discipline/self-regulation of emotions; **e**xtraversion, unlike the more common misinterpretation of extraverts as being outgoing, gregarious people but rather describes an enthusiastic engagement with the external world; **a**greeableness is a form of optimism and a positive outlook on life; and **n**euroticism/negative affect refers to the experience of negative emotions. Big 5 theorists and practitioners propose that people fall within a spectrum on each trait, so some people may be more agreeable, but may still experience negative emotions.

As with the cardinal virtues, the Big 5 traits have reasonably clear links to the 4C model explored through the MTQ measure. The Big 5 are not associated with any specific theorist or researcher, but the model is well-respected in the psychology world as being a strong, reliable, and valid means of understanding significant personality traits that remain consistent across time in individuals.

As we can see, mental toughness has since been built upon a number of different psychological constructs, each with their own bodies of research and practice approaches. Concepts such as resilience, Angela Duckworth's ideas around grit, Martin Seligman's research on positive psychology, Carol Dweck's ideas regarding growth mindset, among many others, are all components associated with mental toughness. Taken individually, each approach has some degree of validity and bear powerful weight in understanding and changing human behaviour, thinking, and emotionality. Mental toughness incorporates components consistent with each of these areas. The act of incorporating a number of different concepts to develop a higher-order approach such as mental toughness carries with it a risk of dilution. If you have too many similar yet uniquely disparate ideas, do you end up with a stew of relatively meaningless ideas, or do you end up with a more focused and comprehensive version of a final product? A number of years of research and hundreds of research articles suggest perhaps more so the latter. Mental toughness is a whole comprised of a number of intertwined parts. Of course, each constituent part is not without fault, and cumulative faults can make for a dodgy superstructure.

For instance, the growth mindset research conducted by Carol Dweck and her associates has not always had positive replication, which is to say that it is possible that the growth mindset research may not be as robust as possible (although I would argue that there is a certain degree of face validity to the growth mindset concept—face validity refers to the degree to which a concept looks like it has value, sort an implicit *feeling* of accuracy). It has also been suggested that positive growth mindset applies best to gifted or highly functional individuals who may be somewhat risk averse, which is to say that it works best with people who are already capable but might need a nudge in the right direction. If true, then can growth mindset research and practice be effectively applied to the majority of the population? Likely, but it is not—like many constructs, including mental toughness—the panacea that many hope for.

Similarly, the concept of grit was popularized in the late 2010s primary through Angela Duckworth's best-selling *Grit: The Power of Perseverance*. Again, there is a high degree of face validity associated with the grit concept— that if we keep working through challenges, we are more likely to experience success in the long-term. Yet it is also possible that grit in itself is not sufficient to explain why some people experience success and others "fail." Specifically, for instance, what of luck? It is possible to lack grit but have luck and that it is the latter, rather than the former, that predicts success. For instance, it is not surprising to know that in general, successful academic performance as measured on standardized tests is often associated more with parental affluence (education, income) and test-taking cleverness as opposed to actual academic knowledge and is, in fact, often due to factors irrespective of classroom interventions. Grit may have a role to play here, to be sure, but it is, in itself, insufficient to explain the complexity of successful performance. Luck matters. A significant issue with grit is the need to know when to stop. There is much to be said for the artist who knows when to abandon their work before inadvertently ruining it. Overemphasizing grit can lead to needless frustration. We need to now when to quit.

So, where does this leave mental toughness, which, as noted, incorporates concepts associated with the Hierarchy of Needs, Locus of Control, the Big 5 Personality Traits, positive growth mindset, and grit, among others? Perhaps it's best and most effective to think of mental toughness as the picture on the cover of a jigsaw puzzle box. The pieces are all there, and each is important, but the picture on the cover provides the guide to putting it all together in a meaningful way.

Mental toughness is a well-known construct in certain fields. Googling "mental toughness" reveals over 10 million hits, largely composed of stories, articles, and other pages devoted to athletic performance. A more detailed search of "images" associated with mental toughness on Google reveals mostly images of athletes, bulging biceps, people sweating, or other similar images of wrecking balls smashing into a brain. Not terribly subtle, but these searches do demonstrate the roots of mental toughness as being embedded in sports performance remains the primary focus of the popular writing, if not the research in the area.

As discussed, the roots of contemporary research on mental toughness lie in sports psychology, and certainly the research has continued to expand in this arena over the years. A search of peer-reviewed publications using "mental toughness" as a key phrase reveals almost 2,000 publications since 2000. The vast majority of these appear in the field of sport psychology and performance. However, mental toughness research has more recently expanded into the corporate world and, more recently yet, is being applied to educational settings.

Mental toughness, as previously noted, has well-researched over the past 40 years, starting with its roots in sport psychology (and even further back, if we take into consideration the existence of mental toughness under different nomenclature over the centuries). But in terms of contemporary research, the concept of mental toughness has been well-validated and researched in a wide variety of peer-reviewed studies. While peer review does not imply perfection, it does suggest that there is a high degree of rigour underlying the studies, which increases our comfort in accepting the results as being accurate and objective. Since the goal of this book is not to provide a comprehensive academic overview of the research literature on mental toughness, but to engage readers in developing a practical and applied understanding of the concept while also ensuring that the concept is represented fairly in terms of what it can and cannot help us with, efforts have been made to keep the writing relatively straightforward. As such, the following section will describe a selection of the contemporary research being conducted in the field of mental toughness. A more comprehensive literature review would be better suited for a more rigorous research-oriented publication. However, for the curious and those with time on their hands (HA!), references to additional research studies are also available in the bibliography section of this book, which the reader can explore at their leisure.

Mental Toughness and Resilience

Mental toughness is comprised of a number of constructs associated with positive psychology, which in itself is not a specific therapeutic or practice-oriented approach, but is a more general way of conceptualizing approaches in psychology. Positive psychology focuses on what strengths and positive attributes an individual brings to any given situation. It seeks not to diagnose, but to support and enhance. One of the most central orientations associated with positive psychology is resilience. Resilience is that combination of mindset, attitude, beliefs, skills, and resources available when facing challenging situations. It is the "bounce-back" factor—how does one bounce back from tough situations? Even traumatic situations? In my clinical work, I often interact with individuals who have experienced all manner of unfortunate situations at school—teasing that morphs into true bullying, judgement about underachievement, social stressors, lack of motivation/drive, feelings of intellectual isolation, and combinations of these and many other factors. Yet some students bounce back from each time they are pushed down like an inflatable Bobo doll, while other crumble like a sandcastle. What makes the difference? Theoretically, provided that all other variables are relatively equal, the answer lies in how resilient one is.

Mental toughness could, in some ways, be considered to be resilience's more assertive twin. Resilience largely reflects how one responds to challenging situations. Mental toughness, on the other hand, incorporates not only *reaction* but also *approach*. Mentally tough individuals tend to seek out challenges, which, should things not work out, require them to utilize resilience characteristics. But it is in the seeking out of challenges that the primary difference between resilience and mental toughness lies. Resilience could be thought of as being somewhat synonymous with coping, while mental toughness would incorporate the beliefs and attitudes that underlie risk-taking behaviours that may elicit coping responses should things not go well. If, for instance, one was to find oneself in an over-turned canoe, one would likely engage in coping strategies ("Well, this is a miserable situation that I'd not anticipated, how will I deal?"). On the other hand, mental toughness incorporates the thinking that underlies the risk-taking in the first place. Why, for instance, were you in the canoe in the first place? Was it an active, positive choice? If so, will the fact that you actively chose this activity make a difference to your response when you find yourself clinging to the up-ended canoe? What if you *had* to be in the canoe because there was no other option available? Does choice play a role in your ability to cope?

Resilience presupposes the presence of risk and challenging situations. In some situations, resilience is forced upon us—in times of stress, what else can we do except be resilient and work though hard things? Mental toughness, on the other hand, does not necessarily presume threat. Quite the opposite, mental toughness becomes engaged when we make a choice to *actively seek out* risk. If our metaphoric canoe trip were forced upon us because we had to get from point A to point B along a river and the canoe was the only valid means of transportation, the resilience becomes imposed upon us when it flips. On the other hand, if we choose to take the canoe out because we want to go exploring and the canoe then flips, the resilience we engage in is largely based on an active choice we had willingly made. It is not, in the truest sense of the word, resilience so much as it is dealing with consequences of self-selected risk.

From a psychological perspective, we think back to our challenged learners at school. Those with learning disabilities and ADHD do not choose their conditions. As such, they must engage in a largely resilient approach at school, which can be exhausting over time (see the next section on hardiness). On the other hand, some people struggle with school because they set very high goals for themselves—they want to be earning grades that they may, in all fairness, not be capable of achieving. However, their desire to achieve those grades is their own self-directed choice so any consequences, both negative and positive, is *earned*.

Mental Toughness and Hardiness

Hardiness is another primary underlying principle to mental toughness that, in itself, is insufficient to explain the complexity of the mentally tough. Hardiness relates to how one resists stress. It refers to stress resistance both in terms of intensity and duration. How intense is the stress and how long can we resist it? It is similar in many ways to acute and chronic illnesses. Acute pain and illness is short-term and often very intense, which requires an entirely different degree of stress resistance than chronic illness, which tends to be less intense (but not always) and of far longer duration. Passing a kidney stone would be considered to be intense—to say the least—but would also be of short duration (although those who have passed one might argue how time *feels* in that situation). My own old friend Crohn's Disease, which I will discuss in a moment, is a chronic illness. It lasts for a long time (and is, in fact, not curable), with periods of high intensity and other times when it is not particularly problematic. Hardiness can be used to explain how an individual could deal with both kinds of pain (acute and chronic), but the presentation, of course, would be wildly different.

Hardiness does not take into account confidence, at least not in the same way that mental toughness does. Confidence, as we will learn later, is largely a mental toughness construct that refers to one's capacity to feel secure in one's own abilities and their ability to persuade others to their perspective. Hardiness is, again, somewhat of a reactive characteristic. It does not directly address the idea that one's confidence is a significant player in how one exhibits hardiness. If, for instance, one were to experience chronic pain, hardiness helps to manage the pain over time. But hardiness without confidence that the pain can be overcome in the first place is likely not particularly effective. It should be noted that hardiness does NOT imply the thinking that underlies a "stiff upper lip/ suck it up" mentality. People who experience chronic pain know that even at their most hardy, they are often exhausted. Nurses often speak of patients who are likely lovely people, but over an extended time of illness and pain, can become immature and whiny. Even those with a great deal of hardiness can glare with disdain and even real anger at a nurse who offers a pain-relieving suggestion ("take a deep breath, make a fist, look at the wall," etc.). These are often otherwise very nice and socially appropriate people who would never scowl in public, now shooting daggers at a well-intentioned health care professional. Where did their hardiness go? In one part, it is simply exhaustion that reduces hardiness. But from a mental toughness perspective, it is also probable that the chronic pain has, over time, taught the patient that no matter how hard they try, they will not be able to significantly reduce their pain. It is similar to learned helplessness thinking. But it is perhaps better explained by the reduction in confidence one experiences after trying different strategies with limited to no long-term success.

On the other hand, if one has a high degree of confidence in their abilities to manage pain, they will experience a greater degree of hardiness, which in turn, enhances their sense of confidence in abilities to manage pain. Again, not to simplify—chronic pain can be devastating and is a very real experience and I wish to be clear that in no way am I suggesting that you just need a good attitude to manage pain. Far from it. Physical and emotional pain are real and can, over time, wear even the most mentally tough individual down. The expression "pain is just weakness leaving the body" is one of the most ridiculous statements ever made and one that, when I see it plastered on a gym wall or, worse, in an office, I have to rally myself to prevent me from ripping it down while yelling "LIES!!!" Of course, the security would be called, and they'd take me away. Again!

Regardless, I would argue that mental toughness can enhance both our resilience and hardiness which, in turn, has a boomerang action that results in enhanced mental toughness.

Mental Toughness and Psychobiology

Of course, few areas related to human psychological performance can be discussed without consideration of the psychobiological aspects of human behaviour. The growth of brain-based research since mid-90s has only accelerated with significant gains in imagining technologies. Contemporary imaging studies have revealed links between mental toughness and different neurological structures and neurochemical interactions. The age-old debate infiltrates these studies—does being mentally tough result in changes in brain structures and chemical changes that are different based on the mental toughness profile of the individual, or is mental toughness the result of such biological components? The best answer in such discussions is that the interaction of biological endowments and environmental factors, while amazingly complex, provides the best understanding of psychological constructs such as mental toughness. Of course, the interaction between the brain and behaviour is enormously complex and it is somewhat of a fool's errand to identify causal relationships in an area of such complexity. However, some emerging research has suggested that mental toughness is indeed related to brain structure and function. For instance, researchers at the Universities of Parma and Modena & Reggio in Italy, using 3D Magnetic Resonating Imaging (MRI), found clear links between grey matter density and higher scores on measures of mental toughness, with specific correlations with confidence in abilities with temporal, occipital, and precuneus areas (which relate to spatial sense, visual skills, and sense of self, respectively). Emotional and life control were also both correlated with higher density of grey matter in the precuneus/inferior parietal lobule, the former of which again is associated with a sense of self while the latter is associated with emotion and perspective-talking/social emotions.

Additionally, the University of Basel in Switzerland is a centre of a considerable amount of research on mental toughness. Research from UB has shown positive interactions between mental toughness and anxiety management, positive sleep habits, test anxiety, enhanced exercise patterns, and overall more positive and consistent approaches to problem-solving. Dr. Lee Crust from the University of Lincoln in the United Kingdom has also been a lead researcher in the area of mental toughness, with numerous publications suggesting correlations between mental toughness and emotional literacy and intensity. Coupled with the work of Dr. Peter Clough from Hull University, also in England, among others, there is an emerging body of research that suggests that (1) mental toughness is a valuable trait that is worth encouraging, (2) mental toughness can indeed be assessed with accuracy, and (3) in using assessment results effectively, mental toughness can be developed to enhance human performance in a wide variety of environments and across developmental stages, from school-aged to post-retirement.

Overall, then, mental toughness is a well-evidenced approach to personal development. One salient example that will speak to many is research emerging from the United Kingdom in particular that has indicated that mentally tough people are less likely to report being targeted by—or taking active part in—bullying. Let's just stop there. If mental toughness is a possible protective factor against bullying—and bullying *only*—would it not be worth teaching *all* students from a young age? Would it not be a significant part of *any* corporate culture? Could it be used as a means of decreasing the incidence of not only bullying, but of many associated power-based conflicts, including professional and sexual harassment?

Additionally, pilot work conducted by researchers in the United Kingdom have also found that mental toughness is also a protective factor in terms of absenteeism—that is, the more mentally tough the individual, the less likely they are to be absent from school or work. Again, think of the benefits of increased attendance to a student's learning, or a corporation's bottom line. The assumption is that people who exhibit more mental toughness tend to have more adaptive responses to stress, and since stress is highly correlated with physical health symptoms, mental toughness can account for a healthier student and working population.

There are many more benefits associated with mental toughness. Various studies cite personal and professional confidence, academic achievement, interpersonal confidence, task completion, team functionality, among others, as all being associated with mental toughness (again, see the bibliography for more details on studies in these areas). I encourage you to think about how mental toughness can be a positive factor in *your* life, while also considering areas in which you might be more mentally sensitive. Mental sensitivity is not, by the way, a universally negative trait. Like most things, we need balance and the idea of "all things in moderation" holds true here. We will discuss the challenges of being too extreme on measures of mental toughness and mental sensitivity in later chapters, but for now, try to focus on where your mental toughness areas, in general—based on the information provided in Figure 1—may lie.

Self-Assessment of Mental Toughness

You can use the following quick assessment to develop at least some sense of your mental toughness profile (although the use of a psychometrically sound measure such as the MTQ Plus or MTQ-48, along with an interpretative session with a licensed practitioner of mental toughness coaching through AQR, for instance, would be a *far* preferable approach to evaluate one's mental toughness).

MENTAL TOUGHNESS QUICK ASSESSMENT		0 = Disagree	5 = Neutral	10 = Agree
Control				
Life Control	I am confident in making and sticking with my decisions			
Life Control	I do not tend to allow others to make decisions on my behalf and I have control over things that happen in my day-to-day life			
Emotional Control	People rarely know how I feel, even though I may have strong feelings about something			
Emotional Control	I am rarely completely open and honest with my feelings at most times			
Control Totals				
Commitment				
Goal Orientation	I thrive on setting goals and feel good when I am working toward a specific goal			

Goal Orientation	Having goals is invigorating and I have little to no question that if I have a goal set for me, that I will achieve it			
Achievement Orientation	I enjoy working toward goals and even if I don't have control over the goal, the work I do to achieve it feels worthwhile			
Achievement Orientation	I rarely have a difficult time working toward goals, even those I may not completely believe in			
Commitment Totals				
Challenge				
Risk Orientation	I enjoy taking risks and view them as being exciting challenges			
Risk Orientation	I find risk taking to be enjoyable and find routine and predictability to be constricting			
Learning Orientation	When I make mistakes, I learn from them and almost never repeat them			
Learning Orientation	For me, learning from mistakes is easy and natural, and I do not have a tendency to repeat them			

Confidence				
Confidence in Abilities	I know what my skill set is and I am comfortable sharing my abilities with others			
Confidence in Abilities	I may have certain skills that others may not, and I am confident that they would be valued by others, so I do not fear being judged if I might make a mistake			
Interpersonal Confidence	I enjoy sharing ideas with others, even people I may not know well			
Interpersonal Confidence	I often have ideas that I would like to share, and happily do so with people, even if I may not know with them very well			
Confidence Totals				

Scoring

For each area, a check in the corresponding box indicates your preference. Total each area. The higher the score, the more "mentally tough" you may be; the closer to 20 in each area, the more "mentally flexible" you may be, while scores closer to 0 suggest that you may be more "mentally sensitive."

Each row is associated with a specific mental toughness characteristic, and again, the same principle applies—closer to 10 suggests more "mental toughness" in relation to that characteristic, scores closer to 0 are suggestive of a more "mentally sensitive" profile, while scores close to 5 suggest more "mental flexibility."

Please note that this is **not** a formal, diagnostic, or even terribly accurate assessment. It is presented here simply as an exercise to get you thinking a bit about how your preferences and tendencies may relate to mental toughness.

Your actual mileage may vary! If you are interested in having a far more detailed and psychometrically sound evaluation of your mental toughness profile, consider approaching a professional trained in the administration and interpretation of the MTQ Plus (my team and I are happy to do this remotely or provide you with a list of practitioners who do this kind of work).

The assessment of any psychological construct—intelligence, academic ability, depression, resiliency, etc.—requires and presupposes the implementation of the scientific method in a broad sense. Why measure something that may not actually exist? The MTQ Plus and associated instruments are theory-driven, psychometrically strong measures. They are norm-referenced (meaning that your scores are compared to others with similar demographic features), with statistically significant normative groups and a great deal of reliability (i.e., results tend to be similar over time, provided that nothing significant has occurred, such as training or trauma) and validity (meaning that the MTQ measures mental toughness, not some other constructs). Scores fall along a continuum (as noted, from "low" to "high" and is not simply categorical, i.e., saying to you either *are* or *are not* mentally tough). The measure is sensitive to individual change, so if you took the MTQ in September and then worked to develop your mental toughness, ideally our scores in April would reflect the work you have done. In regard to scientific validity and rigour, the MTQ has been positively cited in over 250 peer-reviewed studies.

As a psychologist, all of this appeals to me and as a consumer of psychological information, I hope it satisfies you too. There are far too many pop psychology approaches, making too many unverified promises. Many popular measures, such as the Myers-Briggs Type Indicator, among others, are widely used despite the lack of scientific vigor to support their use. Online questionnaires will tell us which friend from TVs *Friends* (I'm Chandler . . . or Ross, sometimes. Occasionally, Gunther.) we are, or which Hogwartian House we would best be suited to (Ravenclaw FTW!). All of these types of measures share a common factor—they are entertaining and fun to share with others, but—to be clear—they are not psychometrically sound measures of any real personality trait. The MTQ measures are well-researched, consistently developed, and have a solid basis of evidence upon which their conclusions are drawn. However, the purpose of this book, as noted, is to gain a practical understanding of mental toughness and while completing and evaluating the results of an MTQ would be a valuable exercise, it is not necessary to understand the concepts or how they apply to you.

It is often best, at least in absence of using the MTQ Plus, to try to understand mental toughness from a personal context. We all have experiences with mental toughness—it's possible you know a lot more about mental toughness through your own intuition and experience than you might first think. To provide some context, I will start with a personal example.

Developing Mental Toughness: When Being Special Doesn't *Feel* Special

When I was 13 years old, I started having abdominal pain immediately after eating, and sometimes even while eating. It was funny at the start—I would be sitting and eating the quintessential teen meal of, say, Kraft Dinner, when, four fork loads in, I would feel rebellion growing in my guts. Specifically, a rebellion in which pain like a baseball bat with nails hammered through the fat end being pushed against my abdominal wall, resulting in an *Alien*-esque feeling, but unlike the Chestburster scene from the 1979 film, the Alien never seemed to leave. It just hung out in my belly, waiting for its next feeding. Once food entered my system—and seriously, it could have been anything—pasta, meat, fruit, even "quasi-food" like Jell-O—the Alien would start trying to get out, pushing its sharp teeth against my abdomen. It could easily knock me to my knees. But not that anyone could see—I would quietly excuse myself, step lightly away from the table until no one in my family could see me, then stagger up the stairs and collapse sideways on the toilet, sweat rolling off my forehead, and then assume the position and let loose.

Sorry for the visual—we are still taking about mental toughness, trust me. But sometimes, we need to detour through some unpleasant scenes in order to get to a happier destination.

My parents were not easily fooled. I had certain tells. I would maneuver the food around into neat little stacks that left lots of white space on the plate, giving the illusion of having eaten more than I had. I would sit sweating at the table before food even hit the plate, trying to figure out ways to look like I was eating. And I'm sure they heard the "thump" noise I would make when I hit the stairs on my way to the bathroom—a collapsing 13-year-old is hard to miss! My time in the bathroom was extensive and rather embarrassing, as we only really had the one place to go—there was a small toilet in our mud room, but rarely used and kind of a last resort. I worried about what my parents thought I was doing in the bathroom all that time—I mean, I was a 13-year-old boy spending 45 minutes at a go in the washroom making all sorts of grunting noises. I know what I thought *they* thought I was doing! But I was simply leaning over the toilet, my head dripping sweat on the linoleum, praying for the pain to Just. Go. Away.

Another "tell"—I was 5'6" and, after a few weeks, and eventually, months, of not eating due to pain, I had dropped from a moderate if slight 120 lbs. to an anemic 87 lbs. I was basically a head on a stick.

School was a bit of a nightmare. I couldn't eat, I dared not go to the bathroom (have you *seen* junior high boy's bathrooms in public schools?), I literally passed out in class due to anemia and fatigue and pain. I was, to paraphrase one of my buddies, "A pale, sweaty marshmallow-head on an uncooked piece of spaghetti." Ah, junior high.

My parents took me to our GP, who looked at me, asked some questions, and said with authority "Stress." So, in those days, "stress" meant that I needed to *just relax*. To this day, the expression "Just Relax" triggers a visceral anger in me that is difficult to describe. Just relax implies blame—it's the individual's fault that they are stressed out and if they would *just relax*, they would be able to eat without pain and start to gain weight. Are you with me on that logic—just relax and the crushing abdominal pain will go away? Maybe this is where my interest in evidence-based practices started. I have yet to find evidence that stress alone causes one's belly to feel as if it were a bag of broken class shredding across raw nerve endings.

So, I "just" relaxed and continued to lose weight and energy and spent more time in pain than not. A second opinion was sought. My folks brought me to a pediatrician who ordered a series of tests, each one slightly more disgusting than the previous. I was injected with chemicals with radioactive tags, instructed to drink liters of thick, warm, chalky Barium (and also had the fun of ingesting it through the "alternative entry point" for an enema-based scan). My mom and I went back to the pediatrician after all of the tests to get the results—I was anxious for something tangible, a "thing" I had that had a treatment. I could not deal with another "stress" diagnosis.

The doctor, in his impeccable British accent (a novelty for us, since my hometown of Charlottetown, Prince Edward Island, is rich in Gaelic-flavored accents impenetrable to almost anyone from outside of the Maritime region of Canada given its folding in of Gaelic, English, French-Canadian; a proper English accent sounded authoritative and comforting in an intellectual sense), he said, "Well, we have an answer. You . . .!" At which point, he gestured to me in a way I can only describe as being an English School Master Point (Minus Pipe) ". . . have Crohn's Disease. It's not common, it's not curable, but we can treat some of the symptoms."

My over-dramatic adolescent brain really only picked up on two ideas. I had a RARE disease! An INCURABLE disease! This . . . this would make me an interesting person! Maybe a Movie-of -the Week awaited!

So, treatment of high-dose steroids and a generally soft diet was prescribed and—it worked! I started to be able to eat without pain, I gained weight. Of course, with steroids there are side effects that certainly did make me an interesting person. My face took on a roundness often described by folks who take high-dose steroids as "moon face" (I thought of it as "Charlie Brown Head"—but the effect was the same—a fluffy, round, acne-filled, sweaty face, quite a departure from the gaunt appearance I had been rocking for the previous year or two). My adolescent mood swings became mood cataclysms. I maintained a fear of food and a paranoid need to be aware of the location of the nearest bathroom at all times. To this day, I can, pardon the pun, sniff out the nearest toilet in almost any environment. And I always hope that it's a fair distance from any social gathering place— my greatest fear is finding that the only nearest bathroom at someone's house is right beside the kitchen or living room—I very much appreciate guest washrooms on different levels or at least, a short stumble down a hall-way, enough distance that no one can hear what happens in there!

I have since had a lot of complications arising from "my Crohn's" (I claim ownership by saying "my" Crohn's—it's part of me the same way my eyes and ears are, so it's "mine"). I spent a memorable 6-month stint on a purely liquid diet—no solids whatsoever. The initial plan was for the fluid nutrients to be pumped into my stomach through a nasogastric tube inserted in my nose, but I couldn't tolerate the discomfort of inserting the tube and wearing the vest with the battery pack/pump combination and and bags of fluid was just too much for me to bear, so I just drank the stuff. I have had four bowel resections, a complete abdominal wall reconstruction due to the various other surgeries, and some of the medications I have used to treat my Crohn's have had side effects contributing to other complicated conditions, along with ongoing issues with anemia/lethargy, difficulties swallowing, and living in a near-constant state of heightened anxiety at even the smallest twinge of abdominal discomfort as a potential harbinger of a full-on flare.

I will say this—through my teen experiences with health-related issues, my family was always supportive. My parents and brother accommodated by atypical eating patterns and frequent absences from family events. They didn't push me to just "suck it up" and get on with things, which is some-thing for which I am eternally grateful. But at the same time there was only so much they could do. Over time, their constant questioning of "how are you feeling" became very frustrating. I understood that they were asking out of genuine concern and empathy, but in my self-centered adolescent brain, I could barely stand the frequency with which they would ask about how I was feeling. I would become angry and strike out, telling them to leave me alone, to stop pushing, to just . . . stop it! Not something I am particularly proud of, but that is the reality of what was happening. I was tired, sick, in pain, frustrated, and just overall miserable. On occasion, when in the midst of a flare, which I have been fortunately avoiding now for quite some time, I still have those feelings. Just leave me alone and let me be miserable.

This is where I am supposed to say that all of this has made me stronger, right?

Wrong.

It's sucked! I'm not shy to say so—but at the same time, I am an optimist by nature and my belief is strongly that pain is a challenge that can help us evaluate our tenacity and willingness to move forward, even if we do so on our knees. So, okay, *maybe* my Crohn's has been a good thing. But I can't help but wonder if there might have even an easier way to get where I am!

The Formation of Mental Toughness—Suffering Not Required

We can learn to enhance our sense of mental toughness through our experiences and every individual has the capacity to learn from experience. Even the most basic organisms have this capacity, if only from a stimulus-response perspective. If you expose an insect to excessive heat, they will avoid that stimulus. That, though a very rudimentary response, is a form of learning. We avoid things that cause us discomfort. That would seem to be a biological basic.

So, why do some people actively seek out discomfort? Jumping out of a perfectly good airplane is not something that I would consider to be a particularly good idea, yet thousands of people do it every year—they *pay* to do it. For fun! Sure, if the plane is on fire, the pilot and co-pilot have both decided to vacate the premises and the tube of metal is hurdling toward this big block of rock called Earth, I may strap myself into a parachute and jump. Maybe. But if the plane is just cruising along, the pilot and co-pilot are chatting in the cockpit about whatever people who fly planes talk about, and there is a serious lack of fire, then, no, I'll not be jumping out a door at 10,000 ft, thanks for asking. I may just grab a seat, strap myself in with a seatbelt and read a book while waiting someone to come by asking if I'd prefer a sweet or salty snack (Frequent flyer note: The answer is always "Both!").

Yet the reality is this: People spend money—lots of it—to jump out of perfectly good airplanes. Happens all the time. What about this behaviour can be explained by mental toughness? It could be argued, accurately, that skydivers have a level of risk orientation that exceeds the norm. Does this mean that only this who are high on measures of risk orientation take risks? Of course not—risk is a broad term with numerous presentations. Public speaking for most human beings is a high-risk activity—even though no one has ever died from public speaking itself (okay, many have died for the messages they share through public speaking—political activists, religious icons, etc.—so, meaning no disrespect). I have a crippling fear of public speaking myself—I'll tell you where it came from and how I beat it later on. It has been paralyzing at times, but I have yet to die from public speaking. (Yet). But, people do die skydiving. Well, more specifically, not so much skydiving but "earth-landing." The assessment of risk and one's personal risk tolerance is the key and will be discussed in detail in a later chapter. This concept of risk orientation is being discussed here as an example of one aspect of mental toughness that strongly suggests the role of self-aware-ness, self-confidence, learning, resilience, anxiety management, and other associated factors. And, most importantly, risk orientation, as with all areas of mental toughness, can be enhanced and developed through effective self-analysis and coaching.

Angela Duckworth's work on grit, Carol Dweck's work on growth mindset, Brene Brown's emphasis on the strength of vulnerabilities, con-temporary ideas of resiliency and tenacity—all of these have a significant value and resonate effectively with mental toughness. But mental toughness could be argued to have a more global and broad-based appeal that is easily understood by most people at a very intuitive level. Kids get the idea of mental toughness when they first learn that life is not always going to work in their favor—the first time that they hear "NO!" provides them with an introduction to the concept of a boundary, which they often process as being unfairness. Unfairness is a big idea for a growing human to assimilate, but it does lead them to the idea that a boundary will not hurt them—that they can continue to push boundaries in different situations as part of their natu-ral capacity to experiment with rules and expectations. And as a result, they learn about the idea of challenge, a core component of mental toughness. Challenges build upon challenges, success and failure start to infiltrate their experiences and they start their journey into the larger world of orienting themselves around goals and the capacity to meet their own goals; their ability to take risks and learn from their ensuing experiences; they learn about their own abilities and develop confidence—or, unfortunately, their lack thereof—in these abilities and they learn to interact with others; ultimately, they learn that they themselves are active and engaged agents in their own lives. At a very early age, they have a true, intuitive sense of their own mental toughness and the mental toughness of others. Traditionally, we have not really had the language to describe this triangulation of characteristics.

Mental Toughness as a Trait, Not a State

The idea of mental toughness as a *trait* stands in contrast to a *state*. A trait is a relatively enduring pattern of characteristics that describe how we approach stress, challenge, and pressure. A state is a temporary response through which we tend to move rather quickly. For instance, if we come home to a flooded basement or if we hear a sudden crash from the room we JUST left our 5-year-old to play, we may enter into a state-response. Often, state-responses are heightened emotional responses and I believe it fair to say that most of us do not make our best decisions when in a heightened emotional condition. As such, we try to avoid finding ourselves in states; however, as human beings, we accept that these states happen from time to time.

As a former school administrator, one of my roles was to manage discipline at school for students with complex learning needs. It was an odd role as I was simultaneously serving as the school psychologist/counsellor. One lunchtime, I was sitting in the school's staff room, likely having deep philosophical and ontological discussions about the pedagogical soundness of contemporary curricular developments (or, maybe, what happened on *The Bachelor* the night before) when we all heard—or rather, *felt*—a loud booming sound. The teaching staff looked at me as if to say, "Aren't loud booming noises YOUR job?," so I went out into the hallway to find out what the ruckus was.

The ruckus was running down the corridor outside of the staff room, a plume of plaster powder trailing behind two grade 9 boys. Scouting the trail of plaster dust led me to a large grade 9-boy-sized hole in the wall just outside of the staff room. I barrelled down the corridor in hot pursuit, eventually finding my suspects sitting on the floor, sweating, out of breath and covered in plaster dust. "It wasn't us!" they protested before I'd even asked anything. "My Office! NOW!" I was shaking with anger—vandalism has always been a button issue for me—it seems so pointless. At least if you are stealing something, you are getting something. Vandalism is just a hole in a wall that needs to be filled. I was apoplectic.

So, the boys scurried to my office. I raged into the office, slamming the door shut and looked up at both of them (I'm 5'6"—these guys were almost a full head taller than me!). I ranted for a bit and then—well, see if you can identify my mistake:

"That hole in the wall will cost $500 to fix! YOU are going to work it off." I grabbed my calculator. "You will provide community service until you have earned the equivalent of $500 . . . so, assuming we paid you minimum wage, that will be . . . " I tapped in some numbers. "50 hours of community service you each owe the school!" Obviously, I'd not needed the calculator—I was trying to make a point about how complex this consequence was.

In any case, did you catch it? What was my mistake? I neglected to calculate (and for this, I should have used the calculator for real!) the time it would take *me* to create odd jobs and tasks, not to mention the supervision necessary that would be required to go into this community service program. In my anger, I applied a consequence that would ultimately penalize me far more than my wall-crashers. But I was committed. So, for the next 20 weeks, I planned to meet these boys daily at lunch with a new task—cleaning tables, putting away garbage and utensils, helping younger students find missing mittens and toques. After 2 weeks, I was running low on tasks. But I was stubbornly committed to my plan of action. Eventually, I acquiesced, but tried to maintain my dignity at the same time. "Turns out," I explained/lied to the boys, "The estimate from the contractor was lower than anticipated—so the repairs were only $150." They were summarily released from their indentured servitude, hopefully never to puncture an innocent wall ever again. In the meantime, I learned a lot about the dangers of allowing a state to overcome a trait.

By contrast to the volatility (and possible tranquility) of a *state* is the more stable *trait*. Traits, while not written in our psychological concrete, are relatively stable and don't tend to change significantly in different situations. A trait of patience is one I try to exemplify, but in the case of the damaged wall, I fell victim to the situation and reacted out of an impulsive state, not a stable trait. As we mature, we hope to see more consistent and positive traits emerge and evolve. Mental toughness is an example of a trait that we wish to have as a guiding characteristic.

Mental Toughness and "Coping" vs. "Working Through"

There can be a tendency for psychologists and others in mental health work to focus on language that includes phrases such as "coping strategies." Mental toughness goes beyond such thinking. Coping suggests a bare minimum. We do not hear of great copers. Effective team leaders are not ones who simply cope with their team. Inspiring teachers do not simply cope with their students. And psychologically healthy people do not simply cope with challenges. Coping is a valuable characteristic, sure, but it is a bare minimum response. When under stress, our coping strategies are engaged, should we have them, and often, this helps us deal with the situation at hand. The higher order activity here is not simply coping but "working through" the situation. Working through things presupposes success and an engaged, proactive approach as opposed to simple coping, which is largely reactive. Coping helps us work through. Working through helps us move forward. Moving forward helps us with learning, and learning is the foundation of self-realization.

The Power of the Situation and Mental Toughness

Another consideration in relation to mental toughness is how we deal with situations. Part of the definition of mental toughness related to how respond ". . . irrespective of situations." This may seem rather impossible—how can we discount the power of the situation? This is a fair criticism. Social psychology teaches us, as does history, that human beings react very differently depending on the situation. Perhaps one of the most disturbing but fascinating examples of this can be found in social psychology research on obedience to authority and the diffusion of responsibility.

Following the conclusion of World War II, when the full reality of the atrocities of the death camps started to emerge in the public consciousness, and the Nuremberg Trials started to ask some very important questions that were resulting in some very disturbing answers, the general public across Europe and North America reacted in a very similar way. In their shock, people would ask, "How could this have happened? Why didn't anyone stop it?

Why did people go along with these horrible actions?" The response given, almost to a person, at the Nuremburg Trials was a variation on the same theme: "I was only following orders." The more self-righteous in the population would exclaim, "How could you follow orders willingly when you knew it would lead to pain and suffering and death of innocents, based solely upon their ethnic and religious background, their sexual orientation, their state of disability?" We have since learned through disturbing but fascinating work in social psychology that under certain circumstances, there is indeed a high probability that almost all of us would do almost exactly the same thing. Simply because of the power of the situation.

Solomon Asch and Stanley Milgram were pioneers of social psychology research on conformity and obedience to authority, respectively. Their studies are still published in introductory psychology textbooks decades after they were conducted and, in fact, decades even after they have been largely criticized for their unethical handling of unsuspecting participants. Asch's work was simple, yet profound. He simply had a group of people sit in a room and state which of three different sized line was closest in length to a stimulus line. The answer was obvious—line #2 was clearly the closest in length to the stimulus line. So, what happens when you are sitting in a room of strangers and asked to state a clearly obvious answer and everyone else starts saying "Line 1." "It's Line 1." "The closest would be, uhm, Line 1." What would you say? Asch found that the vast majority of participants would conform to the group, even though the answer they gave was obviously wrong. If people would conform on such a small issue as the length of a line, what would have happened in more powerful situations, where all of your closest friends and family were also conforming? The implications were troubling.

A student of Asch's, Stanley Milgram took the ideas of his mentor a step further. In his well-known study, he had confederates (i.e., actors who were in on the experiment) pretend to be experimenters who told the "teachers" (the actual research participants) to provide an increasing voltage of shock to a "learner" (also a confederate), who was in another room close by, when they responded incorrectly to questions. The scale on the apparatus that delivered the "shock" (and it's important to note that no actual shock was given, but the learner was to *act* as if shocked, starting with offering a surprised grunt and escalating to yelling, demanding to be released, and ultimately to full-on screaming and eventually, an ominous silence) increased in voltages of 15 v from 15 v (mild shock) to 350 + v (XXX DANGER: EXTREME SHOCK) on the front panel. How far would participants go once the learner started expressing pain, eventually screaming for the teacher to stop, and then, disconcertingly, becoming silent. The only instruction the teachers were given from the experimenters, who were given only the authority is granted by wearing a white lab coat, was "You must continue." The answer was shocking, pun intended. Sixty-five percent of the participants went all the way to XXX (remember, by this point the learner had stopped screaming and only silence resonated from the adjoining room, suggesting that they had passed out or might have even died). The participants were normal, everyday people. They were not psychotic or cruel or even ill-tempered or weak. They simply followed orders.

Beliefs about power and the role of authority, the lack of opposition, the tendency to not challenge authority, and our seeming innate desire to go-along-to-get-along can obviously be extremely powerful motivators of behaviour and we underestimate these forces at our peril.

So, in the case on mental toughness, how can we say that our response to challenge is essentially "irrespective of the situation"? It's actually a relatively straightforward answer—our mental toughness allows us to be flexible in our approaches to different situations, but we have some core tendencies that do not really change significantly across situations. In our conversations, we all have verbal and nonverbal behaviours, tones, phrases, gestures, and so on that form a significant part of who we are in our social engagements. And these forms of communication are relatively stable—but are not 100% predictable in all settings. We communicate differently to our partners in public than we do in private. We communicate differently with young children than we do with teens. We communicate differently in the staff room than we do with clients. And so on. Yet our unique communication style essentially regresses toward a mean, which is to say that there is a core to our style that does not vary significantly. This is what "irrespective of the situation" means. Our mental toughness infiltrates our public and private personas; it centralizes our approach to new situations and allows us to set consistent goals (or not set goals at all, depending on our orientation toward goal setting in the first place).

Since we are unlikely to get fired at home, we may tend to be somewhat more, let's call it "honest" in our interactions with our family. If your teenager is not doing homework, you may become frustrated. You might raise your voice. You might even (gasp!) use "swears" (as the kids call those naughty words)! You may say/yell/scream something like "You NEVER do what you are asked and you ALWAYS ignore me!!!" All *honest*, not all of it *true*. If you engaged in such behaviour at work, you might be facing down your friendly HR rep before the end of the day. "Why do you NEVER do your homework?" is a common exclamation made by many well-intentioned but highly frustrated parents. Alternatively, perhaps you could try something like this: "Dearest Son/Daughter, fruit of my loins, core of my heart, my lovely one, I have become aware that the tasks assigned for you to complete, in partial satisfaction of the social contract in which you are engaged for your right to a proper education, have not, at this point, been completed. I am wondering, since you are such a smart and delightful person, *how* this could possibly be?" Less honest, yes? More rational, but not reflective of your emotions—which is where emotional control becomes an area of mental toughness that one needs to be aware of.

I have learned volumes from my clients over the years about what mental toughness is and how it plays perhaps THE central role in individual success and, unfortunately, in individual failure as well. But remember, we are all capable of learning, which is a key and central tenant of mental toughness; as such, failure is best construed here as being what many folks in 12-Step programs call an AFLO: "Another F**king Learning Opportunity"!

A Warning: The Dark Triad

It is concerning, but perhaps not particularly surprising, to know that mental toughness has been associated with what is referred to in personality psychology as the Dark Triad. Beyond sounding like a supervillain team from a Marvel comic book, the Dark Triad actually refers to the personality factors of Machiavelliianism, narcissism, and psychopathy. Like most aspects of personality, mental toughness is an area that can be bastardized into something dangerous and as such, requires a degree of governance which can keep it from being used for more nefarious means. While the relationship between mental toughness and the Dark Triad is not clear, the fact that there is a relationship at all is concerning and needs to be addressed.

The first component of the Dark Triad is Machiavellianism, taken from the Italian philosopher Niccolò Machiavelli, whose writings centred around themes of manipulation, deception, and an "ends-justifies-the-means" philosophy of achievement. As a character trait, Machiavellianism is associated with similar themes—manipulation, deception, a lack or moral principle, except that which allows for individual success at essentially any cost, as long as that cost is paid by others. It is absent a sense of morality and empathy, with a focus on a moral self-service. People exhibiting Machiavellianism traits tend to care little for those who may be victimized by their behaviours, and pursue their own interests with essentially no regard for those around them. Think of the evil corporation in any Disney film, or most of House Lannister from the *Game of Thrones* series.

Narcissism, on the other hand, is associated with a sense of superiority and grandiosity. People with this particular trait believe themselves to be better than others in most ways, and believe that they are entitled to whatever satisfied their desires. Think of Walter White from *Breaking Bad* or Gilderoy Lockhart from the *Harry Potter* series (played fantastically by Bryan Cranston and Kenneth Branagh, respectively).

Psychoticism is perhaps the most concerning of the Dark Triad, and likely also the most well-known due to its association in pop culture with any number of amoral sensation-seekers who engage in high degrees of risk-taking without thought of consequence for others. Psychoticism is often associated with Antisocial Personality Disorder (APD) or what is often referred to as psychopathy. Numerous examples from film and other media exist, but perhaps the most vivid example would be Dr. Hannibal Lecter from Thomas Harris' series of books about the cannibalistic psychiatrist and the subsequent uneven films and television series, including the iconic and excellent, if disturbing, *The Silence of the Lambs*. Dr. Lecter has no concern for anyone other than himself, and even his own sense of self-preservation is driven largely by an interest in seeing what kind of pain and humiliation he can impose upon others and still get away with.

How does the Dark Triad relate to mental toughness? Like most good things, mental toughness is a concept and set of characteristics that, in moderation, can be construed as being positive and admirable; it has a genuine ability to enhance one's life and the lives of those around us. But, like many things, taken too far, it can be disruptive and harmful. Expecting someone to have high mental toughness and then impose their own values on those around them is problematic at best. Some people simply do not benefit from the intensity associated with a great deal of mental toughness. People who are unrelentingly mentally tough can be simply exhausting. Their optimism can appear false and hollow.

High degrees of mental toughness are associated with characteristics that could under certain circumstances, be associated with the Dark Triad. For instance, it is not uncommon for mentally tough individuals to be highly committed to their goals. Might there be a temptation to use social manipulation and exploitative strategies to help them achieve these goals, especially when there is no trait to govern their behaviour? Might the goal-orientation of mental toughness drive one to use *any* strategy at their disposal to achieve that goal? Might they use their interpersonal confidence to overwhelm and silence others?

Unfortunately, the answer to these and similar questions is yes. Mental toughness can be mutated into an unhealthy, dominant, controlling set of characteristics that harm others. We need something to govern our mental toughness to keep us humble and morally in check.

While not directly addressed in the literature on mental toughness, I believe that ethics can provide this governor. Psychologists adhere to a set of ethical principles that serve to protect the public from any misuse of the knowledge or skills we have learned and practiced over decades. Our code of ethics in Canada, designed by the Canadian Psychology Association (CPA), are a set of guiding principles, not a set of Ten Commandments style "Thou shall" and "Thou shall not" directives. We are expected to, indeed required to, align ourselves with our professional ethical principles in a meaningful, consistent way. Having a code of ethics to which members must be accountable is a core principle of most professions and, it could be argued, ethics are a significant part of what makes a profession a "profession," not a "job." Ethics and morals, while certainly not synonymous, can help us set directives for ourselves in relation to mental toughness.

Mental toughness cannot be codified in the same way that happiness or greed cannot be codified. It is simply a construct, an idea, a way of being, and no specific set of rules can govern what makes one happy, what satisfies one's greed, nor how one can use their mental toughness. We need to negotiate our own set of morals, embedded in our communities, the culture around us, our religious and spiritual beliefs, or sense of common good, justness, fairness, equality and equity, and any number of associated factors. The discussion of what constitutes moral or even ethical behaviour falls well outside of the purview of this book, but it is worth thinking about in relation to the development of healthy mental toughness.

Toughness, Sensitivity, & Flexibility

It is critical to note—and I will be emphasizing this over and over through this book—that there is a tendency to look at mental toughness as being an optimal trait, and the corollary must be that the opposite must be true of those at the other end of the spectrum. For every mentally tough individual, there must be someone who is mentally weak. This is a dangerous misconception we need to eliminate.

Mental toughness largely falls along a continuum, and the range falls from "tough" not to "weak," but to "sensitive." Huge difference! Which would you prefer, a tough steak or one that is more tender? Would you prefer to work with a colleague who is inflexibly goal oriented, or with one who is more sensitive to the needs of the team or the project? Do you want a mentor who is so confident in their abilities that they seem impenetrable? Brené Brown's work on vulnerability and the misconception that vulnerability is a synonym for weakness is a great template for similar thinking in relation to mental sensitivity. Mental sensitivity can be—and *should* be—thought of as being the Yin to mental toughness's Yang. It makes me think of heavy metal and hard rock bands from the 80s.

Bear with me—you'll see the point in a moment.

Many hard rock and heavy metal bands in the 80s became popular due to their melodic but hard-edged sound. A few, such as Iron Maiden, Judas Priest, and eventually Megadeth and Slayer, maintained the hard-edged sound through their entire careers, well into to the 2000s. Others, including Def Leppard, Bon Jovi, Motley Crue, and Metallica, discovered that if they softened their edges a bit, they could reach a larger market. Thus, the "power ballad" became a ubiquitous part of the 80's music scene. Many accused these bands of selling out and being "wusses" (another Maritime-ism meaning "soft like ice cream"), but the sales suggested that they were on to something. And not all of the power-balladry of the 80s was horrible. Even noted heavy metal monsters Metallica played around with acoustic guitars and melodic warmth. Heavy metal, in its most rigid form, could be analogous to mental toughness (strong, powerful, dominant, perhaps lacking in humility) while the power balladeers could be analogous to mental sensitivity (somewhat softer, more introspective, perhaps a bit of more accessible).

Musical analogies notwithstanding, it is important to demythologize mental toughness as being macho, in line with the "rugged individualist" concept dominant in Western culture. By the same token, it is also important to demythologize mental sensitivity as being "weak" and, by extension, not as valuable as mental toughness. The common error often made is that mental toughness is a macho/masculine trait. This is a mischaracterization of the idea. Mental toughness is comprised of values such as perseverance, resilience, honesty, and compassion for self and others. While these are not "feminine" traits, they are not gendered by masculinity either. They simply *are*.

In the middle ground between toughness and sensitivity lies flexibility. The mentally flexible are those who adapt well to varying situations. Some leaders are excellent at being mentally flexible—they can read a room and adapt their behaviour accordingly. They can understand when to pursue a goal and when to let it go. They can take *calculated* risk. Yet even the mentally flexible benefit from coaching. To draw upon mental toughness' roots in sports psychology, it would be easy to argue that the best athletes tend to exhibit more extreme mental toughness, which provides them with the abilities necessary to excel into elite levels or performance. But it also leads them to be vulnerable to different stressors—what, for instance, does a professional athlete do when they lose? What happens when they have to retire from the sport that has been all consuming from them since early childhood? In particular, what do they do when they retire at 28 years of age, or 35? They are often poorly suited for life after their sport because their mental toughness has been unidirectional. The same applies to elite-level soldiers—military service being another one of the areas in which mental toughness research has its roots. Many soldiers who train extensively and serve in combat exhibit considerable mental toughness. But upon entering civilian life, they find themselves ill-prepared for the day-to-day life of living in a noncombat community. Their routine and structure, the intensity of combat are all lost, leaving many service members at a loss in terms of how to adapt to their new reality. It is such situations that mental flexibility can become a powerful ally. Mental flexibility can be an area to which one can strive without feeling pressure to be the "best" at anything, not feeling like a miserable failure because you are "too sensitive," nor need to be a paragon of mental toughness at all times.

Mental Sensitivity

So, what of those of us who are not Navy SEALS, professional athletes, corporate magnates, or traditional leaders in our fields. What of those of us who are perhaps a bit more risk averse, those who avoid goal setting in an effort to limit our sense of failure? Are people who are not mentally tough essentially weak?

Not at all.

Mental sensitivity stands at the opposite end of the scale from mental toughness, but this placement on a scale does not make being more mentally sensitive an area of weakness. Mental sensitivity is best described as being sensitive to risk and challenge. It refers more to vulnerability than weakness. Brené Brown does an excellent job of differentiating vulnerability from weakness—vulnerability, Brown argues, is actually its own form of strength that takes immense courage. The same is true for mental sensitivity, which is best defined as exercising considerable caution in approaching new situations and a hesitancy in taking on new challenges without first examining a wide range of possible outcomes.

The downside to mental sensitivity, of course, if the potential loss of experience faced by those who take no real risks; those who get caught up in risk analysis and who can, under extreme situations, become paralyzed by fear and anxiety about new possibilities. They can tend to look at the future and the world in general as being hostile and as such, do their best to avoid risk and challenge. While they can, as a result, be providers of a great deal of stability and routine, they can also become frustrated with their own lack of progress, while yet others can become frustrated with them when the mentally sensitive do not truly engage with the excitement of possibility.

One of the central points of separation between mental toughness and mental sensitivity on any of the 4Cs is the direction of the effort. For the mentally tough, the energy often appears to be focused outward, toward others and the external world. There is an effort to have an impact that goes beyond the individual. On the other hand, the mentally sensitive tend to be somewhat more focused on the inner world, upon the self (for better and worse). People who would be best described as being mentally sensitive tend to have a heightened awareness of their own performance (or the lacking quality thereof) and their own capacities to contribute to the world around them. However, their focus, if negative, can lead to withdrawal, symptoms of depression and anxiety, and a general fear of the external world. They may feel that, due to whatever their perceived flaws, they will experience failure and, in extreme cases, identify as being failures. However, the reality is that the mentally sensitive can have tremendous positive insights into themselves and others and potentially can make positive changes both in their own lives and in the lives of others. They are not destined to experience only anxiety and fear; rather, they can use their natural sense of trepidation to enhance their own performance and to set more realistic and achievable goals than those at the other end of the spectrum.

An excellent analogy for the highly self-aware, inward-focused individual who may not feel like they have any significant impact on the world around them comes from art. Many artists, regardless of medium, are inward-focused, highly aware of their inner world and they find joy through expressing their inner awareness through their art. The stereotype of the starving artist, the creator who is highly focused on artistic expression through music, painting, sculpture, writing, photography, and other media, may have, at its core, a kernel of truth. The artist who creates with no real concern of criticism or commercial outcomes is driven by an internal motivation of expression of creativity. It could be argued that such individuals, and art history is full of exemplars of such individuals, are actually quite common in the artistic community. An interesting question posed by Neil Strauss, a journalist who has interviewed many of the biggest names in the modern music industry, is as follows: If you could create a piece of art that would be your masterpiece, your *Starry Night*, your *Sgt. Pepper*, your *War and Peace*, your *David*, but no one would ever have the opportunity to experience it—for instance, once created, you had to bury it so that it could never be seen by anyone, ever, would you still do it? Or, to make this hypothetical even more complex, your masterpiece is hidden for all time, but less interesting and lower quality work that you have accomplished would be readily available to the world, would you want that art to be seen by others, who invariably would think of you as a lesser or, at best, moderate talent?

People who fall along the more mentally sensitive range might respond quickly by saying that the fact that they had created a masterpiece is enough. Their success is not measured by the evaluations by others. However, it could also be the case that their trepidation about the perception of their art as being, at best, "okay," might prohibit them from creating in the first place. However, the truly mentally sensitive would be more likely to create works that would not be evaluated by others out of fear of negative evaluations and criticisms. They may create something beautiful, only to hide it behind a curtain, looking at it only by themselves late at night when no one else can be around to possibly criticize their work.

Not all who are mentally sensitive, however, would take the risk associated with creating a truly brave piece of work. Their self-awareness can be so heightened that they are uncomfortable in taking on any risk, regardless of how potentially successful they could be. The undiscovered country of the future inhibits their willingness to explore fully their options. Again there is always an upside and in the case of the mentally sensitive, a part of their profile is that they tend to be stable, predictable, and agents of stability in an uncertain and unpredictable world.

Mentally sensitive individuals tend to be comparatively strong in regard to sensing the mood of those around them. They can be natural empaths, in part due their own interior sensitivity. They have the ability to sense the mood of a room and respond accordingly. Since they tend to be more inward-focused, they may not feel comfortable in working to change the mood of the room, but their natural sensitivity makes them a powerful ally to those who are more outward directed, especially those who lean toward being more mentally tough, who may struggle with both reading a room accurately and doing so empathetically. However, if a mentally sensitive person can clearly articulate to a mentally tough individual the nature of the mood in a group, the mentally tough individual can be effective in modifying the nature of the group's mood. Such a dynamic can be found in many corporations and leadership groups, in which the team leader makes the final decisions, but wisely relies heavily on their mentally sensitive advisors as to how best navigate a path forward that facilitates a way into any new initiatives, especially when those initiatives require emotional change.

Mental Flexibility

Most of us would agree that Goldilocks was a bit of a princess. On one hand, I empathize with her as we share an affinity for inappropriate break and entry. On the other, though, she barges into a stranger's house and immediately starts to complain about the temperature of the food that most certainly has *not* been served to her, then about the quality of her unknowing host's mattresses. However, she eventually does find the bowl of porridge and the mattress that are just right, neither too hot/cold nor too hard/soft. "Just right," she says dopily as she drifts off, unaware of the three bears coming home to discover some whiny Paris Hilton-esque human drooling in her sleep upon the Bear family's best pillow. As much as Goldilocks is a rather horrible person, her search for "Just Right" is one that I believe many of us could empathize with. In mental toughness terms, Goldilocks and the rest of us search to find ourselves in the realm of being mentally flexible.

Mental flexibility is where most of us lie in the normal cure of mental toughness. Neither too sensitive, not too tough. Just right. We can, on average, be mentally flexible while still exhibiting significant mental toughness in some areas and considerable mental sensitivity in others. In fact, it could easily be argued that mental flexibility is in many ways superior to being mentally tough. While mental toughness provides us with the capacity to engage with challenging situations with optimism and excitement, it can also lead us to taking a higher degree of risk than is necessary, which obviously can cause us unwarranted problems. In the same vein, our emotional control can be too rigid, which is associated with being mentally tough, making us somewhat unreadable to others, which can be problematic in almost any social situation in which genuineness is valued.

Presuming that we can fall anywhere along the mentally tough continuum in relation to the normal curve, the mentally flexible are, for the most part, in the average range. Being average in contemporary Western society is unfortunately associated with the risk of being viewed as not being special. Specialness is highly valued in Western society—people strive to be unique and different while at the same time find comfort in being largely invisible. Many, if not most of us, would be almost offended at the idea of being considered to be average is to insult many of us (actually, most of us, since statistically, most of us *are* average!). I would be willing to bet that some readers right now, having read this paragraph, are feeling a sense of defensiveness. "How can I be average? Average is for others, *I* am unique and special." Well, of *course* you are unique and special! But you are simultaneously statistically average. So am I. But being average is not so bad. We are all in good company.

Mental flexibility suggests that, beyond being average, that we can adapt to varying situations effectively. While mental toughness applies irrespective of the situation, the *degree* to which we engage our mental toughness can change based on situational variables. For instance, most people have somewhat different social personas that apply in different situations. They interact with co-workers differently than they do family members and differently yet again with friends. As a lecturer, I interact with my students differently than I do my counselling clients (for which I am sure both groups are quite happy—I doubt my counselling clients would enjoy a 3-hour lecture while my students would similarly find an emotional therapy session to be rather uncomfortable). And I act differently yet again with my family than I do with either students or clients . . . or colleagues, or relative strangers, or extended family, and so on. Yet at my core, I am intransigently me. Even if you fell along the 50th percentile across the board on all of the subcomponents of the 4Cs, meaning that your performance was as high as higher than 50% of the population upon whom the MTQ was normed, there is still a statistical range of error that allows you to be unique. So celebrate your mental flexibility!

Summary and What Lies Ahead

Mental toughness is a contemporary spin on an old concept, but its practical implications are impressive. We have the capacity not only to evaluate and assess individual and team mental toughness profiles, and we can also develop interventions to enhance our performance using mental toughness principles. Since, as noted, the development of mental toughness requires active engagement, and you were promised activities through this book to make you an active participant in the development of your own mental toughness, I have a question for you to consider. Think on this: **Who are you on your worst day?** In the criminally underrated 1999 Mike Judge film *Office Space*, Peter, the lead character who is facing an existential crisis as a result of his mindless job and meaningless relationships, says to his therapist, "So I was sitting in my cubicle today, and I realized, ever since I started working, every single day of my life has been worse than the day before it. So that means that every single day that you see me, that's me on the worst day of my life." The therapist asks Peter if this means that today, right now, is the worst day of his life. Peter replies glumly, "Yeah." The therapist responds with a moment of therapeutic honesty, "Wow. That's messed up."

We've all had bad days, some worse than others, and certainly some of us can recall what we could clearly say was the worst day of our lies. Often, trauma is a part of that recollection, and we know how emotionally powerful trauma memories can be. Our reaction to trauma also tells us a lot about ourselves. I would not be so glib as to suggest that mental toughness is the answer to trauma. Trauma is a complex, powerful, and certainly unique experience to everyone who experiences it, and there is no single approach to dealing with it. However, we can learn from our responses to trauma. It is best, however, if our learning about trauma response is co-facilitated with another, someone who can keep us from feeling guilt when such feelings arise, as is often the case in trauma—we blame ourselves for what happened. The question, though, is not necessarily about trauma. It is about our more general worst days, those days in which we are not firing on all cylinders, days where our energy ebbs, our frustration is high, our irritability overpowering, days when our ability to keep things together falls apart. Who are we then?

A recent worst day for me, to provide an example, involved an unexpected early start to the day due to anxiety-provoked sleeplessness, followed by a lengthy day of counselling in which I felt I was just about 10 degrees off target all day, two staff quitting for different, but fair reasons (one had to commit to her research obligations and could not continue her clinical work and the other's partner had been relocated out of town, so they had to move), and, on top of that, a blustery grey snow was falling outside my office window all day, making me slightly dread the drive home (which is usually a quite enjoyable part of my day as a switch of gears from psychologist to regular-guy-who-happens-to-be-a-psychologist). And, not surprisingly, on that drive home, my little SUV (purchased just a month earlier when my old vehicle blew its engine in the middle of nowhere, British Colombia, which was the last worst-day-lately I'd had until this specific day) was rear-ended by a monster truck, a not-uncommon sight on the wintery roads of Calgary, driven by a distracted, but very nice gentleman. After exchanging information, I got home and collapsed, Archie-Bunker style, into a recliner in our living room and just started at the wall. "What a complete crap day. I hate that I try to do all the right things and all I get are troubles." You could almost hear the mournful blues guitar in the background. "What did I do to deserve such an absolute crap day?," I wondered aloud and somewhat passively to my wife. Quickly, she responded, "Did you stop to think that maybe it wasn't YOU? Maybe—just maybe—it's not always about YOU? The dude who hit you, it was his fault, so his insurance costs will go up. One of your colleagues will have to forego employment to get her research done and the other has to pack up her life because her husband got relocated. Your clients received, at best, your 90% best effort. Is it possible that maybe they had worse days than you?"

Consider my thinking reframed, from victim to, well, chagrined husband. However, I was then able to refocus on my mental toughness to think about things more positively. So, think on it a bit. **Who are you on your worst day?** The follow-up question, of course, is, since the day itself cannot change or bend to your will, **how could you engage your mental toughness to get through it?**

Chapter 2

The 4Cs

An Exemplar of Mental Toughness

Terry Fox dipped a shoe, tied tightly onto his prosthetic foot at the end of a stick of wood that was his artificial limb, into the Atlantic Ocean in St. John's, Newfoundland, on April 20, 1980. But this was no normal sneaker on no normal stick of wood. It was the terminus of his prosthetic leg, which he had been wearing since he lost his right leg to cancer in 1977. The prosthetic was rudimentary, even comical, by contemporary comparison. Made of wood, leather, and a plastic cup and rusting metal hinge, it was a bulky, heavy, inflexible appendage that made Terry's run appear to be a two-step hop-gait. But appearances were deceiving—when he ran, the effort was double that of a runner with two biological legs intact. The dipping of his sneaker and leg into the cold and grey waters that morning was a symbol of a starting point of an intense journey, something Terry had been dreaming of ever since reading a simple magazine article while in the hospital following the amputation of his leg.

That day in St. John's was the first day of Terry's Marathon of Hope, a planned run across the second largest country in the world in an effort to raise money to support cancer research.

Terry had been an elite athlete through his high school and university years, his passion for all athletics eventually being focused on his hunger for basketball. He had earned an athletic scholarship to Simon Fraser University, despite being only 5'10" and not being a particularly skilled player. He was, however, tenacious. His high school coach recommended him almost solely on his character, not his physical attributes or his skills on the court. When Terry was diagnosed with cancer and the treatment led to the leg amputation, his coach dropped by his hospital room, leaving behind a sports magazine with an article about a one-legged runner who was starting to complete in marathons. Idea taken—and then some.

Terry's Marathon of Hope involved running a marathon. Every day. On one leg. Across Canada. To raise money for research for an incurable disease. He actively refused any personal financial compensation and, in a tribute to his character, he refused potential sponsors from capitalizing on the Marathon. He used Adidas sneakers that were provided to him, but did not act as spokesperson for the designer. He used a Ford Econoline van, but never shilled for Ford.

The Marathon came to an end outside of Thunder Bay, Ontario, approximately 5,373 km from St. Johns after only 143 days, and only after Terry was again diagnosed with cancer, this time in his lungs. Perhaps his legacy could be summarized by his famous citation for the reason for taking on this massive undertaking in the first place: "I believe in miracles. I have to." After his death from the lung cancer that stopped his Marathon, schools and communities across Canada and eventually, around the world, have held annual Terry Fox Day runs every September, resulting the hundreds of millions of dollars being raised in support of the search for a cure for cancer.

I could stop there and say, "All you need to know about mental toughness can be learned from Terry Fox" and I wouldn't be far off. He exhibited immense constitutional strength, driven by passion and, many would say, sheer stubbornness. Terry Fox used mental toughness as an expert chef uses salt and pepper—he, like everyone, has access to it, everyone knows how to use it, but there is something about the way a professional uses it that amplifies all flavors.

As noted previously, mental toughness could best be described using the "4C" model—Control, Challenge, Commitment, and Confidence. Fox had each of these in abundance, but here we enter the nature/nurture debate full-on. Are these internal, intrinsic, inborn qualities, or are they learned through experience and through our environments? I would argue that mental toughness is a combination of innate/inborn characteristics that are "battle-tested" through our environments, not only in childhood, but on a day-to-day basis. It could be argued that Terry Fox's exceptional example of mental toughness was a combination of his genetic endowment combined with the nature of his upbringing. By all accounts, he was raised in a competitive but loving family that encouraged the best from all family members, parents included. This upbringing, combined with his genetic endowment of an athletic body, could explain some, but not all, of Terry's mental toughness. There are always intangibles.

As we discuss each of the 4Cs, keep in mind that your journey is not yet compete—you may feel that you perhaps lack in a certain area, or perhaps are too rigid in another. You have a lot of experiences that you have yet to encounter and while past behaviour may be an excellent predictor of future behaviour, it is by no means the *only* predictor. As humans, we are innately driven to evolve and adapt—to steal from a well-known quote from the U.S.

Marine Corps, we are designed to "Improvise, Adapt, and Overcome." The 4Cs provide us with guideposts as to how best grow and develop ourselves and others into more consistently mentally tough individuals.

The 4Cs of Mental Toughness: Control, Commitment, Confidence, and Challenge

The 4Cs, as conceptualized here, are not presented in any particular order. There is no formal hierarchy of quality or importance of any specific component of mental toughness in comparison to any other components. That said, it is important to note that each component is a critical aspect of mental toughness. Perhaps the best way to think of the 4Cs is as each component as being part of a recipe, perhaps for cake (because who doesn't like a good cake!). Eggs are important, as is flour. You need both, among other ingredients, in different balance, in order to make a successful cake. Try making a cake without flour. Enjoy your baked goop! Mental toughness follows a generally similar model—you need certain ingredients to achieve success, but the ingredients can somewhat vary according to taste.

Control

Control is subdivided into life control and emotional control. Described in further detail in Chapter 3, life control refers to the degree to which life is under our control. Life control underlies all other areas of mental toughness, for without it, we are passive agents of life, having no more control over our environment than a sportscaster does over the results of a competition. They can describe what is happening, but the events on the field are beyond their control. On the other hand, there are those who believe that they can essentially control almost all aspects of their lives and, in some cases, the lives of others. The issue, of course, for people who have such views is that rarely do we have total control and even if we do have considerable control, we may not be able to control other aspects of our situation. "The more you tighten your grip," Princess Leia told Darth Vader and Grand Moff Takin in *Star Wars*, "the more star systems will slip from your fingers." Presumption of control can be as harmful as not having a sense of control at all.

Emotional control, on the other hand, refers to one's ability to mask emotions from others when needed. It also incorporates one's ability to affect the emotions of others. Again, a balance is optimal in most situations.

People high in emotional control may appear to be remote, distant, and disengaged—possibly good qualities in a surgeon (do you want a highly emotional surgeon? Maybe—but I like my surgeons to be as "Spock-like" as possible when in the operating theatre!). On the other hand, some people clearly telegraph their emotional state—it's always right there, on their face, in their tone, in their body language. There is a certain honesty in those who are mentally sensitive in relation to emotional control. There is no question where they stand and where you stand in relation to their emotions. But, there can also be some degree of unpredictability. Moods can change, alarming those in the individual's social circle. John McEnroe, the volatile genius of tennis, would be perhaps a good example of an individual with relatively limited emotional control. In many ways, his emotionality made him a better player (though it could be argued that has really just made him famous for yelling at court judges, not for his tennis skills). Again, balance is worth striving for—it is important for us to be emotionally vulnerable and expressive, but we also need to be aware of situational variables in which we may need to mediate our emotional responses. Rolling your eyes and heavy sighing may be an accurate expression of your emotions, but if you are in conflict with your partner, it is unlikely that doing so will be helpful!

Commitment

The belief that we are active agents in our own lives is only a part of our endowment of mental toughness. It does us good to know that we are capable of controlling certain aspects of our lives and the world around us, but it is not enough. We need to *do* something about ourselves and the world around us! Commitment is perhaps well-described as being similar to Greg Reid's conceptualization of "stickability," described in his book *Stickability: The Power of Perseverance*. It is the human capacity to set and achieve goals, even under challenging situations. In regard to mental toughness, it is subdivided into two characteristics: goal orientation and achievement orientation.

Goal orientation is the ability to identify and set goals for ourselves. Such goals can be personal (i.e., "I will lose 10 lbs. by Summer Holiday," "I will drink less alcohol," "I will reach out to my friends more consistently," and so on), professional ("I will take part in professional development to enhance my skills," "I will make junior VP by my 30th birthday," and so on), but can also be in almost any area of human functioning. In my work with students with complex learning needs, goals are often oriented around academic skill development, social skills, executive functioning, and so on.

For the gardener, the goal may be to raise competition-worthy orchids (or perhaps just a nice little herb garden—a goal is a goal!). As will be discussed in later chapters, **there are those folks who are highly motivated by goals and those who may find goals to intimidating. Think for a moment— which are you?**

Achievement orientation is the vehicle to goal orientation's pilot. Goal orientation tells us where we are going and to some extent, how to get there. Achievement orientation is the mechanism that helps us achieve the goals we have set. Again, some folks are highly achievement oriented, putting in plans and making every effort to achieve their goals. Those who are not achievement oriented may have excellent goals, but their efforts to achieve those goals are often lacking or may be inconsistent. I think of the classic image of the 30-year-old, sitting in their parent's basement, playing video games and smoking enough weed to stone Snoop Dog. This same individual may have great goals—designing a new video game, opening a marijuana shop, going back to school to finish their undergraduate degree. But, that's work for tomorrow. Alternatively, they may indeed have positive goals and every intent of achieving them but become distracted easily or may find themselves partially completing many goals but not fully realizing their final objectives.

In both cases, commitment is a central component of mental toughness that acts to set direction and ignite the fuel to help us get there. **But ... even with a destination and appropriate fuel and an engine to get us there, what happens when, invariably, a barrier pops up? How do you deal with barriers to your goals?**

Challenge

Barriers are obstacles to our progress, at least temporarily. These barriers can be managed through the next component of mental toughness, Challenge. Challenge simply refers to how we see and adapt to challenges. A challenge is, at its core, anything that could be perceived as being out of the ordinary that requires us to "stretch" ourselves. It is what happens before resilience; without challenge, there is no need for resilience. It is also similar to Suzanne Kobasa's concept of hardiness, which incorporates resilience and tenacity and flexibility into how we adapt to—and overcome— challenges. Challenge is comprised of two orientations (described in detail in Chapter 5): risk orientation and learning orientation.

Risk orientation refers to our capacity to see challenge as positive risk, and the ability to approach risk with enthusiasm and openness. Risk, in this case, does not imply jumping out of perfectly good airplanes, even with a parachute (although it sort of does, too), but incorporates even the small day-to-day challenges we face in myriad situations. Microdecisions entail risk. Even a simple task—should I have toast for breakfast or should I have eggs—carries risk. What happens if, when making eggs, you find yourself pushed for time? It's easy to bring toast along with you in the car. Eggs, not so much (if you doubt me, give it a go and let me know how it turns out!). The blue tie or the red one? What if the blue clashes with your blazer? Should I have that afternoon coffee? Will it keep me up all night? Risk, risk, risk, and not a parachute in sight!

Learning orientation is, in a way, Part Two of risk. If we face a challenge or take a risk, what happens when things don't work out (invariably, not everything will work out 100% of the time, except in Hollywood and even then, it's not a given—the opening 3 minutes of Pixar's *Up* will shatter the belief that everything works out the way we want . . .). Do we learn from our mistakes? Do we have the capacity to observe our own behaviours and reflect upon what works and what doesn't? Those who have a learning orientation rarely make the same mistake twice. They may make *different* mistakes, but at least they learn in a "one-and-done" manner.

People who are less learning oriented may need many lessons before they truly learn. One of the frustrations I hear from teachers and parents in relation to working with impulsive students is, "I *just* went over this with them yesterday—why don't they get it???" In many cases, teachers personalize misbehaviours of their students when in fact, these are simply impulsive kids who may not be very learning oriented. They know what to say after they have done whatever it was they did to upset the teacher, but they may lack true insight into their behaviour. They have heard "How many times do I need to tell you to sit down?!!" a thousand times (so, there's the answer, teacher—"1001 times, Miss"). They may not really learn, though. At least, not until it becomes part of their own goal orientation and their sense of life control adapts to encompass the reality that they actually *can* control their own behaviour.

Confidence

In terms of mental toughness, confidence refers to our capacity to see through to the end of those goals that we have set, despite challenges and varying degrees of control. Confidence, in this context, is the ability to say "I expect the worse, I hope for the best, I plan accordingly." The Scottish poet Robbie Burns famously wrote, "The best laid schemes o' mice an' men/ Gang aft a-gley." I can say, with confidence, that many of our schemes have gang a-gley aft indeed! But it has not been for a lack of ability or inter-personal capacities; rather, my personal a-gleying has largely been due to my confidence in my abilities in general, and my interpersonal confidence in particular, often not being up to the challenge.

Confidence in abilities, the first of the two components of confidence in mental toughness, is essentially a form of self-esteem. It asks, "Are you worthwhile, and are your skills valuable?" People with strong confidence in their abilities rarely require external affirmations—they just *know* that they have skills and abilities that are valuable and worthwhile. The upside to positive confidence in abilities is that these folks rarely question their deci-sions and are quick to share their knowledge or skill set. The downside, of course, is that often one's confidence in abilities may exceed the abilities themselves. A know-it-all-who-knows-nothing. A balanced confidence in abilities, accompanied by *actual* abilities, makes one a valuable contributor to success.

Interpersonal confidence, the second component related to mental toughness's conceptualization of confidence, refers not to interpersonal *skills*, nor does it suggest introversion or extraversion in the traditional sense. One can be quite an extrovert in many ways, but still lack interper-sonal confidence. Interpersonal confidence refers to the ability to deal con-fidently with challenges from others. They can be introverts, to be clear, but the two are not characteristics that necessarily be shared simultaneously. People who are mentally tough in relation to interpersonal confidence feel comfortable to accept the challenges from others, and to offer their own challenges to others. In a staff meeting, they can appear to be domineering on one hand, but positive and engaging on the other. They tend not to be easily intimidated in social settings. Those who may have lower interper-sonal confidence may be socially adept, but may not feel comfortable with conflict. They can be natural peacemakers who act to avoid conflict as much as possible. In a team, these are the folks who can go for years without saying anything at all in a staff meeting, but work fastidiously behind the scenes in more comfortable social engagements.

My own confidence in abilities is moderate, but my interpersonal con-fidence is rather low. Unless it is a critical issue, I will not share my thoughts or feelings in a semistructured environment. So, how do I manage teaching large university classes (or even small ones)? How do I engage with dozens of clients each week? How can I do media appearances on local television news programs? Simple—I fake it! I'm guessing a lot of my fellow "low interpersonal confidence" folks are out there thinking to themselves, "Wait, what? Faking it is okay?" You bet!

Mental Toughness and You

Now would be a good time to reflect upon your questionnaire results from Chapter 1. You have learned a little about mental toughness and have a better idea as to what it involves. **How are you feeling about your responses to the questionnaire now that you are a bit more informed? Has anything changed?**

I hope that you will keep a few things in mind in relation to your "profile" as we proceed through the following chapters. First, as noted, the measure itself is a simple, informal, psychometrically unsound questionnaire that is designed simply to get you thinking about yourself in relation to mental toughness. Second, even if (and it is a huge *if*!) the personal profile were accurate, and you had some areas to work on, well, good! We all have areas to work on! I remember working with one school administrator who was absolutely delighted to have completed the MTQ Plus to learn that she was at the "top" of the scale for all areas of mental toughness. "Awesome!" she exclaimed. "I'm exactly what I thought I would be and that's perfect because I am a leader and good leaders are mentally tough in all areas, right?" She caught me shaking my head slowly and sadly. "Right?" she asked again, uncertainly. "Nope," I said. "You might want to reflect upon how your staff see you—how the parents see you. And, most importantly, how the kids see you."

She paused and reflected for a moment. "They probably think I'm a real bitch. I set unrealistic goals for staff, I am a know-it-all to parents, and I'm a rigid control freak to the kids." Her self-reflection was swift and harsh, but not completely untrue, and we worked on identifying goals that could help her become somewhat more mentally flexible. For instance, she identified a trusted member of her senior leadership team who was not concerned about the power differential, so had no concerns about challenging the administrator when she pushed too hard. The team member was enlisted to simply ask one question of the administrator when needed: "Is this goal/statement/task necessary for the students or is it necessary for *you*?"

As we proceed through these chapters, keep this in mind—mental toughness is a trait, but one that is flexible and open to change. So, let the change begin!

Chapter 3

Control

Control is perhaps best likened to the psychological construct of "self-efficacy"—our beliefs about our capacities and abilities to do things that can help us achieve our goals. Control, to be clear, is not about the control of others, nor is it a narrow reflection of self-control (which is really just a very basic human characteristic of behavioural inhibition). It is actually quite complex in many ways, but ultimately, control in the sense of mental toughness reflects our abilities to understand the factors that we are capable of controlling, those that are beyond our control, and our ability to control the expression of our emotional responses.

Control and Self-Efficacy

Albert Bandura, a well-known Canadian psychologist, is perhaps best known for his experiments in observational and learned aggression in children, in which kids watched adult models beat up inflatable clown dolls, known commercially as Bobo Dolls. And if anything in the world ever really needed to be whaled upon, it's an inflatable clown doll! As a person living with *coulrophobia* (an intense, irrational fear of clowns), I would happily beat down on Bobo (once I stopped screaming in terror). Bandura's initial work was focused on observational social learning and the results were quite interesting. Children who observed adults lay a beating on the Bobo Doll (which they watched on a recorded video) were far more likely to beat down the Bobo Doll when given a chance, especially compared to those who watched other adults play in a nonviolent way with the doll. His findings here have, like many areas of research in social psychology in particular, been misinterpreted over the years, extending to a hysteria in the 1990s about the role of violent video games and films as being casual factors in school shootings. Again, these relationships were correlational, not causal (after all, is it not likely that those with violent or aggressive tendencies might be drawn to violent imagery in any case, not that such imagery *causes* violent or aggressive behaviour? Not to mention the fact that the vast majority of those who actively game do not act in aggressive or violent ways at all). In any case, Bandura's work had a secondary and, ultimately, perhaps more interesting focus.

Bandura also worked extensively in the area of self-efficacy, which is not, as is often incorrectly assumed, the same as self-esteem. Self-efficacy refers to one's beliefs about their ability to succeed in different circumstances. Self-esteem, on the other hand, is basically how we feel about ourselves, irrespective of our actual skills, abilities, or successes. One can have a great deal of self-esteem but little self-efficacy and one can have significant self-efficacy but low to moderate self-esteem. Self-efficacy is in one part learned through observation of others and how they perform and in one part based on personal experience.

Have you had success in a certain area in the past? If so, that success will likely breed enhanced self-efficacy in that task and, more than likely, other similar tasks. If you make a grilled cheese sandwich and it turns out to be not bad, you'll likely try again with the hopes of improving on your sandwich-making skills. What if, on the other hand, you mess up? Such things are possible. I have destroyed many grilled cheese sandwiches by burning the bread, putting on too much—or too little—butter, choosing a cheese not designed for such purposes (under no circumstances should you try making a grilled dry-grated parmesan cheese sandwich). Failure can breed a sense of incompetence and poor self-efficacy, making it exponentially more difficult to try again. Therein lies the challenge of control.

Self-efficacy is a core component of mental toughness in general and control in particular. Here is a quick example:

> *Linus is interested in dating Sally. Sally has heretofore shown no interest in Linus except (say it with me) "as a friend." He does not like being in the friend zone and wants to pursue a more romantic relationship with Sally. This is not the first time Linus has been in this situation. He consistently finds himself in the friend zone with women in his life. This time, though, he wants to escape that zone and enter the boyfriend zone. In the past, he has been slow to express his desires to his female friends, especially those to whom he is attracted, primarily because he gets nervous around women he views as being sexually attractive. By the time he feels comfortable expressing his romantic desires, he has already been their confidante as they talk about the other guys they have been dating. So with Sally, he wants to try something different.*

Now—YOU play the confidante. What would you suggest that Linus do? Based on his history, his self-efficacy related to the pursuit of romantic relationships is likely low. He may view his previous experiences as being failures out of his control. After all, he cannot force someone to be interested in him (despite what many rom-coms try to suggest otherwise). Additionally, regardless of Linus' feelings toward Sally, if she makes it clear that she is not interested in him in any romantic way, Linus must accept that fact as reality. He cannot force the issue, nor should he attempt to do so. Far too many men think that they can push their way through the "friend-zone," and in doing so, become all that is wrong with male-centric power and control, what has come to be known as *toxic masculinity.*

How can you go about helping Linus enhance his self-efficacy and take the risk of asking Sally out on a date, while also helping him prepare of the possibility that he has a good chance of having to accept "No" as a perfectly legitimate response?

In this, and most, cases, self-efficacy can be viewed as a component of control. Control determines the beliefs we have about ourselves when confronted with challenges. If we have a sense of control, we are more apt to view challenges as having a component of opportunity and to learn from mistakes. On the other hand, if we do not have a sense of control, we tend to view the world as happening *to* us, and we view ourselves as being passive agents in our own lives. If the latter, we can easily find ourselves in deep trouble, existentially speaking (and who doesn't love speaking existentially!). If we have limited confidence in our autonomy and control in our own lives, and we view ourselves as being acted upon by the world, life quickly loses meaning. Why do *anything* if life is just going to happen to us regardless of our beliefs, attitudes, actions, and relationships?

One of the more worrying trends in contemporary society has been the emergence of "incels," literately, involuntary celibates. These are men who harbour great anger toward women because they feel that they are "nice guys" who have been rejected by women. Their attitudes are full of hate and anger, and often manifests as violent and aggressive behaviour and language. These people lack a sense of control, feeling that the world not only happens to them but somehow owes them something. The concept of control suggests that the world owes us nothing and any meaning we find in the world is a creation of our own. Therefore, we can contribute in a meaningful way—doing so is an active choice—and the results of our contributions may or may not be perceived as being positive. But at the very least, since we are largely in control of our behaviours and our ways of thinking, the sense of control itself is what is important.

In Linus' case, you as confidante could encourage him to try something different. After all, his experiences with Sally are unique. It's a relationship, like all human relationships, that has its own specific qualities. While combining certain amounts of certain chemicals under certain circumstances will invariably result in the same results, the same cannot be said for human interactions. We never really know how things will interact. So, let's see if Linus could do an experiment in his approach with Sally. Maybe rather than starting with the confidante role, but still maintaining his integrity, perhaps he could be a bit more assertive in expressing his hopes and desires. Who knows, it may work! It may not, but again, making the attempt is not necessarily a failure, it is an opportunity to learn what does not tend to work and refine his approach.

The Language of Control

It's actually fairly easy to spot people with a high sense of control in their lives. Listen for the language they use. It is often full of sentences containing phases such as "I can do it . . .," "Leave it with me . . .," "I'll give it a go!," and so on. A lack of control is characterized by statements such as "I can do it, *if*. . .," "I'll see what I can do . . .," "I'm not sure I can, but I guess if I *have* to . . ." You know people who say these things—perhaps YOU are a person who says such things. **Really pay attention to your language over the next few days—** when you are asked to do something at work, at school, at home, what is the nature of your response? Is it confident or cautionary? Is it based on belief that you can do something that makes a difference, or do you feel that even if you try, you are unlikely to make any significant difference? Do you use "will" in relation to doing things, or do you find yourself using "if" language?

The tonal shift between expressions of positive engagement compared to cautionary and conditional language is something I see in my clients very frequently. Those with goals of true self-enhancement tend to be people who use the language of positive engagement ("I'll give it a go!"). These folks tend to do "best" in therapy in the sense that they believe that they are actively engaged in their own successes (and failures). After all, that is why they are in therapy in the first place—to enhance their functioning, to be the best version of themselves that they can be. On the other hand, those who use conditional language ("I'll see what I can do . . .") tend to have lower self-efficacy. Indeed, many of these folks are not in therapy of their own volition; rather, they may have been strongly encouraged or, as is often the case with teens, been pushed into therapy by well-intended parties who may not see that not everyone is ready for therapy. However, once these folks with limited self-efficacy are in the therapist's office, we work extensively on developing a sense of control, even over small things. More on how we do that when we discuss goal orientation later on, but for now, a simple technique to engage control in someone for whom a sense of control is lacking, is to focus on even rudimentary and sometimes silly examples of situations in which they do indeed have control.

I recently worked with a grade 2 student who was highly anxious and would refuse to contribute in class, even though she had a trusting relationship with her teacher and was well-liked by her peers. She said that she would not ask questions because that would make her look stupid and she would not give answers for fear of being wrong and, again, looking stupid. So I simply asked, "You must think that I'm really stupid then?" She paused and looked at me, somewhat confused. "No . . . you seem nice and, like, smart and stuff." I accepted the compliment and said, "But most of what I have done with you since we met is ask questions, and if asking questions makes a person stupid, then I must be really dumb!" She laughed. And then said "Ooohhh! You got me!" So we worked on that conversation to facilitate her willingness to ask at least one question per day and work up from there, a plan she agreed with, in no small part because she was also rule-follower and if the rule was "Ask a question," then she would do it. But in challenging her belief that asking questions made one stupid, we opened up a pathway to a new goal.

Do We *Really* Have Control?

One example of developing a sense of control would be thinking about our entertainment viewing and listening habits. For instance, what kind of music do you like? What did you listen to on the way to work? What do you listen to when working independently? And what happens if a song you despise starts playing? Do you sit passively and "let it happen" to you? Or do you change the song? Most of us change the song. Personally, I can bear at best perhaps about four bars of Gloria Gaynor's self-empowerment hit "I Will Survive." No offense to Ms. Gaynor or those who enjoy the song—I simply Cannot. Bear. It. Same with Rick Derringer's "Rock and Roll Hootchie Coo" and the collected works of the Black-Eyed Peas. And in all fairness, my musical tastes are not for everyone (or even anyone, as my preference leans heavily toward progressive rock, a genre which features inscrutable/*Jabberwocky*-like lyrics, multiple time changes, and epic song lengths). But regardless of tastes, we have control over what we choose to listen to (for the most part—family road trips with little ones will invariably start and end with infinite replays of "Bananaphone" or "Baby Shark"). Point being, we have control over the songs we are listening to, the shows we watch, the books we read. If we can control even those small things, then we have a template of choice and control that we can use to build on to develop an enhanced sense of active and engaged control over our own lives. The world no longer *just happens* to us; we become active agents of change in our own worlds.

To go back to the pining Linus, his past experience has been characterized by what he would describe as being full of failure. We could challenge Linus to reframe his thinking, that his previous experiences have been a series of experiments. We conduct experiments not to prove something but to explore. Data collection is a part of this process.

Linus' past experiments have resulted in a rich mine of excellent data— he knows what doesn't work, so there is no need to replicate previous experiments. And, he can now form a new hypothesis. His hypothesis, if coming from a space of low control, might be "women don't like me that way." He could test this hypothesis with Sally, but what would be the point? He would likely act in a way to confirm this particular hypothesis. However, assuming that he has a positive sense of control, he might develop a hypothesis such as "*Some* women don't like me that way, but Sally is a new opportunity to show that not *all* women have that response." If this is his hypothesis, he can now test it using a new or different procedure. Perhaps the new procedure is to act sooner, to be open and honest about his feelings, to ensure that she is aware of his romantic, not plutonic, feelings. And, if the experiment results in a happy dating relationship, great. If not, he has learned and now can refine his procedures for future experiments. Should Sally shut him down with a "I like you as a friend" response, he also has the freedom to continue to pursue a plutonic relationship with Sally (presuming she is interested in any kind of relationship), or not. Worst-case scenario: He learned and now can adapt in the future. Do not assume that I am saying that this is easy work! Heartbreak is heartbreak, our emotions are powerful and sometimes overwhelming. Most of us have been friend-zoned (and have friend-zoned others) many times, and it hurts to only be liked "as a friend" when we want more. But we learn, we adapt, and we overcome. All to the better for many—a happy, committed partnership incorporates the best possible aspects of the friend zone with the additional benefit of a rich romantic life.

I should note here that control, in mental toughness language, is not about the control of others, what Nietzsche referred to as the Will to Power. Will to Power, described very briefly and clumsily, is perhaps best understood as being the desire to exert control over others, in one part to protect oneself and in another, to feel power. This Will to Power stands in contrast to Viktor Frankl's Will to Meaning, which Frankl described as the human desire to have meaning and purpose in life. From a mental toughness perspective, Frankl's concept is closer to the control component than Nietzsche's. Again, this distinction is important since the entire concept of toughness tends to rely on an understanding and misconception that to be tough, one needs to have power and use that power to protect themselves and control others. Of course, mental toughness as we are using it here is far more about understanding oneself and how one interacts with the world. Control is simply a subcomponent of mental toughness that characterizes our beliefs about how actively engaged we are in our own lives and our personal emotional responses.

From a mental toughness perspective, control is subdivided into two areas: Life Control and Emotional Control.

Life Control

Life control refers to our beliefs that we are active agents of change in our own lives. Most people can quickly acknowledge that they can only control certain aspects of the world in which they operate. However, we all know people whose sense of life control is rather extreme. They can be of the belief that they control far more than they actually can. This belief can actually become somewhat narcissistic and, in the extreme, almost comical. 1982's *National Lampoon's Vacation*, is a great example of life control taken to an extreme. For those unfortunate enough not to have seen this 80's classic, Chevy Chase plays Clark Griswold, a husband and father who wants, above all, to take his wife and teen children on a holiday road trip to the mythic Wally World (a thinly disguised Disney World). Between the departure from Chicago (where Clark pulls the "Family Truckster" out of the garage, scraping all of their luggage off the car's roof) to the arrival at this final California destination (where Clark uses a plastic BB gun to kidnap John Candy's security guard character after finding Wally World closed due to maintenance—remember, this was the 80s and there was no way to check ahead), Clark and his family experience myriad complications. Their car is spray-painted with graffiti and ultimately jumped across a ramp in Death Valley; they inadvertently killed a dog and lost an aunt (who is strapped, sitting, to the roof of the Family truckster after she passes so that she can be dropped off at her family's home for a more dignified ceremonial disposal); Clark has a brief dalliance with a younger woman, steals from a hotel cash drawer, eats a urine-soaked sandwich, and falls asleep at the wheel. Among other adventures.

Through all of these shenanigans, Clark maintains a focus on his ultimate goal, despite any number of challenges. He believes that he can control the situation, despite all evidence proving otherwise. He is the very model of "I've got this!" thinking. Life control, in this situation, is perhaps too strong, too powerful, and does not permit for flexibility.

The "I've got this" mentality is deeply embedded into our thinking in Western culture. I certainly fall victim to this arrogant and inflexible thinking pattern—and have certainly played the Clark Griswold role in all sorts of areas of my own life, including the mythic road trip. I have (more than once) lost my passport in different countries; I have run out of money halfway across the country as we hauled our travel trailer along a very similar route to the one followed by Terry Fox (though with more calamity and far less valor). I've run out of gas in the middle of the wilderness and in the heart of the prairies; I have very nearly had one of the wheels of our trailer fall off and roll right on ahead of us on the most densely travelled highway in Canada. My enthusiasm, like Clark Griswold's, was often mine alone and not shared with my passengers. It was an enthusiasm based in optimism and misplaced positivity; it was certainly not based in any sense of competency. Yet, my response to any of these (mis)adventures was almost always the same: "I've got this."

Unfortunately, in the previous paragraph, I used the pronoun "I" a lot. But in reality, I was travelling with my wife and stepson. Collectively, "we" were on this road trip. So my assurances of "*I've* got this" soon fell on increasingly incredulous ears, and even worse, I was involving others in a variety of calamities based on my own erroneous belief that I could control more aspects of reality than I reasonably could.

A lack of life control, taken to the opposite extreme, is equally problematic. The corollary of "I've got this" is "I've not got this—I've got *nothing!*," implying that the individual has little, if any control, over things that happen in their lives. Life happens *to* them. They are passive observers, taken along for the ride that life offers, for good and bad. When good things happen, they are attributed to luck, chance, and fortune. When bad things happen, well, bad things just *happen*, don't they? Especially to *me*. In my clinical experience, people who suffer from depression in particular seem to be very sensitive in relation to life control. The idea that they can be actively engaged in their own lives is often uncomfortable and foreign to them. If they try to effect change, they can become stalled coming out of the gate with a simple thought "Yes, I can make a change . . . but what happens *when* I fail?"

There is a considerable amount of psychological research supporting the idea that one of the key features of depression is a sense of not having control over one's choices or actions. Most of us have experienced states of depression, days in which we feel lethargic, a lack of drive, and generally negative attitudes about ourselves and our capacities. This is normal and, arguably, a helpful mood state in that it provides us for context for understanding positive feelings—a comparison point, if you will. Major Depressive

Disorder (MDD), on the other hand, is a psychological condition in which the individual experiences symptoms of depression over an extended period of time, more days than not, and of such intensity that it has a negative impact upon their social and/or occupational or school-based functioning. While there is certainly a neurochemical process that often contributes to MDD, as with most psychological disorders, there are numerous and complex sociobiological factors involved. A lack of life control could certainly be seen to be an underlying factor to MDD, be it causal or correlational. When a person believes themselves to be inert and passive in regard to their own lives, it only makes sense that they may view their sense of life control to be quite low. There is hope, though, in that if one understands that life control can be enhanced, then perhaps one's mood can be too.

An approach to enhancing life control may involve creating small points of control. The idea of life control may be overwhelming to those with MDD. It's simply too much. So, what are some smaller aspects of life over which most of us have control? From an existential perspective, we all make a choice, every day, to continue to live. Simply living—moving from one breath to the next—may, in some cases, be sufficient to provide some degree of control. Of course, the corollary to this daily choice to live is that since we made that choice, we are responsible for anything and everything that happens to us. This sense of responsibility may be overwhelming to a person experiencing depression, but it is also highly possible that a sense of personal responsibility may lead to a sense of positive engagement. As one of my clients with depression and substance use issues said after we discussed this existential choice "If I'm responsible for my life because I choose to live, then I'd better do something worthwhile with that choice." This was a subtle shift in his thinking, which had previously been guided by statements such as "No matter what, nothing will get better and I have no choice in that—crap just seems to keep happening to me."

Learned Helplessness, Negative Cognitive Triad, and Right-Sizing a Gym

Renowned psychologist Martin Seligman's early work on Learned Helplessness, accompanied by Aaron Beck's exemplary clinical work around the Negative Cognitive Triad, provide us with a framework for understanding the mentally sensitive in relation to life control. Seligman researched how dogs, when given electric shocks, would initially engage in escape behaviours to avoid the pain; when they were conditioned to experience pain without a means of escape, they would no longer even try to escape, even when a clear means of avoidance was presented. Seligman associated the dog's learned helplessness to human thinking and behaviour. If, after a time, you have not been able to successfully avoid the pain of depression, then why bother even trying. Even the attempt may result in negative assessments of one's own capacities, resulting in further avoidance. This is broadly what Aaron Beck referred to in his well-known Negative Cognitive Triad. Essentially, people with depression often have negative thoughts about themselves, their current situation, and the future. "I suck, my situation sucks, and it's only going to get worse." Obviously, people who find themselves in this way of thinking may not be capable of thinking about the aspects of life that they can control. "I've got this" is a concept both foreign and incomprehensible.

However, as noted, mental toughness, including life control, is malleable and, to a large extent, coachable. We can enhance our sense of life control to a nice balance in which we can see and act upon those areas we can have control and let go of those that we cannot. Reframing is one strategy therapists and coaches use to assist individuals enhance their sense of life control.

In the film *Hoosiers*, Gene Hackman plays the coach of a small-town basketball team in rural Indiana. He is a fierce competitor who believes in fairness and commitment to team goals. As the team improves, largely due not to individual skill but rather team cohesiveness, their record also improves to the point where they make the state championship tournament. Upon arriving in Indianapolis, the players are in awe of the large gym, the stands, the sheer spectacle of the arena compared to the tiny rural high school gyms they were used to playing in. As they stare open-mouthed at the size of the auditorium, Hackman's character pulls out a tape measure, quietly walks to the free throw line and has one of the players take the other end of the measure to just under the backboard. "15 ft. Same as our gym in Hickory." He has another player measure the height from the floor to the rim of the net. "Same as our gym in Hickory." He puts the tape measure back in his pocket and walks away, saying in the same quiet tone, "Let's get dressed for practice." One of the players, previously awestruck by the immense size of the arena, yells out "Victory!," his words echoing in the empty stands.

Hackman's character took a negative set of beliefs—this is too much, we can't do this, *this* is out of our control,—and with calm, rational thinking, and a calm, peaceful tone, *reframed* the anxiety and fear into hope and optimism. What had been a challenge was now an opportunity. Life control works on the same principles—we need to ask ourselves and those with whom we work—to what extent can I control this situation, and to what extent is the situation out of my control. Rarely is the answer 100% in either direction.

Life Control and Mindset

Carol Dweck's work on the concept of mindset has been a very popular approach to psychology, education, management, and any number of other areas of personal growth. I believe that the popularity of her work is due in no small part to the basic and intuitive truth she speaks of. It is really just basic common sense. If we believe we can learn from our experiences and have a "growth mindset" in our approach to the future, we will be more successful. A "fixed mindset," on the other hand, leads people to become stuck in rigid and inflexible patterns of thought that are rarely helpful and inhibit growth of any kind. So, pretty straightforward, yes?

Apparently not.

People with fixed mindsets are notoriously difficult to work with in most environments (work, school, families), and are particularly challenging clients in counselling settings. I have had no small number of clients make statements along the lines of "That's fine for *you*, but there's no way *I* could do that," "I've already tried that and it didn't work," or, my personal favourite fixed mindset statement "Why bother???" (the properly trained clinical ear can actually hear the additional question marks—parents and teachers have this skill too!).

I vividly recall working with a male client who was struggling with interpersonal relationships at school. He was an extremely bright boy with some really neat interests, but no one to share them with. He burned through his few friendships quickly, largely due to his controlling nature. He was very much a kid with a fixed mindset who believed that if others were playing with him, they needed to play by the exact same rules as he did. No variation. He would also perceive even the slightest bit of conflict as being bullying behaviour. His list of bullies—no lie—was basically the entire class list of students in his grade. *Everyone* was a bully. When asked about how this student or that had bullied him, he would say that they "made him feel bad about himself" or that they "talked about him behind his back." When pressed about how he knew that they intentionally acted to make him feel bad or how he knew that they were talking about him behind his back, he would say "I just know that's what they do. And *everyone* does it *all the time*." Everyone. All the time.

In our first, second, third—well, almost every session, this boy would say to any challenge to his perception of being bullied (and to be clear, he was indeed bullied on a few significant occasions and we worked on that trauma eventually with success, but that bullying was with one student and only in certain limited situations, not *everyone all the time*) "Yeah, but . . ."

(another favourite expression from the fixed mindset dialogue guide!) ". . . it happened before in grade 1." In every session, he referred back to a bullying situation 9 years ago in which another boy hit him twice (once on the playground and once in class). This situation, as I understood it, was dealt with effectively at the school. But this boy had created and lived in a fixed mindset—once bullied, always bullied.

After our second session, I asked his mom to come in to chat. After discussing the perception of bullying and separating actual bullying from perhaps imagined harms, she stopped me by raising her hand, popping up her index finger in a very imperious manner and said "Yeah, but—*what about that time in grade 1?*"

I could imagine the dialogue at home around interpersonal relationships—both mom and son were fixed in a time long past and could not move forward. Granted, I fully acknowledge the role trauma, particularly childhood trauma, plays in our beliefs about the fairness and justness of the world. But I was puzzled as to what they were hoping to get out of therapy, given that they were both fixed in grade 1. I decided that rather than continue to bash away at their conceptualizations of what constituted bullying, I chose a far more passive yet deeply interactive approach. I re-focused my energy and I listened *hard*. And I listened actively.

Over time, they continued to tell their story, and it was almost always the same story. People who have experienced trauma often feel a strong need to tell and retell the trauma story. So, they did. Over and over. And eventually, but gradually, the story became just that—a story. No longer a real, here-and-now experience, but a story that one tells over dinner and then moves on. They had worked through their fixed mindset into a much more growth mindset in relation to developing successful interpersonal relationships by moving through and past the trauma by transforming the trauma into a story. In doing so, we eventually incorporated some of the experimental language discussed earlier. "Yes," I would say. "You were bullied in grade 1. What evidence do you have to suggest this is still happening? Let's experiment—next week, choose one day at random and make note of any situations you believe to be bullying in nature." Once done, he brought the list to me—a fairly short list, as it turns out, because he was, after all, a boy in grade 9 who didn't like to do homework! But the list itself had very few incidences and for each one, we developed alternative hypotheses.

I asked, "You wrote that some girls walked past you and then started giggling. What are some alternative hypotheses beyond them bullying you or talking about you behind their back?"

He thought for a moment. "They might have just been stupid girls giggling about stupid girl things."

"Okay, possibly, fair enough—we'll hold off on the work around developing a positive attitude toward girls and women until later, but let's keep going."

"They might have seen something funny after they walked by?"

"Sure. Anything else?"

He reflected once again. "Well, one of them had her phone out—maybe they were giggling about something they were watching on the phone."

So now, with some alternatives, we could engage the growth mindset. Over time, his experimental thinking was a great help in decreasing his anxiety and fear of being bullied. He eventually stopped accusing others of bullying him, which in turn resulted in more positive relationships with the others in his classes. But the fixed mindset was not completely gone, and given the co-rumination he shared with his mother, it was not surprising to see it return 3 years later when, in his grade 12 year, he had a conflict with a science teacher.

"He hates me. He's so unfair. He *always* gives me bad marks and *never* listens to me."

We've been here before, I thought. *Always* and *never*. But the same corrective pattern worked. Listen. Let the experience become a story. Reframe. Develop hypotheses. Test the hypothesis. Learn and adapt. Limit the fixed mindset, embrace the growth!

Life Control and the Locus of Control

Julian Rotter was an American psychologist who studied at the famed Brooklyn School under Solomon Asch, the guy with the three lines we discussed earlier. Rotter became interested in the idea of intraindividual control, specifically to what extent individuals took responsibility for their own successes and failures. He developed a model referred to as the Locus of Control (locus referring in this case to the *source* of control). The Locus of Control was, according to Rotter, typically either internal or external. An internal Locus of Control indicated that the individual felt personally responsible for their own actions and emotions, while those with an external Locus of Control attributed their successes, failures, actions, and emotions to external factors (including factors related to specific situations, uncontrollable variables, and luck). Neither internal nor external were viewed as being a superior Locus of Control; they both had positive and negative attributes. For instance, if a person had success, they could attribute their success to internal factors (hard work, dedication, intelligence, etc.) or external factors (the task was easy, my employer likes me, etc.). They could, alternatively use internal and external attributions in describing their perceived failures (internal: I am weak, I lack intelligence, I am unlikeable; external: I was lucky, the task was easy, anyone could have done it). Sometime, combinations are necessary "I did poorly on the test because I didn't prepare well (internal), so next time I have to study harder because I know the instructor doesn't like me (external)."

Locus of Control is deeply integrated into the life control component of mental toughness. An internal Locus of Control is valuable when we experience success, which allows us, to develop a stronger sense of life control. The external Locus of Control focuses on situations beyond our control. Again, our attitude toward these situations is a prime factor. If, for instance, our home is flooded due to a broken pipe, we have little control over the situation. Yes, we can learn, but that may be of small comfort as you stand knee deep watching the flotsam and jetsam of your basement man-cave (or she-shed, if you will) drift by as you wait on hold for your insurance company. We are allowed to get upset. However, one sure way to *stay* upset is to focus primarily on external factors. Someday, our luck will run out. The external factors will become overwhelming. It's in our learning (discussed later in the learning orientation portion of the Challenge chapter) that our hope lies. And hope is a precursor for optimism which, in turn, is a precursor for control, both life and emotional control.

The Godfather's Michael Corleone is an exceptional example of how one's Locus of Control ties into life control. If you haven't seen *The Godfather* films, or read the books, first of all, what's *wrong* with you? Sorry, movie snob moment! Rather, *film* snob moment!. But if you haven't, or need a reminder, here's a quick summary. Michael is the youngest son of a mafia family led by Don Corleone. Michael is the hope the family has of becoming a legitimate, noncrime-based family. He joins the military in World War II, is well-respected, and has a strong desire to live a decent life away from the criminal one lived by his family. Through a series of calamities, Michael becomes the new head of the family and continues their crime-ridden ways, taking them to new levels of corruptness. Michael is an individual who, I would argue, had an external Locus of Control. Life happened to him. Though he was an active participant in some pretty unseemly actions, he would consistently resent his family and external circumstances for his situation. His goal of "going legit" was always compounded by some external factor—his oldest brother getting shot (like, a thousand times), his middle brother being a nebbish pushover, his first wife getting blown up, his second wife leaving him—none of these things were *his* fault. As he said to his wife, Kaye, by way of abdicating his responsibility and connection to the nefarious actions he and his family had taken "That's my family, that's not me." Had Michael been in therapy (perhaps not the worst idea in the world!), a nice follow-up question Kaye might have asked would have been "Well, okay—so who *are* you?"

We also see the Locus of Control in action in sport. The football place-kicker who blames the holder for holding the ball incorrectly ("Laces out!"); the golfer who blames the wind for a duffed shot; the Tanya Harding's who blame the broken bootlace. On the other hand, there are those with an internal Locus of Control who attribute success and failure to essentially the same thing: themselves. Michael Jordan, Wayne Gretzky, Lionel Messi, Serena Williams, Alex Rodriquez all failed somewhere along their professional path. Jordan was famously cut from is high school team. Gretzky missed penalty shots. Messi, a multi-million dollar soccer player, misses penalty kicks. Serena Williams repeatedly suffered racist comments, even after proving herself a champion on the court. What a bunch of losers! In all honesty, if there is a group of failures and losers that most of us would want to hang out with, it's folks like these!

Though fictional, perhaps one of the best examples of an "athlete" who exemplified the internal Locus of Control is Sylvester Stallone's Rocky Balboa. Here's a boxer who got beat up. A lot. But almost never did he beat himself up in the same way that those with an external Locus of Control do. Rather than blame his poor training conditions, his quasi-abusive trainer, his poverty, his lack of opportunities, he accepted these conditions as being outside of his control, focusing on the one thing he could control: himself. A favourite quote comes from late in the *Rocky* series of films when Rocky is confronting his adult son, who is embarrassed by his father's punch-drunk mannerisms and who wants to step out from his famous father's shadow. Rocky confronts his son with some truth bombs: "You, me, nobody's gonna hit as hard as life. It ain't about how hard you hit. It's about how hard you can *get* hit and keep moving forward. How much you can take and keep moving forward. That's how winning is done!" That, friends, is life control.

Emotional Control

"Bottling up emotions is unhealthy. You need to express your emotions!" This is perhaps great advice in film or on a sitcom, but in reality, we all bottle up our emotions, and we do so effectively and for many good reasons. We need to. Like all things, containment of emotional outbursts is a healthy thing to do *in moderation*. Same rule applies to expression of high emotion—in moderation, it is healthy and, on occasion, necessary. But to suggest that it is always unhealthy to bottle up emotions is counter to human nature and also counter to what we understand from psychological research. There are many downsides to being fully expressive of emotions, the primary of which is that we are social creatures. If you have ever been yelled at by a dissatisfied customer, or even simply been given the finger by an irate driver, you know that to receive unfiltered emotion from another, especially anger, is to become defensive, which, in turn, is rarely a healthy state of being.

I live in a city where a heavy snowfall can seemingly arrive out of nowhere. One morning, I woke up to look out the window to see almost 2 ft of fresh snow that had fallen overnight, with no sign of a break. And I had to get to work. So, I rushed out the door and, after an extensive shoveling session complete with old-man like muttering, started driving. The roads were treacherous, but manageable, until I arrived at a hill about a kilometer from the school I was working at that day. I was running late for a meeting with parents of a student I was working with and was anxious to get to the school on time or, worst case, a few minutes late. As I drove up the hill, I saw that the snowplow had piled the snow high on the right side of the road and it encroached into the driving lane, so I had to switch to the left lane quickly. But the moron driving next to me was matching my speed exactly and was not allowing me to move in, and the person behind me hadn't yet seen the ending lane ahead. So, I laid hard on the horn. The driver next to me looked over, made quick eye contact, and just kept going at the same speed. I honked, honked, and HONKED! I started yelling and gestured in a most certainly unfriendly manner, middle finger raised angrily. The driver looked over at me and then back to the road. I lost my mind! I slowed down as best I could, rode over the snowbank, and my Land Rover slumped over into the left lane. Once the lane opened up, I roared past the offending driver, honking, swearing, and providing helpful sign language to assist with the clarity of my commentary, using my left hand to shake my fist and slam my middle finger against the window. The driver was now behind me. I turned off to make my way to the school. The car followed me. I turned into the school driveway. The car followed closely behind. "Oh, great—road rager!" I thought. I pulled in to park and lost sight of the car. Once I was in the school, I found the meeting room and was relieved that I was not late as the mother I was to meet had not yet shown up.

Don't get ahead of me.

Sure enough, I set up my MacBook and opened the student's file to review my notes and the door opens. In walks the mother. Yup, the very driver I'd been swearing and gesturing at. She looked at me. I looked at her. We took a moment. I broke the silence with a smile and said "Well, THIS should be awkward!"

Sometimes, honesty is the best, seriously!

In expressing my rage, I put myself at risk. Perhaps bottling up my emotions would have been preferable to my outburst. Well, there's no *perhaps* about it. So, let's let go of the "bottling up emotions is unhealthy" thinking. The psychological act of compartmentalizing emotions is actually a potentially healthy defense mechanism. Defense mechanisms also get a bad rap across the board, but playing a defensive game is, on occasion, exactly what is needed when we feel under threat. The ability to mask one's emotions from others as needed and the ability to affect the emotions of others are the core components of the mental toughness idea of emotional control.

What Is Emotional Control?

Emotional control can range from masking our own emotions to attempting to control the emotions of others. In the case of the former, there are certain advantages to masking emotions. My example of the aggressive driver (me) would be an example of what can happen when one does not mask one's emotions. This sort of reaction happens all the time with children, largely because they have not yet learned how to mask their emotions or why they should in the first place. Playgrounds, gyms, parks, classrooms, change rooms, hallways, and, in particular, the online world can be crucibles of "honesty," in which kids say and do mean things to one another. To use the experiment analogy, some kids, if not most, experiment not only with learning prosocial and positive experiences, but they also experiment with how to hurt others. Happily, most kids will learn quickly that when they hurt someone else, their own unhappiness at the result is sufficient for them to cease and desist with any future hurtful behaviours. We are not, in general, a people who see the benefit in hurting others so, largely, we do not do so on an ongoing or repetitive basis. However we do have to learn this lesson, and in doing so, people do get hurt.

It's not uncommon for adults to say "Kids can be cruel" when reacting to how "honesty" can be hurtful, but in creating an honesty-at-all-times-in-all situations culture, we create an arena in which hurt is inevitable. Again, using out sense of life control, we can conceptualize the harmful, but perhaps honest, words of others as being out of our control, so we can redirect our energy to developing a positive response to such hurtful statements. However, children have not yet developed a sense of life control and as such, largely rely on an external Locus of Control and have a poorly developed internal Locus of Control, making them more vulnerable to hurt. In what seems to be a paradox, they must learn to mask their emotions, which is direct dishonesty, in order to become emotionally healthy. In the child's mind, and in the minds of most adults, the paradox is essentially this: It is bad to lie, but I must lie to protect my emotions, so in lying to protect my emotions, does that make me a bad person? This thinking can lead us to negative emotional states. It may seem cynical to focus on the need to mask emotions—after all, we are encouraged to express ourselves honesty and by masking our emotions, we are actively being dishonest, in a sense.

For most of us as adults, the experience of getting hurt is unpleasant, so we protect ourselves. We defend ourselves. One of the most effective ways to defend ourselves is to mask our emotions—if someone tries to hurt us, a basic but effective means of stopping further hurtful behaviours is to limit or hide our reaction. We believe, often correctly, that if someone tries to hurt us we want them to stop, our best bet is to show no negative reaction. By showing no reaction, perhaps the person will stop trying to hurt us, which presupposes an intent on their part to create a reaction. Why someone would want to elicit a negative reaction has often puzzled me, but regardless of intent, the reaction to a nonreaction is frequently exactly what happens. The aggressor, more often than not, will lose interest and just leave.

We also have the option to respond to ongoing aggressive or unpleasant and provocative comments or behaviours in a proactive manner by saying "It bothers me that you would say/do that to me. I would appreciate it if you would stop," which is a logical and rational, nonemotional response. However, we do not always respond in such a rational manner. This is because the human brain, from a developmental perspective, is strongly centred more so by emotion than logic, in part because developmentally and evolutionarily, emotion has been part of our lives longer than logic. We are born with basic emotional responses (fear, happiness, etc.) which become more complex over time. Logic only enters the picture when we enter higher levels of cognitive development, often throughout toddlerhood. So, we frontload with emotions, followed by logic. And when our logic is challenged, we can rely on emotion simply because it's comfortable and familiar to do so.

Sometimes, children feel caught in an emotional-logical bind that carries into adulthood: I am supposed to be open and honest about my emotions, but when I am under threat, a good way to defend myself is to mask my emotions. This is a lesson I learned from a young age. My family, as I have noted, is very religious. From a young age, before I could read, our bedtime routine involved sharing of Bible stories. In my elementary years, I had Bible comic books (Jesus was, of course, a handsome, tall, bearded white man with flowing robes, more Greek god than what Jesus would have really looked like historically). There was no aspect of life that did not tie back into religion. Naturally, religion became the lens through which I viewed all things. And I became a bit of a pious little twerp! I would be very quick to judge, but lacked the ability to turn the lens to my own behaviours. I eventually became some weird sort of social safety barometer in my friend community. If there was a party or other social events and I was going, then it would be okayed by my friend's parents because if Brent was going then it must be good and wholesome. Yeesh.

I also became a relentless people-pleaser. There was nothing worse than disappointing someone. I would go to great lengths, including lying, to please others so that I came off looking worth of praise. Unfortunately, these traits can become highly engrained in our personalities and I continued to have a residual need to be liked, even if it required dishonesty or misrepresentation. I have misled people in the past simply because I want them to think better of me, the fact that telling the truth might actually lead to a more genuine appreciation of my character not really occurring to me. My fear of judgement overwhelmed my desire to be honest and a person of actual, not artificial, virtue. I eventually learned, and continue to learn that not all things require judgement, either from ourselves or from others. Subtle judgement was something I now can see as being rather formative in my later tendency to be holier-than-thou. I have continued to work on this particular aspect of my own mental toughness. Again, a work in progress.

In terms of being open about our emotions when under threat ties directly into our upbringing. My parents worked hard to provide my brother and I with what they honestly believed—and continue to believe—to be a strong sense of morality. Unfortunately, a side effect of a moral upbringing is the tendency to become constricted emotionally. It's hard to be honest when you have done something that may be perceived as being morally wrong and be fearful of judgement. It's easier and safer to not communicate or even to lie (itself not particularly moral, but better than feeling judged). This became a habit through much of my life. Rather than communicate honestly, I would "shade" my language to make things seem better than they were, typically so that it worked out in my favour. Without realizing it, I became manipulative in my language. My desire to exert emotional control over others was way more powerful than my need to exhibit the same kind of control over my own emotions. Although I did manage to do that fairly well too, resulting in a pattern in which I would disregard my own emotional truth for some convenient explanation I would offer myself to justify any morally questionable behaviour. I have worked hard on developing a far better balance of emotional control over the years and, as in all things, still have work to do. But at least now, it is honest work and if the work becomes "dishonest," I have a partner and other strategies to catch myself before I start treading down dangerous paths.

In adulthood, this bind can cause conflict in relationships, but when addressed directly, can be a very positive characteristic in communication. Letting others close to you know that sometimes, you are not in a place in which a fully open emotional conversation can occur communicates not only honest but also emotional vulnerability, both of which are at the core of trusting relationships.

At work, we mask our emotions because in many situations, to do otherwise would scuttle our careers. We have ALL had moments in which, were the adage "bite your tongue" been literal, we would have sliced clear through our tongues years ago. Bosses expect too much or provide poor leadership. Coworkers chatter on inanely. Subordinates don't do what you want them to do the way you expect them to. Clients are unreasonable. If we lost our minds every time we experienced heightened anger or fear or other such emotions, we would be spending a lot of time trying to update our resumes!

Emotional control, then, can be conceptualized as being both an adaptive and healthy construct that is actually prosocial in that it allows us to maintain a functioning society. Imagine if world leaders were actually honest with one another! We'd be living in some sort of post-apocalyptic nightmare of honest emotions and bloodshed. So, three cheers for emotional control!

Emotional Control as Camouflage

In my clinical work, I have had the opportunity and genuine pleasure to work with a number of "twice exceptional" clients—these are clients who have been diagnosed as being gifted (a diagnosis that I have certain troubles with as it implies "smart," and high intelligence and "smart" are not mutually exclusive) and "something else," typically ADHD, Learning Disabilities, Anxiety, or Autism Spectrum Disorder (ASD), or combinations thereof. I am not a fan of the phrase twice exceptional as these clients are often better described as being complex-exceptional. Many students with gifted profiles become experts at camouflaging themselves, and even more so when ASD or other conditions are in play. They create complex camouflage systems that make them essentially invisible in many situations. But the camouflage, though complex, is thin. A peek under the cover reveals the vulnerable and often frightened individual beneath. These clients do their best to hide their emotions, which they often find to be overwhelming and difficult to understand in the first place. They have learned through bitter experience that societal expectations of honesty are not universally true—and these are people who typically place high value on the integrity of truth. The subtleties of reality—when to be truthful, when to tell a white lie, when to deceive, when to hide emotions—are all foreign concepts. If we are expected to be honest, be honest.

The work complex-exceptional clients often do in therapy focuses on developing an understanding of how and when to use camouflage successfully, especially in clients with ASD. People with ASD, particularly girls, can actually be exceptional users of social camouflage. They can observe their social environment and essentially mimic the vocabulary and social interactive play that occurs. I had one adolescent client who could talk for hours about a favourite anime series. She knew characters, themes, plots, sequences, everything. And she and her friends would talk about this series for hours. But she had a secret. She had absolutely no interest in the series. She overheard other girls talking about it one day and, as is common with people with ASD, took it upon herself to become the foremost expert in everything there was to know about this specific anime. As with the most effective camouflage, she took a look at her surroundings and then used materials to which she had access to conceal how different she actually was. As mentioned, my clinical experience has been that girls with ASD tend to be much more effective users of camouflage compared to boys with the same condition. This goes a long way to explaining why so many girls are not diagnosed with ASD until they are into their early adult years.

For those of us who do not have ASD, camouflage is often simply an analogy for emotional control. I have seen this approach work well with complex-exceptional clients, and it also works for most folks across different situations. The core of the camouflage model is that the exterior can change based on the situation, but the core, the person below the camouflage, is the "true" individual. That person doesn't really change. They share their true selves with select few, typically only those who they trust implicitly and completely. Therefore, the integrity of their individuality remains intact while, at the same time, they learn to more successfully navigate the complexities of the social world.

Many species camouflage for protection and, in some cases, while hunting, and humans are no different. Our camouflage tends to be more social in nature. In the same way a chameleon changes colour to mimic its background environment to evade detection, people control their emotions to make them invisible to others in an effort to protect their egos. We have all done it, starting from a very young age. Remember when you were in elementary school and your teacher would call on that one student who didn't do their homework? Maybe that was you! It was certainly me. In such situations, kids would do what is simultaneously logical and ridiculous—they would avoid eye contact and take a sudden and heretofore unwarranted interest in their shoes. The thinking here is obviously "If I can't see you, you can't see me." We learn pretty quickly that this approach really doesn't work, but that doesn't keep us from trying it again and again, even though adulthood. I still catch myself doing it—my annual meeting with my accountant is not something I look forward to, not because I am in trouble . . . but because I *feel* like I am. As such, I don't think that, to this day, I've ever made eye contact with my accountant. He probably thinks I'm up to something. I'm not, I just feel like I have not done my homework and if I can't see you . . .

While such thinking may seem ridiculous, it does make sense. Human nature is to avoid that which causes us anxiety (i.e., threat). Anxiety is an emotional reaction to threat, so our behaviour when threat is perceived is guided by a desire, an impulse to reduce the emotional arousal. Whether the threat be real ("The roof! The roof! The roof is on fire!") or simply perceived ("The smoke I smell is from the toast I burned earlier") makes little difference, which partially explains why so many people have difficulties with anxiety. Their amygdala, that nut-sized part of the brain that, at its most basic level of functioning, supports us by identifying and evaluating threat, is very sensitive, almost like a sore tooth that we do not want to antagonize, so we avoid biting down on it. The amygdala perceives threat sometimes where none exists, resulting in a physiological threat-response that has us preparing to flee from something that doesn't truly exist, resulting in enhanced sense of threat (if we can't see the threat, it must be hiding—how scary is *that?*).

It should be noted that camouflage is only necessary when hunting or being hunted. It is not necessary when we feel safe. In our more trusting relationships, the true self can emerge. In an environment in which judgement is limited—or nonexistent—or when there is a strong, mutual trust, there is less need for emotional control. Our need to exert emotional control is largely contingent upon our feeling of safety. As such, it is important that we seek out and engage in trusting relationships (which, in turn, requires the capacity to take risk, something we will discuss later in the challenge chapter). When our interpersonal needs are met in a safe and mutually trusting manner, the need for camouflage diminishes significantly for obvious reasons—there is nothing to hide from anymore. Absent trust, and should judgment become a significant part of a relationship, our need to hide will become increasingly important as a protective measure.

So, we camouflage. In social situations, we try to fit in or, in some situations, try too hard. We will discuss social engagement when we learn about interpersonal confidence later in this book, but for now, it is important to understand that emotional control often is a significant factor in our social engagements. We also try to exert emotional control externally; rather than trying to camouflage and control our own emotions, we work to make a difference in the emotions of others.

Emotional Control and Jedi Mind Tricks

Emotional control not only entails the masking on emotions in situations in which doing so is healthy and prosocial, it also incorporates the ability to energize and find the enthusiasm in others, which has the dual benefit of making others feel more positive about themselves while also providing us with a positive and potentially never-ending source of virtuous energy.

In *Star Wars*, we are introduced to the idea of the Jedi Mind trick. Obi-Wan Kenobi described the mind trick essentially as using the Force to influence the "weak-minded." Again, if you haven't seen *Star Wars*, please put this book down and watch the films (in the recommended order of IV-V-I-II-II-VI-VII-VIII-IX) so you can join the rest of us here in the 21st century. While Obi-Wan used the mind trick on a pair of Stormtroopers to let them know that the droids they had in Luke's land speeder were "not the droids you're looking for," it is implied that the ability to control the thinking of others could also be used in a positive manner. In fact, I believe that in using the mind trick to deceive, Obi-Wan was actually tapping into the nefarious Dark Side of the Force, but that's a debate for another time!

In social psychology, we refer to the Jedi mind trick as simply being persuasive communication. Persuasive communication is something we are all familiar with, perhaps not by that name, but certainly we have all experienced it. Ever seen a commercial or an advertisement? Yes? You have experienced persuasive communication. If not, please let me know your secret! A commercial-free life sounds like one I'd like to live!

Persuasive communication is the social psychology description for the means and methods that humans use to persuade others to do something that they may not otherwise do, or to strengthen their behaviour in a specific way. When used effectively, persuasive communication can truly change the world. Politicians use persuasive communication extensively and perhaps overwhelmingly. We can become inundated with political messages, particularly as election seasons come and go. Our lives, almost from waking every day to closing our eyes at night, are saturated with persuasive communication. Our iPhone alarm wakes us up and, for many people, the first order of business—even before we fully open one eye—is to check our phone for notifications from social media and email. Think on this for a moment: Before our second eye is even cracked open from sleep, the other eye is gathering information, including advertisements and clickbait articles.

Advertisers, at least the good ones, use marketing based on solid psychological principles. One of the keys to understanding persuasive communication is to understand the appeal that persuasion holds for us. We tend to think of ourselves as being unique, independent thinkers, and to some extent, we are. But, on the other hand, we are also somewhat lemming-like in our tendencies to want to fit in. Advertisers take advantage of both of these ideas. Advertising, much like the Jedi mind trick, we assume only works on the weak-minded. This is incorrect. Anyone involved in selling, from Apple-and Amazon-sized corporations to local mom and pop shops, would not spend huge proportions of their budgets on marketing if it didn't work. Marketing works and when it is based on effective understanding of persuasive communication, it works unbelievably well. Even psychotherapy utilizes persuasive communication techniques to facilitate client change. Hopefully, though, we are more open and transparent in our use of persuasive communication than advertisers are!

Emotional control suggests, in part, that we wish to fit in and one way to do that is to be like everyone else. Marketers using effective means of persuasive communication understand this desire to fit in—they tell us we *will* fit in, our appearance will be acceptable, so long as we use their styling products; our homes will be judged as being acceptable so long as we use the correct design materials; our vehicles will get us from A to B in style so long as we buy their vehicles; and so on. The desire to fit in, though, is only one component of emotional control that is affected by persuasive communication.

After all, who wants to be just like everyone else? Am I not a unique, special individual? Again, marketers understand this side of emotional control as well. If you wear these clothes, not only will you fit in, but you will also actually exceed expectations and become desired! If you use this styling product, your unique beauty will shine through (but not so much as to ostracize you—you will still conform to socially accepted values and expectations around appearances—yours will just be a *bit* better).

Persuasive communication is not in the sole domain of politicians, corporations, and marketing teams. We *all* use it, and frequently. Even basic techniques work to help us persuade others. A slight nod, for instance, shows that we agree with what the other person is saying, making them an ally, encouraging the say more of the same sort of things. Allies are easier to convince and persuade to our perspective, so a slight nod can ease further communication, making the other person more susceptible to agreeing with you. Very basic, even unconscious, but something that people with a high degree of emotional control do without even realizing it. It is a subtle action, but one loaded with intent.

Another example of using emotional control to affect the moods and emotions of others would be showing empathy. We like to be empathized with—it makes us feel understood and accepted, not judged. Empathy can be expressed very easily and very subtly—for instance, a simple "That sounds rough" shared in a concerned but not condescending tone when a friend shares a trouble from work or home elicits a positive response on an unconscious level: "this person gets it—they understand me!"

Corporate, military, and athletic leaders all use emotional control and persuasive communication. However, I am not sure how often emotional control is addressed in job interviews or in board rooms. There might be some degree of discomfort in asking people about how they deal with big emotions. We ask this question of kids often, but rarely leaders. So, some worthwhile, but perhaps infrequently asked, questions that might be of benefit to leaders might include the following:

- How do you control your emotions when you are upset?
- How would someone even know you were upset?
- How do your emotional reactions colour your interactions with your team?
- Do you encourage people to express not only ideas but also emotions?
- What is your approach to camouflage?
- What are your strategies for expressing big emotions with colleagues?
- Have you ever lost control of your emotions? If so, what happened?

Some of the best teachers I have had the pleasure of working with exemplify effective emotional control in their classrooms, resulting in few, if any, disciplinary issues, and having highly engaged students enjoying maximal learning. They exhibit strong emotional self-control (camouflage) without losing their honesty and vulnerability. As a result, they typically have highly predictable, but generally moderate emotional responses. Kids know that this teacher will not go off the rails if someone acts out or if their homework is not completed. This leads to an enhanced sense of trust and a resulting environment in which confidence is nurtured and risk-taking becomes far more comfortable. At the same time, these teachers actually affect the emotional state of their students and colleagues. Their positivity and enthusiasm is, quite literally, contagious.

Emotional Control: An Essential Component of Success

There have been a wide variety of studies focusing on the myriad complex factors underlying the broad concept of success. Specific research has been conducted that examines factors related to success for students and teachers, business executives, work-teams, athletes, those in military service, among others. While no clear consensus exists, partially due to the numerous complicating actors in conducting such research (starting with defining "success" for each group), meta-analytic studies have suggested that many of those factors we often associate with success are actually far less relevant than we think. In relation to student success specifically, socioeconomic status and home environment have been identified by Australian educator John Hattie in his comprehensive analysis presented in *Visible Learning* as actually being among the *least* significant factors in student engagement in learning success (though American educator Alfie Kohn would suggest that socioeconomic status and parental income would be the among the most predictive factors in relation not to student engagement but in student performance on high-stakes standardized tests), with the ability to self-assess one's own knowledge (i.e., self-awareness) leading the list of predictive factors associated with student engagement and ultimate academic. The other top factors are consistent with positive teacher—student relationships. His list is, in part, as follows:

- Student self-assessment/self-grading
- Response to intervention
- Teacher credibility
- Providing formative assessments
- Classroom discussion
- Teacher clarity
- Feedback
- Reciprocal teaching
- Teacher—student relationships fostered

Home environment and socioeconomic status are among the lowest leading factors. Obviously, it would be foolish to suggest that these are not significant factors. We know that society is not fair and that many people have social-cultural situations that do not need them to have the same struggles and challenges that those for other SES groups may have. It's easier to have "success" if you do not have to fight against racism, homophobia, classism, ageism, ableism, among other areas of possible challenge, nor does having money hurt when seeking out a quality education. Hattie's work is far from perfect and has been criticized, as all good research should be, but even if he is close, the trends are clear. The most important factors relate to *professional practice* (the ability to practice response-to-intervention, reciprocal teaching, the appropriate use of formative assessment, and so on) and *quality relationships* (teacher credibility, teacher clarity, reciprocal relationships).

Studies of student performance have indicated that, all things considered, the most accurate and universal predictors of student success (not just academic success, but also social and emotional wellness, resiliency, willingness to take on challenges, etc.) have little to do with advanced pedagogical techniques, educational technology, aesthetically pleasing learning environments, quality of senior administration leadership, family income, class size and composition, or any number of other factors that have come and gone as educational trends are wont. While each of these approaches play a role in student wellness and success, the most consistent, effective, and perhaps least expensive approach to enhancing the quality of the educational experience are the *professional qualities* of the teacher and the *quality relationships* that exist between the student and teacher.

The teacher as leader is largely responsible for the development, maintenance, and enhancement of a positive relationship with students, which in turn is the best predictor, overall, of *student success*. Student success itself is very difficult to quantify and it is perhaps a fool's errand to try to do so. Is success a measure of future career satisfaction? A love of learning? An ability to engage in society through the most basic functioning of literacy and numeracy? A passion for athletics or the arts? It is almost impossible to describe exactly what success means in most contexts, so perhaps our best option is to allow for individual definitions of success, which is then facilitated through *professional practice* and *quality relationships*. Professional practice will be discussed in more detail when we address confidence in abilities. Positive relationships are a component of both emotional control and interpersonal confidence within the mental toughness model.

To return to the idea of measuring success from an academic/school-based angle, we can say, based on extensive research into reading, is that one of the best predictors of *reading* success is tied to two other factors—parental educational level and presence of books in the home. Of course, a degree and a bunch of books does not mean that you will have kids who are strong readers. The research in this area is largely correlational, not casual, meaning that there is a relationship between educational level and the presence of books and reading ability of children, but it is not a cause-and-effect relationship, since there are a lot of other variables at play. Parental engagement, modeling of reading, parental presence (which in lower-income families may be less frequent not because of a lack of love, but the financial reality of needing to work more outside of the home) are among these other factors. But for educational leaders and budget makers, you could do worse than train teachers how to develop positive and nurturing relationships with their students if you want a good return on your investment. Learning about mental toughness would be one way to enhance quality relationships between students and teachers. There are many others, but ultimately, no specific program or course will fully prepare teachers for the rigours and joys of positive relationship development. Again, emotional control supports the development of such relationships by allowing for a trusting relationship to be built on a sense of predictable responses on the professional's behalf. If the student trusts the teacher to keep their emotions in check, they can learn to take more risks and therein lies the core of a trusting, quality relationship.

Of course, the role of emotional control in no way is limited to the school environment. From a leadership perspective, the role of professional qualifications and quality relationships is critical to the enhancement of emotional control and, subsequently, effective leadership practices. For instance, an executive who is well-trained in their area of practice and who is a good listener is more likely to have a successful team than someone who know little about their content area of the area of practice or who is prone to emotional outputs or, similarly, emotional stoicism that prevent team members from feeling that the leader is approachable. Of course, there are exceptions. Based on news reports and other readings, it would likely be unfair to say Mark Zuckerberg does not understand the technology underlying Facebook; however, one could also say with some degree of confidence that his emotional control is perhaps on the far end of the normal curve, given his tendency to appear somewhat remote/robotic in his public presentation. On the other hand, there are numerous examples of corporate success stories in which a leader from another field has come in and turned a large organization around from failure to success by using their own emotional control as a lever.

In *Mindset*, Carol Dweck gives the example of GE chairman Jack Walsh as having a growth mindset. However, he also clearly had a positive sense of emotional control. He did not have a great deal of experience in GE's product or service line, but he was relationship-oriented and even when he had to make difficult cuts, he was aware of the human factors, not just the color of ink on the corporate annual report. In Zuckerberg and Welsh's situations, emotional control played a significant role in their successes and their challenges. If it can be true for multi-billionaires, can it be true for us normal folk? Why not!

A practical activity to think about, not just for teachers/corporate megastars, but for *anyone*, be they in a leadership role, including parents, or just as normal human beings, is to **identify an individual or a personal characteristic that *really* annoys you**. Teachers can usually identify "that kid," the one they struggle with. They may have great empathy for this student, but at some level their human response is that this is the student who they hope is absent tomorrow (but never is!). For employers, it's the staff member who is in our office daily complaining about some real or imagined slight, or the one who always asks "why" when something needs to be done (without offering an alternative approach). For parents, it's not so much the individual child, but rather a characteristic of the child. The child who argues *every little detail.* Or the child who whines. Or takes forever to get their shoes on *every single time.*

Now, once you have this person or characteristic in your mind, turn your notion about them on its head. Approach them in an *opposite* manner than your usual manner. If you are dismissive, hoping that they will just go away, try engaging them by learning something new about them. If you get angry, find a way to engage your humor. For instance, your son takes 20 minutes to find and tie his shoes. Race him! Video record him and share the video later on as a sitcom (of course, do this in a way that is not demeaning or sarcastic—engage their humor too! A neat idea might be to provide commentary—kids might take to this as their TikTok moment!). I often ask teachers to identify the one student with whom they have the most difficult time connecting, and then on the following day, find out one new thing about that student that they had not previously known. I tried this myself with a few clients that I found to be challenging and found one who was *that* client: the one whose answer to most queries was "I don't know" or "I already tried that," or "That won't work—are we done yet?" I discovered this client to be an avid reader of Chekov and Dostoevsky and was reading Tolstoy's *War and Peace.* Obviously, I'd missed a huge component of who this client was and his interests and values. In another situation, I took a risk by being open and genuine with a client who I found unpleasant to work with—I saw him as being arrogant, sexist, racist, close-minded, homophobic, and bombastic in his "religious" views. So, after careful consideration, I had an honest moment and shared my feelings about our relationship with him. His response? "No sh*t! You think *I* like *you*? You're pretentious, disengaged, and seem distracted all the time when I'm talking. What kind of psychologist can't even focus when that's what they're getting paid for?"

He was right—in his case, I was disengaged, which led me to appear to be pretentious and distracted. I struggled with focus. We had a genuine moment of truth and in doing so, I earned the client's trust by taking a risk and as a result, I could become a much more effective therapist. Therapy is not the only place for this kind of sharing of emotional control; however. It can be utilized in any human relationship. As noted, we will talk about risk-taking later, but emotional control is a necessary precondition for taking risks and for expressing our emotional condition. Sometimes, expressing emotional truth can be not only risky, but also truly scary. We can learn from others, even in tough situations, about the role of emotional control and how to shape and modify our responses. Even thinking upon our own histories and experiences can guide us.

As an educator, I have had the opportunity and genuine pleasure of working with a lot of great human beings. Some, less so . . . but that's my issue. I appreciate the honesty some teachers express, but also know of the power implicit in honest expression of emotion. It is important to note that while most teachers tend to be enthusiastic and idealistic, they are, at their core, deeply human. As such, they have their less than stellar moments. In juniour high, I had one teacher who, having left her classroom of unruly grade 8 students to fend for themselves while she went to get something copied, re-entered the classroom, narrowly being missed by a pencil that had been thrown, with force, toward the door. The student who threw the pencil had no ill-intent, just goofing around while the teacher was out. This was not a particularly popular teacher, one who was quick to anger and not terribly approachable. At least, that was the common view among students. She lost it. "Whoever threw that pencil," she roared, "Will be sitting with me every day at lunch until the end of the school year! WHO DID IT?!" We were stunned into silence. No one said anything and, of course, we all found out that our shoes were *really* interesting! She then made a statement that she ended up committing to: "Unless whoever threw the pencil comes forward, your end-of-the-year field trip will NOT happen." We usually had a fun off-campus day planned for June, and this year was no different—and now, this highly anticipated day could be lost. Still, no one said anything.

Class resumed, the teacher still fuming. After class, two to three students stayed behind. Later, we found that each of these students had altruistically taken it upon themselves individually to claim guilt, even though none of them had thrown the pencil. Better for one person to miss the activity day than everyone. Altruistic or not, the teacher's emotional control had worn thin. She accused each of the students of lying, covering the tracks of the real offender, and conspiracy. So, we not only lost the activity day, we had to spend the day, as a class, doing math. Math as group punishment . . . maybe that's why I maintain a generally antipathic attitude toward fractions.

We had seen this teacher at perhaps her most human, though we did not recognize it at the time. Certainly, teaching appeared to be a challenge for her. She seemed deeply unhappy and, as noted, was not a favourite among her junior high charges. From her perspective, someone had purposely thrown the pencil at her, with prejudice and purpose, to hurt and humiliate her. Again, had she been in a position of stronger emotional control, she could have mediated her response and perhaps, scored some "cool points" from the students. Not that scoring points is a critical feature required of teachers, but an honest, vulnerable moment may have been more advantageous than an angry, impulsive response. Of course we've all been there. We have all had our emotions get the better of us. Through emotional control, we ask ourselves—hopefully, anyway—why am I reacting like this? Why the intensity? How will others perceive my intense reaction and will that possibly make things worse? Without emotional control, these questions do not even occur to us.

As an experiment, try this: **Next time you are angry, clench a fist**. Focus on the fist itself, the tenseness of the muscles in your hand and forearm. Take in a deep breath, tightening your fist as you inhale, tight as you can. Keep the fist tight and exhale, then inhale again, clenching your fist even tighter. Do this four times. By now, your fist should be shaking, your muscles tight, your skin becoming cold. Then, as slow as you can, exhale and gradually release the tension. Very slowly. Four exhales, each time gently and slowly relaxing the muscles. Notice the physical sensation as your muscles slowly relax and blood returns to your hand. The stiffness of the muscles as oxygen returns to the cells. Focus all of your energy on making the fist, holding it, noticing it, and then relaxing it. The whole process should take about 60 seconds or so. Now, notice your emotional state. Still angry? Probably. *As* angry? Maybe—but maybe not. By shifting your focus, the emotional control has an opportunity to do its work and reduce the intensity of the emotion. You likely won't eliminate the emotion, nor is that the goal. Anger is a perfectly valid and useful emotion and you are encouraged to feel it. It can become a problem when you lose control of it, which usually happens when the intensity increases. By engaging emotional control through the fist exercise, you create a subtle shift from intense to moderate. This shift allows your emotional core to open up and your higher-order thinking, embedded in your frontal cortex, can activate, allowing in turn for enhanced problem solving and reasoning. All because you made a fist.

Pretty neat mind trick, yes?

Emotional Control and the Human Condition

Sometimes, the best understanding of human emotion comes from instances in which the absence of emotion is central. Deep Blue, the chess-playing computer system, was defeated by world champion Garry Kasparov in 1996, but only after much controversy. After Deep Blue won the first match, Kasparov drew and then eventually beat the computer, but Kasparov maintained that the IBM programmers had made alterations to the operating system after the first match; essentially, they taught Deep Blue about Kasparov's strategy. Yet Kasparov won, not only through his obviously superior game play, but also because he could make intuitive leaps that Deep Blue couldn't. It was limited by its programming and, by extension, its programmers. Emotion played a significant factor in this challenge.

Emotional control sometimes fails us and when this happens, as it does, the consequences can range from minor discomfort to global trauma. Who hasn't, in a moment of anger, said or done something they have come to regret? I would be willing to wager that many readers have done so within the past 48 hours. I certainly have. We often lose our emotional control around those with whom we are closest—we allow them the privilege of seeing us at our worst. I often speak with parents who are extremely frustrated with their teen's moodiness. Adolescents, with their not-yet-finished brains, are highly emotional, yet they rarely display their rage and fury and depression and anxiety in front of their peers or teachers. In fact, many teachers are flummoxed when parents tell them that the quiet and respectful student they see in their classroom is a Hulk-like rage demon at home. Parents can be patient, but in their vulnerable moments, a simple eye roll can light a fuse that results in a huge explosion. And if you haven't had the joy of experiencing a full-on adolescent eye roll, you are missing out on one of life's great emotional roller coasters!

So, your lovely teen has just rolled their eyes at you. They sighed as if you were some new sort of idiot, one who cannot possibly perceive reality as they see it. So, you lose it on them. And over time, these interactions become insufferable frustrations in themselves. So, why are teens so *mean* to their parents sometimes? The answer is a paradox, one that parents struggle with but one I truly believe in—many families, including the teens themselves—have validated this perspective, which is that effective parents have created emotionally safe environments in their homes. The teens have absolutely no question, on a very intuitive and deep level, that their parents love and trust them. So, if there is love and trust, there can be true honesty, which, unfortunately, is sometimes ugly and unpleasant. But where else can the adolescent truly be themselves? At school and with friends, they must put up barriers of artificiality to protect themselves emotionally and socially. No such need in a truly loving home. So, take heart, parents of adolescents—you've done a great job if you have an eye-rolling, head-spinning, emotional cave troll living with you!

And parents of younger kids who cannot fathom their little ones losing their emotional control as just described . . . wait for it.

We see the same issues related to difficulties with maintaining emotional control in all sorts of relationships. Partnered couples often express antipathy toward their partners, which to some extent can be helpful. Honest expression of emotions can let your loved one know exactly how you feel. But, as noted, those with lower emotional control may become too expressive, and repetitively so. This sort of highly emotional dynamic can lead to frustration on both parts, especially since living in a heightened emotional state can lead to feelings of threat and uncertainty, which are unsustainable over time. Exercising emotional control in our communication with our partners can be very difficult work, but highly rewarding as in doing so, we develop a truly honest yet trusting and safe environment to express emotions effectively.

As a science fiction/fantasy junkie, I could provide any number of examples of "the other" who tries—and usually fails—to understand human emotion. Perhaps the best known is Spock, the first officer and eventual captain of the Enterprise on *Star Trek*. Spock was "impaired" by his half-human genetic makeup which made emotionality an embarrassing part of his desire to be consistent with his logical Vulcan side. This discrepancy between emotion and logic was a point often explored on the show and the subsequent films. He was created as a counterpoint to humanity, an observer of human behaviour and emotion through a highly refined sense of logic. It was Spock with whom I identified as a kid—I never wanted to be Captain Kirk; Spock was my jam. Logical, detached, but on occasion, highly emotional and a keen observer of humanity.

It is interesting to note that when *Star Trek* returned to broadcast television in the 1980s as *Star Trek: The Next Generation*, Spock's surrogate human-observer was an android, Data. Data, unlike Spock, was an artificial life form with no emotions to control, but, unlike his predecessor, Data desperately wanted to experience human emotion. Both Spock and Data provided commentary on emotion. I bring those characters up as examples of how we often view our own emotions and the emotions of others. Sometimes, when we have had a very strong emotional reaction, we may react, not unlike Spock, by thinking that the intensity of our response was "illogical." Having an internalized Spock or Data can help us identify and understand our emotional control from a less passionate perspective which, in many circumstances, exactly what is necessary.

Human beings struggle, we get frustrated, we get angry, we get sad. But those with a positive sense of emotional control acknowledge that these emotional states are just that—states. Temporary and changeable. Not intransigent traits. So, for teachers, employers, parents, mentors, and others in leadership roles, they view others in the same way—when an individual is upset, they attribute the negative emotional outburst to the situation, not the individual's character. In doing so, they provide a gift or vulnerability and recognition to all individuals in their charge and indeed, to all of those in their orbit. They provide hope.

Emotional Control and Collective Conflict

On a grander scale, what happens when emotional control is not exercised by those in positions of power? We have seen human history as being filled with conflict and rarely is such conflict tempered by strong emotional control. "We" hate "Them," "They" hate "Us." Simple conflict and difficulties with communication and values lead not to understanding and compassion, as would be the case if emotional control were factored in. Rather, we become distrustful and protective. And ultimately, these feelings lead to a sense of threat and anxiety. On an individual basis, we can learn to manage these emotions; from a global perspective, it is difficult to exert emotional control as a collective.

Do not presume these comments as being a naïve, oversimplistic approach to global conflict. Obviously, there are innumerable complexities involved in any system that includes humans, and emotional control is only a very small cog in this machine. But it is one that perhaps has been overlooked overtime. The emotional component of collective conflict is important to recognize, as ultimately, it is individuals who make decisions. We do have safeguards, but again, social psychology research suggests that we make poor decisions both as individuals and as groups.

Emotional control is not unlike trying to keep a highly agitated dog on its tether. Regardless of the reason for the dog's agitation (extreme anger, anxiety, or excitement), it's important that their leash be secure. If we lose control of the leash, we lose control of the dog. If the leash is frayed and worn out, it risks being torn apart. Our emotional control is similar in that we can try to keep our emotions in check but if we are tired, we can lose our grip. If our control is frayed and worn out, it can break. And, on the other hand, we can exert *too* much control, resulting in a need to always be on in relation to emotional regulation. This is true of us as individuals and on a more global scale. International conflict can be initiated by even petty squabbles when leaders become deeply entrenched in their viewpoints and do not have the emotional control necessary to reconsider their options.

Again, not to diminish the vast complexity of conflict but, at the end of the day, it is emotional control, or the lack thereof, that can lead to some pretty devastating global consequences. In the age of heightened connectivity, the role of emotional control becomes even more critical, as collective conflict has become a central part of our daily lives through enhanced access to information and the rise of social media.

Emotional Control and Social Media

Honest moment—no one will know except you and me, and I am not telling anyone. **How much time do you spend on a daily basis consuming media?** I mean, for fun/enjoyment/relaxation? If you've a pen handy, write down the number (it'll be in hours, don't worry—you're only human!). Now just sit and look at (or create an image in your mind of) that number. How do you feel about it? Are you proud of the number—is it a number you have earned and feel that you deserve? Are you ashamed of the number? Do you want to crumple up the paper and toss it out? Before you do anything, think about—or write down—what you *do* with that time. Again, be honest, it's just you and me, and again, I'm not telling anyone!

Maybe do a pie chart of your media usage. Or just a list with a rough percentage next to each item. How much time on Twitter? Facebook? Instagram? Snapchat? YouTube? TikTok? Given the changing nature of social media, by the time this piece is published, you'll likely be into some heretofore unheard of new platform that you use to connect with others. What about gaming? Mindless surfing on Pinterest or different meme sites? I'm not talking about work-related media, though for many, it is the work-related media that is the most absorbing and in many cases, the most problematic.

Still feeling like you are proud of your numbers? Or perhaps you are even more ashamed than you were when you just thought of the about of time you were spending on a daily basis. Maybe this will help—I'll show you mine, based on yesterday!

Total Media Screen Time: 6 hours

- **Facebook:** 2 hours (scrolling through stories, articles, links, videos, and a couple of images of friends and family)
- **Twitter:** 2 hours (scrolling through news stories, opinion pieces, articles supporting my preconceived notions about work, etc.)
- **YouTube:** 1 hour watching concert video footage of prog rock band King Crimson
- **News Sites:** 30 minutes (local, national, international stories, in many cases, variations on the same stories I'd seen on Twitter, news from my hometown)

- **Memes:** 30 minutes (some pretty good ones of potatoes shaped like non-potato things; cats)
- **Email:** 30 minutes (not producing anything, just seeing what is coming in)

And if you add that up, you'll see that I lied. Okay, it was closer to 7 hours. Not including watching the first half of *Mad Max: Fury Road* in bed. Nothing like an extended post-apocalyptic car chase scene with dozens of screaming Australians blowing each other up to get one into a nice sleep mode.

Am I proud? No. Not even a bit. But nor am I ashamed. One of my most hated expressions is "It is what it is." (after all, what else would it be? Anyway . . .). In this case, my media consumption was what it was. It's neither good nor bad; the screen time itself is not positive or negative. The *impact* of the screen time, on the other hand, is certainly not particularly positive. Much research has been conducted into screen time and while there are advantages to gaming and social media, our poor brains, particularly developing brains, are ill-equipped to deal with the level of stimulation and immediate gratification that screen time provides.

In relation to emotional control, our capacity to control our emotions can be eroded by excessive screen use. What is excessive? Depends. Various factors come into play, including the nature of what we do with our screen time, the time of day we use it, the duration of how long we are on screens, the frequency we check our screens, and perhaps most importantly, how we feel when away from our screens. Emerging research, and my own clinical practice with high school and university students, suggests that preventing young adults from checking their devices can result in anxiety levels equivalent or even higher than those associated with high stakes testing. If our emotional control starts to crumble in absence of our devices, we need to wonder about the stability of our emotional control in the first place. Perhaps, even if we feel confident in our emotional control, if we experience high anxiety in absence of our devices, perhaps we are not as in control of our emotions as we would like to think.

The other significant consideration in regard to emotional control in the age of heightened and easy access to screens and media is that our online personas can often take on a somewhat less optimal and perhaps even dark tone. Wander into any anonymous chat board for evidence of people who let their more base nature run free. Absent social control, their personal emotional control appears to be absent, but their desire to control the emotions of others is high. People will say all sorts of things online that they would never say in real life and it could be argued that this said online may actually not be reflective of the actual views of the individual. Anonymous chat boards can be a place to experiment with opinions and to take social risks, but perhaps not in a particularly healthy way. Emotions can become intensified and with no way to filter outside of disengaging from social media contact, we tend to pick up on only those emotions that we can sense through a screen with little opportunity for a true sharing or communication of social subtleties.

To develop a good sense of social control online, we would be wise to adapt those strategies that work for us IRL. Specifically:

- Avoid high-conflict situations to begin with. If you know that engaging with someone with an opposing political opinion, use caution as what could start as a healthy exchange of ideas can devolve into name calling quite quickly

- The truism of no-go areas for family dinners can hold true for online engagements as well—so limit conversation of religion and politics

- If you wouldn't say it to a person's face, probably don't say it online

- Know that there is a permanence to online communication that does not exist in real life. In a conversation, if you say something inappropriate, you can apologize genuinely and immediately and the offending comment is often forgotten. Online, your words leave an indelible footprint will last way longer than your anger or mood at the time you typed it. Ask anyone who has lost their career based on ill-stated Tweets (there are numerous examples of celebrities who, after a single tweet, have become *persona non gratis* in their fields).

- Step away. In face-to-face conflict, often the best bet is simply to acknowledge and take on an agree to disagree stance and then just leave. Hard to do that online when notification bubbles keep popping up, eliciting a need to respond.

- There are currently about 7 billion people on the planet. Many of them disagree with you. And you disagree with many of them. And that is what makes the world an interesting (if conflictual) place to live. But there is little to no value is raging against every single opposing viewpoint.

- Gene Roddenberry, creator of *Star Trek*, developed as the core of his show the concept of *IDIC*: Infinite Dimensions in Infinite Combinations. His philosophy was that if we accept that there are infinite ways of looking at things and infinite ways to *choose* to exist, then we can develop empathy and compassion for everyone, even the most heinous person. That would include you online nemesis who believes that their sports team is better than yours!

- Know your limits: If you start rage-typing in the comments section of a political story in Twitter, it's time for a break. If you are a person who does not normally swear, but find that your responses to online debate are expletive-laden, perhaps go get a sandwich.

- Try an experiment: Delete your social media apps for a week (or a day). Don't delete the accounts themselves, just the apps. See what you end up doing with your spare time when not flipping through screen after screen of—whatever it you scroll through!

Emotional Control and Language

Emotional control is enhanced when we can identify—using actual words—our emotions. Human languages are limited, however, in how accurately we can describe our emotions. It's analogous to describing colours—there are a lot of words used to describe the various shades of red, but most people only know so many. To me, red is light red, dark red, red, crimson, scarlet, burnt umber (I think), and that's pretty much it. Google tells me that there are 40 or so words in the English language that describe the colour red. My limited vocabulary makes it difficult to express what I mean when I see a specific red. In fact, our thinking is largely limited by our vocabulary. Most humans think in terms of language and images. When thinking about our emotional response to others, often there is a significant limitation on our ability to describe our feelings not only to ourselves but also to others. When I work with children, the use of language is extremely limiting, largely because they have not loaded their emotional word bank fully, so they use words like "good," 'bad, "happy, "mad, "sad," and so on to describe feelings that we, as adults, might describe using more advanced vocabulary. But the underlying emotional state is the same. We are just better at using language to describe emotions. But we remain limited, which in turn, limits our ability to exercise emotional control. How can we control something we cannot even name?

In my therapeutic work, I tend to use an existential approach, even with children. Existential models address deep intrapsychic pain and joy in the larger context of our existence and, in many cases, while such concepts are essentially beyond the scope of a child's language development, they may not be beyond their capacity for understanding. A good way to access this emotional core without focusing on emotional words is to use analogies. Analogies have the benefit not only of providing some distance between the client and their actual lived experience, making many people feel much more comfortable with sharing their sense of reality with the therapist; they also allow for higher-order emotional processing that is not limited by language. Rather than talking about how one felt about being criticized by a teacher or supervisor, which the individual may feel as humiliating, stressful, embarrassing, and so on, we can talk about how a character from film or literature may have felt in a similar situation. Superman, my personal favourite superhero, has a wide range of exceptional powers, but I believe the true core of his power, his real superpower, is restraint. He knows his power and how to set boundaries to prevent himself from hurting others, while also knowing when to allow others to solve their own problems. Not all situations require a superheroic response. Peter Parker, photographer for the *Daily Bugle* in the Marvel comics, regularly gets berated by his boss, J. Jonah Jameson, who demeans and humiliates Peter for the most insignificant mistakes. How would Peter feel about that? What if Jameson knew that Peter was actually his hated nemesis, Spider-Man? How would Spider-Man respond to Jameson? Why hasn't, after all of these years, Peter just unleashed his strength on Jameson?

Because "with great power comes great responsibility." Peter knows that he must restrain his emotions. He must, in effect, exhibit emotional control. This analogy works well for younger individuals and, due to the popularity of the Marvel movies through the 2010s, with a broader range of adults. Without this analogy, it's likely that we could talk with someone about working for a bully who would describe their emotional response as being "upset" or "frustrating." While valid descriptors, these emotional words do not present the richness that analogy can, resulting in problems with expressing emotional control.

On the other end of the emotional spectrum is joy. **Take a moment and try to describe *joy*.** It's kind of hard to do. We tend to list synonyms—happiness, pleasure, contentment. But none of these are accurate in themselves—they are dry, analytical vocabulary-list words. Now try the same thing, but use an analogy from film, literature, music, or sport. The band and crew singing "Tiny Dancer" on the tour bus at a low moment in *Almost Famous*; Anne's excitement in almost all situations, but particularly when allowed to go the ice cream social in *Anne of Green Gables*; the upbeat and impossible-to-frown-to rock-pop of Queen's "Don't Stop Me Now"; New York Yankee Lou Gehrig's farewell speech after being diagnosed with ALS "I consider myself the luckiest man on the face of this earth." *These* are true experiences of joy, expressing the range of emotion, the complexity of joy in ways that words could not.

In many analogies, we find that joy itself is often found when it is least expected. When working with others who struggle with emotional control, it is valuable to bring this to one's attention (without being too Pollyanna-ish about it). Phases such as "It's always darkest before the dawn" and so on are not particularly helpful nor true and certainly not likely to engender someone at a low point to say "Hey, that's right!" Using analogies is an effective way to elicit both personal emotional control and to engage positive emotional responses from others. Everyone has something they identify with—it need not be fiction or music or sports—it can be personal connections or personal experience. Humanistic psychologists speak of the "peak experience," those moments in which we are truly on top of our game, when we fell that we are truly at our best. These feelings, though transitory, can be reflected upon as moments to strive toward again, knowing that we will never really hit that particular high again. We may hit other highs and other peak experiences, by never one the exact same. Again, this gives us motivation to try new things, to experiment.

Wrapping Up

Control can be viewed as being comprised of life control and emotional control. Life control relates primarily to our own sense of control over our own lives—are we active participants who are actively engaged in our lives? Or are we subject to fate? Or somewhere in between? Emotional control, on the other hand, relates to our ability to control our own emotions and to have an influence on the emotions of others.

Of course, if one were to take the MTQ Plus or similar measure of mental toughness to find that they were, for instance, low on life control, might this person feel hopeless and might such a finding simply just confirm their feelings of helplessness and hopelessness? While such a response is possible, it is absolutely critical to remember that mental toughness can be enhanced through effective coaching and dedicated self-improvement. Knowing what your areas for growth are is usually the first step in a journey to become stronger in those areas or, where necessary, to circumvent areas of difficulty is that is a preferable and more effective approach.

Characteristics of the components of control in relation to mental toughness are perhaps best summarized as follows:

Life Control	
High	**Low**
• "Can do" attitude • Recognize limits of control without self-blame • They are capable of making changes • Have an active role in their own lives and lives of others (but also have limits) • Willing to try new things • Optimistic • See opportunity • View challenges as positive • Seek out motivation • Recognize obstacles and develop methods to overcome them • Good planning skills • Strong organizational skills • Can "operationalize" challenges into manageable plans • Tend to be effective multitaskers • Set effective priorities and stick with them within reason • Adaptable • View failure as an opportunity to learn • Can take on too much • Intolerant of those with lower life control • Can be perceived as being control freaks • Micromanage others • Intimidate others • Overplan • Set unrealistic goals for others • May fail to see/act on improving their own weaknesses • Overfocus on their strengths • Overconfident	• Not overwhelming to others • Not pushy • Allow others' space to work independently • Encourage *others* to take risks • Fatalists—victim-oriented • View life as hostile • View situations as happening to them • Passive • Blame self/others for circumstances • Make excuses • Low accountability • Avoid taking responsibility • Pessimistic • See failure as an option and as an end itself • Unwilling to take risks • Actively seek excuses • Procrastinate • Use cautionary language ("If . . ." "But . . ." and so on) • Difficulties with setting priorities • Easily overwhelmed • See themselves as passive victims

Emotional Control	
High	**Low**
• Able to manage their own emotional responses • Effectively camouflage intense emotional reactions as necessary • Have a good sense of emotional balance (i.e., while camouflaging their emotions, they do not neglect their own need for emotional expression and well-being) • Difficult to provoke • Not easily annoyed • Deal well with difficult people • Mask anxiety effectively • Deal well with bullying behaviour • Unlikely to be bullies themselves • Empathetic • Compassionate • Approachable • Socially well-liked • Can be *too* controlled (perceived as being robotic or distant/cold) • Can be perceived as being *too* optimistic/high energy • May not make great leaders as they can have difficulty in communication and connecting at a genuine level	• Reveal emotions to others, perhaps *too* much and *too* honestly • Easily effected by the moods of those around them • Can let the negative moods of others have a negative impact on their own mood • Struggle with criticism/feedback • Require external affirmations • Feel that things happen to them • Lack a sense of control over their own emotions • Blame others • Overemphasize the negative aspects of emotions • Underemphasize positive emotions of others • Can lose control of their own emotions easily • Easily hurt/angered • Can misread positive affection as more than it really is • Self-critical • Blame self when things go wrong • Emphasize character over situation when things go wrong • Perceived as being unpredictable and therefore, difficult to approach

Chapter 4

Commitment

"Every corpse on Mount Everest was once a highly motivated individual. So maybe settle down."

—Unknown

Motivational speakers make much of goal setting and working hard to achieve goals. Often, they delve into what might best be described as delusional thinking. They will say "You can do anything that you put your mind to." Well, I have tried really hard and I will not ever be capable of being 3 inches taller. Nice try, motivational speakers! We all have limitations and to suggest otherwise is harmful thinking. It is important to have goals, to be sure, and it is important that we have the initiative and work ethic necessary to achieve these goals. But to say that we can achieve any goal we set for ourselves, essentially becoming whatever we want to be is bordering on dangerous thinking. Such thinking is often destined to do little but set people up for disappointment which, while a potentially valuable learning experience, can also be devastating. Making commitments to reasonable and challenging goals and having the endurance to do what is necessary to achieve those goals is admirable and arguably lies at the core of human initiative. However, as individuals, we have certain limits and we need to be aware of these as well as being aware of our strengths so that we can make the best decisions leading us to success.

I have worked with many young adults who experience considerable disillusionment when they do not immediately meet their career goals upon graduation. They have built up a mythology, supported by well-intentioned parents and teachers, amplified through pop media, that once they have jumped through all of the necessary hoops, they will experience success—the dream job, the great car, the attractive partner, the nice home. When these things do not come to immediate fruition, they experience, perhaps really for the first time in their lives, a sense of bitterness. They were of the belief that if they did everything as expected, then the reward would be inevitable. But sometimes, the world does not work that way and if they had not experienced significant disappointment earlier in their lives, they may not have any resilience with which to rely on to regroup and engage in more realistic planning.

I recall one student who wanted to study music in university. To do so, he had to have his high school diploma and meet the minimal acceptance requirements of the university. However, this student, despite my advice as his post-secondary advisor and counsellor and that of his teachers, focused solely on his performance portfolio. He was a strong performer and could command a stage with ease, but he was so focused on his performance that he let his other courses slide. Ultimately, he did not pass his math course and was not accepted to his university of choice. Nor had he made plans to study elsewhere. Upon receiving the news, he stormed into my office with his "thanks but no thanks" letter from the university gripped tightly in his hand. "This," he yelled, shaking the crumpled up roll of paper at me, "is YOUR fault! You are supposed to plan for my university and you never said that I needed math to get in! Now what are you going to do about it?!"

Fun fact—math was required for admission to almost all university programs in Canada at the time and this point was noted repeatedly to all students from grade 9 through grade 12. I had also sat with this student numerous times to advise him of the need for him to do well in all of his classes, because music still required that he meet the standard for admission, which included math. I had numerous conversations with him and his parents, various emails, and all sorts of planning documents, all of which were recorded and submitted to the student and his parents. In any case, not being used to being yelled at by 17-year-olds, I stood and quietly closed the door.

"Actually, what are *you* going to do about it?"

Unsurprisingly, he started to cry. I understood his frustration and anger and fear. He needed a target for his high emotions and I was it. Fair enough. But the question I asked remained. Despite knowing what his goal was, he did not do what was necessary to actually achieve that goal, despite the advice of numerous adults, ranging from his parents, his teachers, the university advisors, and me. A hard lesson that he could not get by on charm alone, nor on his skill as a musician. He needed to regroup and that was a hard path, one that conflicted with messages he had learned to believe, often from pop media, but also from other well-intentioned adults in his life. He had been told that he would make a "great musician" and that his future as a performer was bright. These messages were coupled with any number of stories of musicians and other artists who had success despite not having any formal training. He tended to ignore the fact that some of his favourite musicians had, in fact, studied their art extensively and most had university experiences that facilitated their growth in their field. Sure, there are always stories of those who achieve success in the arts with limited to no training. But invariably, there is still a great deal of work involved. Our societal messages are often conflicting and confusing for our young people, it is perhaps not surprising that we see those who do not have mental toughness feeling unhappy with their lives when things do not fit the narrative they have been told.

Developing a sense of commitment to goals and the wherewithal to achieve those goals is a central tenet of mental toughness. Without goals or a sense of achievement, the rest of the 4Cs rather fall apart. There is no directedness to challenge, there is no need for control, there is no sense of confidence without a sense of commitment.

Plans *Gang Aft Agley*

"The best laid schemes o'mice n'men/ aft gang agley"

—Robbie Burns, Scottish Poet

I had personally set some pretty high goals for myself when I was in my 20s. For some reason, I felt a need to accomplish a lot, quickly. So, I had academic goals, relationship goals, financial goals, lifestyle goals, and so on. Most of these were unrealistic or, perhaps more accurately, premature. I started university straight from high school at 17, married the first girl I had dated for more than 6 weeks by the age of 21, had my second degree at 22, a third by 25. My wife and I had planned to have children as soon as I started teaching, we were looking at houses, it was all very exciting. At no point did I stop to think about *why* I was in such a rush, but in any case, I was trying to pack a lot of living into a short period of time. And I was deeply committed to all of these things happening fast. I worked hard at university, taking full spring and summer courses (ending up with a double major in psychology and English Literature), my wife and I were not immediately successful in having kids, so within a few months of trying, we had a fertility consultant working with us. Again, this was after only a few months of trying—we barely gave it a chance, we were both in a rush.

By 25, my marriage was over, no children, there was no house, not even on the horizon, little money, and I was living in a city where I knew no one. I had three degrees and no job. In retrospect, while my goal orientation was high—I wanted to achieve a great many things and had clear targets—my achievement orientation lagged behind. The achievement orientation powers our goal orientation. The ability to make goals tangible and enact behaviours that get us closer to our goals is the focus on the achievement orientation. So, I had to re-evaluate my sense of identity in light of a number of deeply intrinsic goals associated with my sense of self, from husband, father, man who can provide for his family, professional, etc., to divorced student with no money in a strange city. No wife, no kids, no job, no house. All of this happened over time, to be sure, but the loss of identity was still rather shocking since I had spent a lifetime, or least my adolescent years, thinking I knew who I was and who I was going to be.

Over time, I re-evaluated and I learned. There really was no rush. Unfortunately, my learning orientation, which we will discuss later, was such that I require more than one kick at the can to truly learn, so I set a new goal to have my PhD completed and be registered as a psychologist by 30. Again . . . why? What was the rush? I had, on the other hand, perhaps learned my lesson too well in terms of relationships. I studiously avoided long-term romantic relationships, refusing to allow myself to experience the hurt and pain associated with my failed marriage. And I do find that phrasing interesting, a "failed" marriage. The marriage itself didn't fail. I failed my marriage. In any case, I was not at all interested in putting myself at emotional risk again, resulting in a number of short-term relationships that I left quickly, even if there was potential for exploration for a deeper connection. In fact, the moment it seemed like there could have been a deeper connection, I would bail. Happily, I eventually found myself taking a risk which resulted in my current relationship with my wife who, God loves her, puts up with my shenanigans and tolerates the most frustrating of my personality traits, including a shocking lack of attention to detail. For instance I have successfully lost my passport on three separate occasions (see how I reframed losing a passport three times into a "success" story!), once shortly before a return flight from Washington, DC to Calgary, Alberta, which necessitated her flying back alone while I relived the plot of *Planes, Trains, and Automobiles*, flying from DC to Boston, then to Buffalo, then renting a car at 1 a.m. to drive across the Canadian border to Toronto, then catching a flight to Calgary, all before teaching a class the following morning essentially straight from the airport. Even the most basic of activities with me is a high-risk adventure due to my probably unwarranted wildly optimistic attitude. Fun times, and she is still married to me—go figure!

The emptiness that we experience upon completion of a goal, especially when we have no new goal to supplant the previous one, can lead us into some pretty dark places. Nature abhors a vacuum, as the saying goes, and what does one do when a goal is met or, even worse, when a goal is met but then falls apart? Ideally, we set new aspirational goals and set out to achieve these new and exciting opportunities to explore our capacities. Unfortunately, in my case, I filled the void of a failed marriage with work. Work can be a rewarding experience and make no mistake, I really enjoyed (and continue to enjoy) my work. Yet it may not, and should not, be expected to fill the emotional needs associated with an intimate human relationship.

My efforts to become a better person have been full of stumbles and falls. Falling seven times? Got that beat by a factor of dozens. But, I have remained committed to becoming a better person. My work life remains an area in which I need to develop a better sense of balance, but that goal is one I am constantly working toward achieving. When engaging in mentally tough behaviour, we have to do hard things. And in doing hard things, we become stronger and hopefully, others can learn that despite our failings, we can continue to set new goals for ourselves that shape us into more effective human beings.

Identity Status and Development

"Who are you? (Who, who, who, who)"

—Pete Townsend of The Who

Each of us has a sense of personal identity to which we aspire. However, our path to that sense of ideal self is rarely easily traversed. In fact, it is often in our stumbles that true growth lay. In terms of my own development, the trajectory from a person who had been highly value-driven to a person who was essentially a wreck was rather shocking to me. It was humbling to be a person who valued a strong, committed marriage (as I had learned from the excellent example set by my own parents, who not only had a successful marriage, but also worked together every day!) to a divorced 25-year-old. I have since experienced any number of self-inflicted challenges, as most of us have, and my previous commitment to a sense of identity had fallen apart and had to be rebuilt more than once.

It is interesting that this sense of existential crisis is actually pretty common in adulthood. James Marcia, a Canadian researcher, proposed a model of identity development for young adults that built on the work of Erik Erikson, the well-known psychologist who proposed a lifespan approach to human social and emotional development. Erikson's work continues to be taught in introductory and developmental psychology classes, its longevity likely due in no small part to its cohesive and logical/common sense approach. For instance, in young adulthood, Erikson proposed that we go through a phase which he called identity versus role confusion. The healthy person develops a sense of individual identity after exploring alternatives to their sense of self. It relies on an ability not only to explore but also to commit to a pathway. Those who experience role confusion do not satisfactorily explore options in terms of identity (things like spiritual beliefs, career options, educational values, sexuality, and so on), or, if they do, they do not make any commitments to aspects of identity, leaving them in a sort of existential free-fall. Since the time Erikson initially developed this theory, it is worth noting that the model, while designed around the idea of young adulthood, could be considered to apply to children and older adults as well.

Marcia's work capitalized on the ideas of exploration and commitment. Specifically, he proposed that the degree to which individuals explored different aspects of self and the extent to which they committed to these factors suggested a specific identity status. He proposed the following matrix:

Commitment

		Yes	No
Exploration	Yes	Identity Achievement	Moratorium
	No	Foreclosure	Identity Diffusion

Specifically, a psychologically healthy (or, in our terms, mentally tough) individual would be one who had experienced challenges, explored a range of options related to a sense of cohesive identity, and has made a firm yet flexible commitment to these options. The areas that Marcia suggested that we explored and committed to (or not) included vocation, sexuality, religion, political beliefs, and so on. As such, it is possible to fit into more than one square in the matrix. You could have engaged in a deep exploration of your vocational options and made a reasoned commitment to one of the choices in that area, but you may be in the process of exploring your sexuality while also being foreclosed in relation to religious and spiritual beliefs.

Many adolescents and young adults are in the moratorium phase in that they are actively exploring aspects of their identity, but have not yet made any commitments. In terms of mental toughness, the moratorium status implies risk-taking along with the goal and achievement orientations. We need to feel comfortable to take moderate risks in order to truly become independently functioning human beings. The risk of not working toward goals, not taking risks and not having a strong sense of achievement, is to find oneself either foreclosing on a specific areas, often based on parental or community expectations, or to remain in a state of neither exploration nor commitment (identity diffusion). Mentally tough individuals need to have the freedom to explore options. Unfortunately, many well-meaning parents prohibit their children from doing so. They do not want to see their kids make the same mistakes they did. I urge parents to draw upon their own wisdom when thinking about placing potentially unhealthy limits on exploration. Your kids are unlikely to repeat your mistakes—they are quite capable of making their *own* mistakes!

Of course, adults want the next generation to learn from the benefit of their experiences. And this is a fair and reasonable expectation both in terms of the larger societal aspect (we do not want to repeat historical mistakes that have had devastating effects on our species and planet) and the microunit of the family. That said, it is important for children, adolescents, and young adults to experience their own mistakes. They need to explore their own sense of identity to fully achieve a sense of independent self. Mental toughness, specifically the concept of commitment, is central to this evolution of the individual.

I have worked with a fairly staggering number of young adult clients who, upon being asked "what do you want to do when you finish high school" have absolutely no sense of how to answer. Many say, "I don't know . . . university?" as if I had asked them the name of a place as opposed to a course of action. Of course, there are those who, from a very young age, know exactly what they think that they want to do "when they grow up." These people kind of scare me. For a 14-year-old to say "I'm going to be an engineer" is a bit disconcerting. Why? How do they know? What IS an engineer to them, anyway? And in many of these latter cases, what is the source of their rather immature and premature commitment to this vocational goal? I'll give you a hint. It is more often than not parents who are themselves engineers. This is the path to foreclosure. A deep commitment, prematurely made, to an aspect of identity that is almost certain to be a source of frustration and perhaps even bitterness as the individual matures. So, in many cases, when I have a high school student who says, "I don't know" in response to questions about what they want to do after high school, my response is often "good for you!" Adolescence is a time of exploration, to start to set goals and develop a sense of how to achieve them, not a time to commit to someone else's goals.

Other areas of exploration include religion and sexuality. In children of parents who have highly rigid religious beliefs, especially when those beliefs are shared by the community in which the family lives, there can exist a hesitancy for the young adult to truly explore their options. They may be criticized for questioning their faith, or for challenging dogmatic thinking. Many people are religious not because of a true faith or personal relationship with a higher power, but because that is what they were taught by their parents. While there is some degree of validity to making commitments to parentally influenced religious beliefs, the potential for harm does exist. Part of the challenge here is that individuals who base their religious beliefs upon parent or community teachings may only have a very narrow view of religion, and as a result, see those who have differing views as being fundamentally flawed. History and indeed, contemporary society, is replete with examples of those who have, due to their foreclosure on religious beliefs, ostracize or act in discriminatory ways toward those with differing belief systems.

As I have noted, I come from a very religious family. My parents and brother are the types of Christians who rarely miss church services, who actively engage in the social aspect of their faith, who view most things through a lens of faith. I respect that and certainly, while I was being raised, shared in that experience. My social life was one part embedded in my friends at school, the other was through my church youth group. Over time, I have become less observant of some of the more dogmatic aspects of my church's faith. As a younger adult, I explored other aspects of faith and came to understand that Christianity is one way of conceptualizing the world, but perhaps not the only way. In time, I explored other faith heritages and alternative explanations of reality, including science and existential philosophy, and found commonalities more so than I did differences between varying perspectives. In general, all faiths and quests for knowledge seemed to lead back to the same central question: "What is life all about, anyway?" Christianity, the faith of my childhood, remains the one I associate with because it has a resonance for me that goes beyond simple adherence to ritual. But I have also learned that there is validity to other perspectives as well. As the minster who married my wife and I put it, "Religion is simply the voice of God speaking to us in different languages." That's cool! But I had the opportunity and freedom to explore and commit to my own religious perspective. Others do not always have that chance.

Sexuality is another area of exploration that has more recently become more open in western society. There are more and more models in pop culture and in society in general of those who are not heteronormative. Sexuality has become a valid area of exploration and is increasingly accepted, thought certainly not universally so, as falling along a spectrum as opposed to a dichotomous paradigm. While there is work yet to do, and not all communities are accepting of the concept of a range of sexuality, there has been some positive traction that appears to be promising of a positive and more accepting future.

The "C" Word

For many, commitment is the "C" word. Even within the 4C model of mental toughness, commitment is the one "C" that stands out because it requires action. Once can *think* about challenges, one can *have faith* in their sense of control, and one can *believe* in their confidence. But to commit is to *do*. Commitment is, in many ways, the transmission of the 4C vehicle. Extending that particular analogy, challenge could be seen as being the engine that provides motion, control is the operator who sets direction, confidence is the fuel that gives challenge its energy and makes progress possible. Without commitment, we have a frustrated driver with a full tank of fuel and a high-quality engine that is disconnected from any means of propulsion. Commitment makes us go.

The two components of commitment in the 4C model are goal orientation and achievement orientation. Both are critical to achieving our highest degree of potential, but I urge readers to exhibit caution when considering the concept of potential. I have read hundreds of report cards and heard a similar number of teachers and parents make comments about their children, saying "They're a great kid, but they are not meeting their potential." Potential is used like a finite, achievable outcome, something one can somehow "meet." So let me ask you a question:

Have *you* met *your* potential?

I trust that if you are being honest, the answer will be no. Of course not, it's a ridiculous question. It is ridiculous on one hand because the premise itself of being able to meet an unknown quality is not even a fair expectation. It is ridiculous on another account in that if one were to meet their potential, they would almost immediately start to set a new goal that would exceed their current potential. Our potential is a running river, impossible to seize upon in a moment because it is constantly changing. So maybe we could rephrase our comments. Instead of saying that someone is not meeting their potential (because we understand the inability to meet one's potential to be true of all people), we could perhaps say something along the lines of "the student's performance does not appear to be consistently applied in a way that leads them to success on specific tasks." Yes, I admit, it doesn't roll of the tongue quite as nicely, but at the same time, it is more actually descriptive of what is likely happening and as educators and parents, accurate descriptions can help us find better ways to support our kids as opposed to glib sayings that carry little meaningful weight and are, in fact, potentially damaging. If you employer were to say that you were not meeting your potential, but provided no further descriptive information, you would likely have an emotional reaction that would do little to help inform your goals nor the steps necessary to achieve them.

As we learn to set reasonable goals, we ideally also learn how to go about achieving these goals. It is in the combination of goal setting and the achievement orientation that we can see the eventual fruits of our efforts. But it is not an easy path, especially if we set high standards for ourselves. If we do set a goal that is reasonable yet challenging, our sense of achievement and accomplishment tends to be higher. We need to take advantage of the opportunities we have to achieve our goals, and be aware of barriers, including fear of failure/judgement and anxiety, that may prohibit us from moving forward.

No one ever said setting and achieving goals would be easy. Again, our Latin friends had something to say on this issue: *Ex Nihilo Nihil Fit.* Nothing comes from nothing. In order to achieve a goal, one must work hard. And the underlying message suggests that a goal worth setting is a goal worth working toward, but at the same time, any goal should in itself be one that challenges us. Again, we see the common themes of mental toughness—commitment, challenge, confidence, control—having an interactive relationship.

Goal Orientation

"Stay on Target"

—Gold 5 on first Death Star trench run, *Star Wars*

Surrounded by enemy fighters, being shot at by cannons while frantically racing toward a very small target, it's not surprising that Gold 5 needed to remind his wingman to keep his focus on their objective. There were a few distractions! In *Star Wars*, as in life (as is often the case!), it can be difficult to stay focused on our goals, even when those goals are critically important to us. We can lose focus, become distracted by external events, or even by our own uncertainty and fear. We can find ourselves beset on different sides by factors that distract us from even the most critically important goal.

To maintain focus, it is important that our goals have intrinsic value. Those who are higher in relation to goal orientation tend to find ways to set personally meaningful goals or, when working toward goals that have been set for them (for instance, academic goals that parents set for high school students or quarterly sales goals set by managers), they can find ways to make a personal connection, often from an emotional perspective. For instance, a sales goal in itself may not be intrinsically rewarding and as such, may leave us susceptible to distractions. I am not in sales, but in my business, we always have reports to write. The report-writing process is not one I particularly enjoy, so I can find myself distracted by, well, pretty much anything. I am particularly susceptible to news show bloopers on YouTube, Lord knows why, but I cry laughing and can be lost for hours.

If, on the other hand, we can focus on the positive emotional reaction we get from simply achieving a goal, the sense of completion or a job well-done, then we are more likely to experience success with having that extrinsic goal. The emotional connection enhances our focus.

When we work toward any goal, it is advisable to focus on the process as opposed to the final result. If we get too focused on achieving a goal, we may not attend to the process required to get us there, and the process itself is often even more important, ultimately, than the goal itself. For instance, using the sales goal example, if in our journey to achieve a quarterly sales goal that has been determined by a manager, we find a way to connect with our clients in a more effective manner, then the long-term benefits of the ability to connect will ultimately be more important than meeting the quarterly goal itself. Of course, we need to be mindful of the reality of external goals. We are not going to maintain our employment in an organization if we do not consistently meet goals, even if we learn a lot about the process. Students will not be able to get into university if they do not meet the basic grade standards, at least, despite how much they enjoy the learning process. So the end results are important, to be sure. But the process is also very important and it is often in the process of setting and working toward goals, as to achieve the goals themselves, is where true happiness and success lie.

"It doesn't matter if you win or lose, it's how you play the game" is a well-known trope in sport, although as we transition from recreational to more competitive sport, NFL coach Vince Lombardi's observation "if it doesn't matter who wins or loses, then why do they keep score" becomes a more accurate reflection of reality, for better or worse. "It's how you play the game" is interestingly absent from post-game interviews in professional sport because in professional sport, it *is* often about winning the game. This is a reality. It is true in sport, education, the workforce, relationships, and it would be foolish to suggest that the achievement of goals is not important. The suggestion here is that perhaps it is possible that the value of the journey itself can often be underestimated, resulting in a hesitancy to take risks and to find alternative paths to goal achievement. A lock-step approach to achieving goals reduces creativity and can result in a somewhat depressive cycle in which we seek only the ends, not the means to get there.

Gööals

Of course, sometimes we have goals that we have no reasonable ideas as to how to go about achieving. Have you ever had the misfortune to assemble IKEA furniture? If not, allow me to describe the process. You have a box full of materials, parts, and tools (well, actually *a* tool—a small Allen wrench/hex lock bit of metal) and a booklet of black-and-white sketches, the cover of which features an image of the completed piece of furniture you are wanting to build, which is usually named something presumably non-sensical in Swedish. You sort the materials and parts in an orderly fashion and then look at the instructions. Oh, I should note that there are no words on the instructions, just a series of increasingly complex images showing the desired progress of the project. Invariably, the first image is designed to give the user a false sense of hope. Smiling cartoon figures helpfully show you the basics. "This will be easy" you think as you put a wooden dowel into a predrilled hole. By page 3 of the instructions, you have started to drink straight vodka and considering simply burning the semi-complete heap of plastic and pressboard as a sacrifice to the old gods of Norse mythology. Also, do not try assembling IKEA furniture with someone you love, because by the end of the project, it is likely the only one of you will be left to tell the tale. Between dishwasher loading and building IKEA furniture, I believe that couples therapists will never be short of work. I kid. Mostly.

It is worth noting that IKEA furniture is named as it is and the instructions are provided as they are largely because the founder of the company, Ingvar Kamprad, had a learning disability that made reading and remembering item names difficult. So he started naming products based on the pre-existing names of things (for instance, IKEA's best-selling piece of furniture is the Billy bookshelf, named after and IKEA employee named Billy; the Äpplarö outdoor furniture series is named after a Scandinavian island). The instructions are purposely language free and have simple drawings so that ideally anyone could follow them, regardless of their ability to read in any language. This approach is actually a highly creative way of achieving a goal of making simple furniture easily accessible. Yet even when the process is made simple, it does not always work for everyone. The same could be said about goals. Or, in IKEA-speak, Gööals!

While IKEA furniture provides us with a clearly stated goal through the image on the front of the instructions, the process can be deeply frustrating and even damaging to relationships. The analogy, to be clear, is that even with a specific, targeted goal to which we can focus our energy, and even with knowledge of the steps necessary to achieve the goal, the actual process can be highly frustrating and challenging. However, there is always the opportunity to learn and, as such, the opportunity to grow which in itself is a valuable goal.

Goals and Telephone Poles

When setting goals, not only is it important to imbue them with personal meaning and to value the process to achieve them, but it is also important to keep them realistic and do-able. Returning to Terry Fox for a moment, his stated goal was to a raise a million dollars for cancer research through fund-raising by running across Canada. Of course, his Marathon of Hope has since far exceeded that goal which, from our current perspective, was quite modest. But to run across Canada to do so? That is an admittedly fearsome goal. Canada is a huge county, full of nasty weather and difficult terrain. Yet, this was somehow seen by Terry as completely achievable. How? He, like many long-distance runners, broke the journey into far more achievable smaller goals. Waking up thinking "I'm going to run across Canada" would send most people scrambling back to the sane comfort of bed. "Today, I'm going to run a marathon" would likely have the same effect on most people. "Today, I'm going to run a marathon on one leg." Forget about it. But Terry's mantra was "Today, I'm going to run across Canada, starting with a marathon today, which I will run on one leg, but I will measure my achievement as my ability to run from one telephone pole to the next." He often spoke of his focus as being even as limited on one step to the next. It's similar to the idea of "How does one eat an elephant?"

One bite at a time. How does run across the second largest country in the world? One step at a time.

Of course, Terry did not achieve his goal of running across Canada. But I doubt that anyone has ever heard of Terry Fox and thought "What a failure! Didn't even achieve his goal." Of course not—he far exceeded what almost all human beings are capable of despite technically not meeting his goal of running across Canada. The goal orientation does not suppose the actual achievement of goals; rather it expects that one can set challenging goals that we can strive toward and in so doing, learn more about our own capacities.

Achievement Orientation

Individuals who are highly achievement oriented then to be motivated to what is necessary to achieve their goals, regardless of if they are set by themselves or others. Of course, the more intrinsic the goal, the higher the motivation to achieve that goal and the more satisfaction derived from the achievement. If we set our own goals, we are more likely to persevere through challenges and overcome barriers that may stand in the way of our goals. We can be more focused on achieving our goals, although those who are more achievement oriented will likely do what is necessary regardless of the goal being intrinsic or extrinsic.

The Darkness and the Light of the Achievement Orientation

There is a need to engage mechanisms to prevent individuals from being *too* single-minded in their pursuit of their goals. History is replete with highly achievement-oriented individuals who have caused immense damage. Single-mindedness and an intense focus on achievement can be a powerful combination and like all things, power requires a governor to ensure that it is manifested in a helpful and positive manner. We have discussed the need for a moral governor to help regulate our mental toughness and this is particularly true of the achievement orientation. A strong and positive sense of morality and a code of ethics (personal and/or professional) will support and guide a sense of achievement, limiting the risk associated with an unchecked single-mindedness.

For instance, a corporate leader may present as being highly achievement oriented. They will strive toward success, and encourage those on their teams to share in their desire to attain their goals. However, what if the goal is best achieved by eliminating the competition by whatever means necessary? The achievement orientation could serve to embolden the leader and their team to use unsavory and perhaps even ethically questionable means to eliminate their competition, thereby helping them achieve their team goals. What checks are in place to prevent this sort of situation from happening? Most professions have codes of ethics, and there are laws and guidelines established in the corporate world to govern the behaviours of those involved in trade. There are, of course, any number of examples of those who abuse the systems in which they work to achieve their goals. In David Fincher's *The Social Network*, the foundation of Mark Zuckerberg's Facebook empire is examined and does not paint a flattering picture of the social media guru, who is depicted as being socially inept, egotistic, arrogant, and largely amoral. This critique may, however, be lost on some who might view the multiple billions of dollars that Zuckerberg acquired. There is certainly a mixed message here—on one hand, the film depicts Zuckerberg is a social isolate who is a petty and ultimately small man who is driven by insecurity and fear, but on the other hand, he does have his billions to assuage his loneliness.

In any case, the achievement orientation, on balance could be viewed as being a significant contributor to human success. It is not particularly helpful to establish goals if one does not have the wherewithal to go about achieving those goals, which is where the achievement orientation comes into effect. Achieving goals in any endeavour, from playing video games to creating great art, requires an achievement orientation. There are those who have a high goal orientation, but who may lack in their achievement orientation. Such individuals set goals for themselves, but experience ongoing frustration because they rarely actually achieve their goals. They can tend to give up easily, especially when faced with setbacks or barriers. Their ability to maintain a strong and consistent goal-oriented focus is limited. As a result, they can experience frustration and self-recriminations. They can blame themselves, others, and their situations for a lack of success.

One example would be from the world of addictions. Addictions can range from substances (alcohol, illicit drugs, prescription medications, and so on) to specific behaviours (gambling, sex, shopping) and most contemporary science indicates a disease-based model that underlies almost all addictive responses. This disease-oriented model has significantly enhanced our understanding of addictions and has gone a long way, though not as far as we perhaps would like, toward reducing stigma associated with addictive behaviours. Alcoholics are seen not as weak-willed, soft-minded fools who cannot learn a lesson. Rather, we understand the addictive mechanism from a neurophysiological and sociocultural perspective. Genetics are accounted for, as are socioeconomic status, trauma, and other contributing factors, most of which are not within the control of those afflicted with the disorder. Such an understanding has allowed us to create new treatment models that have been far more effective, yet not curative.

Regardless of societies' changing attitudes toward addictions, those who suffer from alcoholism and other addictions remain deeply ashamed of their conditions. They may choose to live with their addiction as opposed to seeking out help because of the fear of judgement associated with not only help seeking but also the very nature of their addiction. How can any strong-willed, intelligent person be trapped by a bottle? The thought seems ridiculous. So they choose, against their own better judgement, to continue with their addictive behaviour even though help is truly a click of a mouse or a call away. From a mental toughness perspective, it is possible that even though they may have a goal of cessation of their addictive behaviours, their achievement orientation is perhaps not up to the task, for any number of reasons. Perhaps they have tried to stop before and have not been successful. This lack of success can erode at a sense of achievement. The goal remains, but the ability to persevere to that goal is impaired by previous failures. Alternative approaches are attempted. Many alcoholics report their numerous attempts to stop drinking. Switching from hard liquor to beer or wine; drinking only on weekends; drinking only after dark; drinking only with other people; drinking only with food; these and many others are attempts cited by those who have tried to stop or at least curtail their drinking, typically with poor to no positive results. The comment has often been made: "I can stop drinking any time I want, as long as it's next Tuesday."

While it would be foolish indeed to suggest that mental toughness could cure addictions, it could be conceptualized as being a positive counteracting characteristic than can have a small role in helping one attain and maintain sobriety. Setting a goal of being sober may be too much for some people with addictions, but the AA saying "one day at a time" is essentially predicated on the commitment model. The goal, obviously, is to not drink for one day. The achievement is to do so for one day only. Tomorrow, the goal is reset and we can look back on our achievement of the preceding day as a moment of pride and encouragement. It is in this way that many people have overcome addictions.

To be clear, this is a highly simplistic perspective and in no way does it suggest that one simply develop mental toughness to overcome addictions. Again, mental toughness can be a positive contributing factor, but in itself is unlikely to make one sober. A positive achievement orientation need not necessarily be an overarching personality trait, but rather can be a part of a positive growth-oriented mindset that supports us in moving forward and achieving our goals. A positive learning orientation is also embedded in risk—we are more likely to engage in actions that lead us to the successful meeting of our goals if our risks pay off positively.

There are times when the pathways to our goals are beset with barriers. How do we go about overcoming these barriers when it feels like no sooner do we overcome one setback then we are faced with another? Perseverance is a critical aspect of the achievement orientation. Overcoming challenges requires a sense of drive and an understanding of the intrinsic value of goals. In our personal lives, we are constantly facing barriers. We want to exercise, but find it hard to make the time, so we end up falling for quick, ineffective gimmicks that end up as glorified dust collectors. Who among us does not have a set of weights, an exercise bike, some sort of athletic gear lying about our homes, sullen remainders of our good intentions but lower achievement orientation at the time? Unused guitars, ancient kitchen appliances, books with unbroken spines, woodworking tools still in their boxes—whose home is not littered with such detritus? We have all fallen victim to our own aspirations and feel the ensuing guilt when we don't follow through. It might be more helpful, however, to feel a sense of positive pride in how our earlier ambitions that made us purchase these things in the first place. Reconceptualizing guilt for not using something to a more positive feeling of reclaimed pride and hopefulness that maybe *today* is the day I will use that stationary bike is a far more helpful and engaging process than sitting in guilt. But doing so requires significant effort and a willingness to let go of our guilt, which is really hard because by maintaining guilt, we have a built-in free pass. If we don't try, then we cannot fail. This kind of thinking is antithetical to the achievement orientation, which instead focuses on doing what is necessary to achieve our goals.

As an experiment, at the end of this paragraph, stop reading. **If you are at home, take a moment to put the book down and take a walk around and find THAT THING.** THAT THING is the thing you got on Amazon or somewhere at a time when you were feeling highly motivated to make a change. Maybe it's a breadmaker. Maybe a set of weights. Maybe a musical instrument. A book you haven't yet read. Find it and give it a dust. Make it a priority. And really focus on what you were feeling when you purchased it. Think back to the optimism, the hope you had. Relive the hope, eliminate the guilt you have experienced since for not having used it. Guilt is not a particularly helpful emotion. In general, it does not advance us. It does not make us go. Paragraph is over—go get THAT THING.

Welcome back. How did that go? Ideally, you had a feeling not only of positive reminiscence but also, perhaps a renewed sense of achievement toward a new goal. Maybe not, but maybe! In any case, you have brought THAT THING back into your awareness and have tried to focus on an emotion other than guilt and as such, hopefully this has been a useful exercise in reframing negative emotions.

The No-Win Situation

Literature and film are replete with no-win scenarios. These are often contrived situations in which the hero finds themselves in a situation for which escape appears to be impossible. Indiana Jones running away from a huge rolling boulder with no visible means of escape. Frodo and Sam on the cliff of Mount Doom, exhausted, without water, their mission apparently at a point of failure. The entire conceit of *Sophie's Choice*. Each of these situations indicates that while there is a goal in mind, the situation is set up in such a way that there is no way to achieve the goal, perhaps at all, and certainly not without risk. The *Kobayashi Maru* simulation from *Star Trek: The Wrath of Khan,* is set up as a classic no-win situation in which the *Enterprise* either attempts to rescue a damaged ship per its primary mission or it is attacked and destroyed by enemy vessels. In any choice the commander makes, there will be loss. Of course, there is always a solution (as Captain Kirk found, cheating is sometimes an option!), but sometimes some solutions carry some very negative consequences.

One need not look to classic no-win scenarios to find dilemmas associated with the achievement orientation. **Barriers of all sorts exist. The question is do we have the wherewithal to overcome those challenges?** Sometimes, the barriers may seem overwhelming and indeed, may be associated with considerable risk and may not seem to be worth the effort. If you lose your job, is it worthwhile engaging in retraining in a new field, or is that too much effort, too high risk? If your marriage is failing, do you engage in counselling? There is a risk that your ego may be challenged or that it may not work, so do you avoid and live in the conflict? Those who are more achievement oriented may be more likely to face the challenges head on so as to enhance the probability of achieving their goals. In long-distance running or hiking, it is often suggested that you remove anything that may be uncomfortable as soon as you notice its presence. Feel a pebble in your shoe? Stop immediately and get rid of it because if you don't, it will only become more problematic the further you go. The analogy here is clear—if there is something unpleasant that is preventing you from achieving your goal, do what you can to make your journey more comfortable.

Which, of course, brings us back to morality. The balance between removing an unpleasant, prohibitive obstacle does not imply that if a relationship is not going the way we want, we bail on it. I certainly have my history of doing so and have learned that there is more value in working through challenging times than running away from them. In the short term, sure, avoidance is reinforcing and oddly pleasant. But in the long term, avoidance simply leads to more avoidance, resulting in isolation and a lack of true engagement in life. Obstacles are not always bad, but in the case of removing an unpleasant obstacle in order to achieve a higher goal, it is the goal itself, not the obstacle, that one seeks to overcome. In a marathon, the goal is not to see how fast you can run a marathon with a pebble in your shoe; the goal is to see how fast you can run a marathon.

Knowing When to Stop

We all know people who enjoy setting and striving toward goals. Many of these people continue to set goals long after they have passed their peak, and those wiser among them adjust their goals accordingly. We also know those who keep the same goals despite having passed their optimal functioning, resulting in occasionally uncomfortable, frequently cringy moments. The singer who at best can hit a mid-G striving for a high-C? The characters in Bruce Springsteen's *Glory Days* reminiscing on their prime days, now in the distant past. The middle-aged man seeking to maintain his youth with a questionable hairpiece or a woman trying to recapture her youthful beauty by engaging in extensive plastic surgery. The singer, the *Glory Days* seekers, the hairpiece guy, and the plastic surgery beauty queen all personify the residue of achievement orientation left unfulfilled. Again, if the "potential" is not met, the risk lies in having people striving toward unrealistic goals that are inconsistent with their developmental pathways. That is to say, if we do not re-evaluate our goals on an ongoing basis, our striving for achievement is aimless and ultimately a source of frustration itself.

Returning to Nike's *Just Do It* slogan, what happens when "it" remains undefined or is unachievable. We find ourselves in positions in which we do not know what it is that we are striving toward and as a result we may not know when to stop. Similarly, what about when we do know what our goal is and despite numerous attempts, and different approaches, we still cannot achieve it. Do we keep striving or is it perhaps wise to re-evaluate the goal itself? Knowing when to stop is a critically important but largely undervalued skill. Many artists know this intuitively; they have the ability to know when one more stroke of the brush, one more note, one more word will be too much and may serve to detract from their vision. Athletes know the same thing, when a certain angle on a shot or twist of a muscle or pull-back on a backswing will result in impaired performance. As a psychologist, I know that I need to focus on when to stop, when to keep my mouth shut and truly just listen (despite all sorts of words desperately crying out to be said trapped behind my firmly shut mouth). Sometimes, the achievement orientation is best served by inaction.

Arrival Fallacy

In some cases, we work hard to achieve our goals and, upon achieving them, feel a sense of emptiness. The goal itself provided us with a sense of purpose and without our goals, we find ourselves free-floating, ships in search of a port.

In psychological terms, this emptiness is often the result of the arrival fallacy. The arrival fallacy is the phenomenon that occurs when we set goals for ourselves that serve not only as directives of future-oriented behaviours, but as destinations in themselves. The arrival fallacy is often the result of thinking that starts with "Once I achieve X, I will be satisfied," where X is any number of potential goals (a specific job, an athletic performance, a relationship, a house, etc.). Once I earn a million dollars a year, I will be happy. Once I have an attractive and intelligent partner, I will be happy. Once I shoot par, I will be happy. The commonality among these valid goals is the contingency factor. Happiness is contingent upon the goal. Recall earlier, we discussed the need for the process, not just the product, as being an important part of the goal setting and achieving experience. The arrival fallacy and contingent thinking explains why the process is important. If the goal itself is a prerequisite for contentment, then we run the significant risk that we may never truly be happy. We may never achieve the goal we set and as noted, it is human nature to set new goals up completion of other goals. "If/then" thinking does not serve to elicit contentment. The pleasure is in the process.

The arrival fallacy does have implications for most of us at some point. Who has not been disillusioned upon achieving some sort of goal? Ever have a birthday party that left you feeling somewhat uncomfortably despondent because it did little but leave you pondering the passage of time? Or maybe just not getting the kind of cake you wanted? Maybe your dream car just didn't have the acceleration you had hoped for. The dream job turned out to be underwhelming. The 72-shot golf game just left you angry about the short putt you missed on the seventh hole. Even that burger you'd been craving all day was just a bit dry. Life is full of potential disappointments!

On a small scale, we are mostly quite capable of overcoming the disappointments and the arrival fallacy plays a minor, inconsequential role. On the other hand, multiple disappointments accumulate over time, leading to more significant problems; similarly, single but overwhelming disappointments can be crippling. The protective factors that prevent us from sliding from disappointment into depression are those resources we establish over time—positive, supportive relationships, healthy lifestyles in which sleep, nutrition, and exercise are all well-attended to, a meaningful life beyond those smaller disappointments that allow us to experience success or, barring success, at least hope for success (or the perception thereof).

Wrapping Up

Characteristics of commitment in relation to mental toughness are perhaps best summarized as follows:

Goal Orientation	
High	**Low**
• Enjoy setting and working toward goals	• Goals and targets, exams, tests, assignments are intimidating
• Targets motivate them	• Tend to avoid as opposed confronting difficult situations
• Goals provide a source of drive	
• Can effectively articulate goals	• Avoid responsibility
• Tend to be objective/target-oriented	• Have difficulties with performance management
• Set personal bests and seek to better them	• Will try to ignore goals and targets
• Visualize success and *feel* it	• Avoid setting goals and targets
• Like being tested—see testing as being an opportunity to show what they can do	• Fear that a lack of immediate success failure will expose them as "failures"
• Will prioritize effort and activities	• Tend to distract attention from the goal
• Prepared to do what it takes to achieve goals	• Use "but" a lot ("I would have done it but . . . ")
• Maintain focus	• Tend to be easily distracted and struggle with re-engaging on task
• Deliver on time	
• Have a strong sense of conscientiousness	• Easily bored—won't commit time and effort
• Can overcommit	• Find working to a goal stressful
• Can fail to see that others aren't motivated in the same way	• Often adopt a minimalist approach
• Accept responsibility	• More likely to be late for things (avoidance)
• May miss doing things that are equally important or more pressing ("odd" sense of priorities)	• Can be flexible
• May "manage by numbers" (difficulty with setting priorities—first things first can be TOO literal)	• Open to alternative approaches to goals since they tend not to be highly committed

(continued)

Goal Orientation	
High	**Low**
• Can be single-minded in pursuit of goals • Tend to stick to their word • Set high standard for themselves and others • Can be seen as being rigid and lacking in empathy	• May have creative thoughts in goal attainment (not constricted by fear of not achieving goals) • Can be empathetic should goals not be achieved • May feel imposed upon by the goals of others • Can have an "I can't" as opposed to an "I'll try" attitude (even if evidence points to the fact that they can!) • Can blame others for a lack of success

Achievement Orientation	
High	**Low**
• Enjoy breaking things down into smaller components • Will work hard and for extended periods to achieve goals • Maintain focus • Diligent • Have a tenacious and consistent work ethic • Good at prioritizing • Can persevere on even unpleasant tasks • Tend to overwork • May miss out on alternative priorities • Can be rigid in their focus • Can be viewed by others as being overachievers • Take on too much responsibility (even the responsibilities of others who are completely capable)	• Easily overwhelmed, especially when more than one task at a time is required • Struggle to maintain focus over time • Willing to acquiesce to others even when they are capable of achieving a task • Tend to see tasks as being beyond their capacity and give up relatively easily • Difficulties with setting effective priorities • Find working to a goal to be stressful • Fear goals in general • Blame others • May skip/avoid/be late for work/school

(continued)

Achievement Orientation	
High	Low
• Take on too much responsibility (even the responsibilities of others who are completely capable) • Enjoy celebrating successes (their own and those of others) • Find goal achievement to be highly rewarding	• Minimalist approach to tasks—willing to do the bare minimum • In absence of goals, can be very relaxed and easy-going • Can be counted on to find easier pathways where necessary

Commitment requires foresight. We all become prognosticators in a sense, trying our best to predict the future (goals) by setting a direction in our behaviours (achievement). It is important to recognize that goals can be either internally or externally set and our commitment to achieving those goals is largely contingent upon how we feel about them. The emotional component is critical. If we do not feel that a goal is worthwhile, it becomes very difficult to engage in behaviours consistent with achieving the goal. Yet we all have goals that might seem uninspiring or overwhelming that we need to achieve, so finding a source of intrinsic motivation is important. Again, the focus here is on the emotional connection to the goal, more so than what we think about a goal. If we can find an emotional connection, it is far easier to engage in achievement-oriented behaviours that will help to get us where we need to go.

Chapter 5

Challenge

Problems v. Opportunities

We have all had those moments upon waking. The alarm blasts us into a semi-daze that could only loosely be referred to as being "consciousness" and we start to put together some rudimentary plans to get the day started. Like automatons, we initiate our morning routine, swinging (or dead-lifting) our legs out of the bed, staggering to the bathroom to get started on our self-care routine of teeth-brushing, showering, shaving, applying make-up, and so on. By the time we emerge from the bathroom, we are hopefully a bit more aware, but perhaps only barely . . . until we jump-start the morning with a caffeine rush. Coffee runs next only to water and tea in terms of global popularity, and gives water a solid run for second place in North America. I have never developed the taste for coffee, so my go-to for a caffeine rush has long been Coke (which, in my more recent years, has transitioned to sugar-free Coke Zero—there's a LOT of sugar in Coke!).

Now caffeinated, we start the day's journey of raising a family, going to school, working, or whatever it is we do. And little do we know it, but we have just embarked on a brand-new series of potential problems. Car not starting, traffic, bus is late, bus is early, coworkers are upset about something, boss is angry, teacher is in a "mood," kids are cranky—you name it. Yet here's the interesting thing—*every day*, we get up and face these problems, which is a really hard thing to do. Yet, we do it. Every. Single. Day. How can this be, when we know that our fight/flight/freeze response would most often make us want to avoid all of these problems? And who hasn't fantasized about just pulling up stakes and hitting the road for a shot at a new existence? Like the protagonist in Bruce Springsteen's *Hungry Heart*, some of us fantasize about taking a wrong turn and just keep on going. Yet most of us don't take Springsteen's protagonist's journey of abandonment and escape; instead, we keep coming back to difficult situations for more. Why?

Of course, the answer often lies in mental toughness. It takes a great deal of mental toughness, particularly a positive approach to problems, to face each day anew. A significant component of mental toughness that helps us face the problems of daily life relates to our perception—is our day full of problems or, perhaps, is it full of opportunities? As Homer Simpson called it when Lisa told him about a Chinese word that meant both crisis and *opportunity*: "Crisitunity!" We'll stick with the non-Homer version; *challenge* is the component of the 4C model that helps us to see the possibilities in problems.

Challenge refers to how we differentiate situations that we encounter on a daily basis, both the micro-stressors ("I'm out of toothpaste!") to more significant acute stressors ("My child is sick on the day I have to give a presentation at work"), to even more chronic stressors ("I am behind—and have been behind for months now—on my credit card payments"). Some consider such difficulties to be threats (and indeed, in many cases, they are correct in that perception), while others view the exact same situations as being opportunities. Being out of toothpaste could mean bad breath all day or an opportunity to try out that old baking soda hack that appears online from time to time; a sick child is no one's idea of a good time, but perhaps if they are resting, you could find some time to fine-tune the presentation, enhancing it beyond what you were prepared to present today; credit card debt is, of course, a huge source of stress, but there might be an opportunity there to think about consolidating your debt or make a budget. Naturally, many readers are right now thinking "Sure, easy to say—and not very realistic!" And you are right. Changing one's mindset is hard, ongoing work. But it also needs to be based in reality. There is no advantage to living with your head in the clouds of optimism. We need to be realistic optimists if we are to develop our sense of challenge.

We all know people who avoid challenges, and we also know those who actively seek it out. Both groups can encounter difficulties. By avoiding challenge, we put ourselves at risk—not in the traditional sense of risk-taking, but at risk for missing out on some of the most excellent experiences life has to offer. The date not asked for. The raise not requested. The feedback on a test avoided. Avoiding challenging situations breeds more avoidance, so people start to actively avoid any and all challenges and their lives become quiet, passive, and unsatisfactory. Others who are more risk-seeking, on the other hand, may also be at risk themselves for taking on too much. They may take inappropriate risks, or risk too much. The dates asked for and agreed upon, but without factoring in any real attraction to the other person. The raise asked for despite previous poor performance. The test feedback that, upon review, elicits anger toward the course instructor. Perhaps we can reflect upon the Goldilock's story. Goldilocks, while not a great role model, at least we could safely say that she was a risk-taker (though arguably, not a thoughtful one!).

Challenge and Learning to be Helpless (and Hopeful!)

Challenges occur all the time, and sometimes they can be too much for us to manage. All of us have had depressed moods in which we struggle to find the energy or motivation to do even the least challenging tasks. Getting out of bed is overwhelming. Deciding about what to watch on TV is a guilt-ridden ordeal than makes us regret even trying in the first place. Even the concept of "guilty pleasures" is a source of stress. So what if I like ABBA? It's hardly a guilty pleasure to appreciate some of the best pop music ever written. I love the music of Yes, despite of what critics have had to say about the band as being excessive and overwrought twaddle over the span of their career. I don't care—I like their music! To suggest guilt in relation to harmless enjoyment speaks volumes about why so many people experience depressive moods. If we cannot even enjoy our simple pleasures, how can we hope to find joy in the more significant areas of our existence?

Depressed moods are not uncommon and I believe it is fair to say that we can all empathize with such difficult times. Depression as a clinical disorder, on the other hand, is a completely different beast. People who have Major Depressive Disorder often have the same experiences described above (lethargy, lack of motivation, feelings of hopelessness and helplessness, etc.), but not just for a day or two . . . they have it for weeks at a time, sometimes even months and for some, even years. It's chronic and recurrent. Unpredictable and insidious. And widely misunderstood as being an issue of motivation and a lack of capacity to embrace challenge. Allow me to be clear—mental toughness can help people approach challenges as being opportunities, but it cannot cure depression. It can, however, be used as a tool to support those who may struggle with depression (or those who have depressed moods) in concert with more intensive psychotherapy and social support. In some cases, medication can be effective as well. I have had any number of clients indicate that their depression responds well to medication in that it does not eliminate symptoms, but it does allow them to view some of their challenges in a more optimistic and positive light, leading them to become more actively engaged in working through their challenges.

So, it could be argued that mental toughness is a tool with which we can, to some extent, alienate depressive symptomology but again, mental toughness development in itself should not be viewed as being sufficient for treating depression.

Martin Seligman's work on learned helplessness provides a good example of how we can examine challenge in response to adverse conditions. Seligman's famous (and ethically questionable, at best) experiments, involved placing dogs in kennels that were bisected by a fence, low enough that the dog could jump from side to side of the kennel with ease. On the floor of the kennel, one side had a normal concrete floor; the other side had a metal grid through which electric shocks could be delivered, enough to cause pain, but not enough to damage the dog's paws or skin. Seligman would place the dog on the metal grid and then run a current through the floor. The dog's escape instinct would initiate, and they would jump over the fence to the safety of the concrete floor. This pairing of electric current and escape behaviours occurred over a number of trials and the dog learned to escape the pain quite effectively. Then, in the second set of trials, Seligman raised the height of the fence to a point that the dogs could not jump over it, essentially cutting off their escape route. Then he again would run a current through the metal grid. The dogs would jump, howl, whine, and eventually they would tire and just lie down and take the shock. Finally, Seligman returned the fence to the initial, escapable level and again, ran the current through the floor. The dogs that had now been conditioned to simply take the pain and would not even try to escape. They would simply ignore the obvious escape route. They had learned that no matter what they did, they could not escape the pain, so they might as well just take it.

This phenomenon Seligman referred to as learned helplessness and is an underlying, albeit partial, explanation of depression. People with depression often do not seek out support because they believe that no matter what, nothing they do will help. They become unwilling to take a risk. Seligman's follow-up work focused on *learned hopefulness*—a leading concept in the field of positive psychology, an area of psychological theory and practice in which mental toughness is deeply intertwined. If we can learn helplessness, can we not learn to be hopeful? Seligman and his colleagues have found that yes, such thinking is certainly possible and, in fact, may be more true of the human condition than helplessness. Again, we see echoes of Seligman's work in the mental toughness model, specifically in relation to challenge and the two underlying concepts associated with challenge—Risk Orientation and Learning Orientation.

Risk Orientation

"The future has not been written. There is no fate but what we make for ourselves."

—Kyle Reese, *The Terminator* (as quoted in *Terminator 2*)

In *Terminator 2*, the lead characters find themselves in a pickle—they learn that the future can be changed, but their actions may not lead to a specific future, just a changed one. Their conundrum—do we take a specific action knowing that the future is unwritten—is one we all face daily. We are all time travelers and we all struggle with the uncertainty of fate. Does what we do make a difference, as we discussed in relation to life control? If so, are we then masters of our own fate? And if we are, does that not create a reality in which we have ultimate responsibility for our own actions and their consequences? Scary, big questions, but questions worth asking. But to the timid, to those who do not take risks, these questions become much smaller, less scary, but also ultimately less meaningful. If my choice is to not take a risk, to play it safe, then my lack of action, while still a choice, does not carry with it the same weight as actually taking an active risk. Rush's *Freewill* contains the lyric "If you choose not to decide, you still have made a choice." The concept of freedom to choose—or not—is heady stuff, and can result in an almost existential paralysis in which we feel that the consequences of choices are simply too overwhelming, so we choose not to decide. Which is, obviously a choice with its own consequences.

Philosophical questions aside, the risk orientation component of challenge focuses on the willingness an individual has in relation to actively deciding to take risks. The question to you is: **What is your comfort level with risk?** Risk should always have some degree of consideration of potential outcomes as part of the process, perhaps more so than other areas of mental toughness. Risk can lead us to some fantastic opportunities, but at the same time, unwarranted risk can lead us to disaster. Charlie Brown, despite his downtrodden demeanor, is a constant risk-taker when faced by Lucy and her football. In the *Peanuts* comics, Lucy would always hold the football for Charlie Brown to kick, always withdrawing it after having convinced him that *this time* will be different, just take a chance, you'll see, *this time* I won't jerk the ball away, leaving you to spin out and fall on your back. Poor Charlie Brown never really learns that it is Lucy's nature to lie and that no matter how optimistic he may be, she will *always* pull the ball away at the last second. Yet he always takes the risk.

The classic example of the *Titanic* also comes to mind, though risk is really associated with any human endeavour, from setting the alarm clock at night and trusting that it will go off to the more grandiose activity of constructing and launching an "unsinkable" ship. The *Titanic* risk was associated primarily with both arrogance and overconfidence in design. The maiden voyage, as we all know, was beset with disaster in no small part due to the high degree of risk taken in setting sail and the attempt to make the transatlantic crossing as fast as possible while at the same time, vastly underestimating the risk of the proverbial iceberg, with its massive, invisible, frozen mountain lying beneath the surface. The *Titanic* hitting the iceberg was truly a collision of metaphors. Unsinkable human hubris running afoul of the hidden and unknown unconscious. Unwarranted risk can be as, if not more, damaging as not taking the risk in the first place. On a sidenote, Rose could have taken the risk of shuffling over on that door and just maybe Jack could have lived. A discussion for another time!

Risk-oriented individuals actively seek out new and often exciting ways to engage with the world. Among sayings, one of my least favourite, and one that speaks poorly of those who use it frequently, is "if it ain't broke, don't fix it." I will grant that *perhaps* this proverb could be true when speaking of a favourite recipe, but little else. Experimenting, trying new things, taking risk—these are all a part of human evolution and growth. "If it ain't broke" is a low bar to set. Arguably, if our ancestors had the same mindset, it's unlikely we would have evolved at all. If our prehistoric ancestors Glargh and Glurg were coming back from hunting with an "ain't broke, don't fix" mindset, Glargh may have said: "Y'know, Glurg, carrying this deer we just strangled to death all the way back to the cave, where we will eat it raw and then die of food poisoning is the life for me!" No need for a spear, or bow and arrow, or fire. Or language, for that matter—Glargh could have simply gestured to Glurg! But language, tools, hunting gear, the wheel, and fire all improved their lives—and all involved risk. Somewhere in our history, someone thought something and then tried to grunt it out in a way that conveyed meaning. This was a risk—what if no one understood? What if they decided to beat that first language-user for just being different? Risk-taking assumes that, while perhaps not broken, things can be improved. All things. And all relationships. But to make improvements, changes are necessary, and change is risk.

Go West—But Maybe Plan a Bit Too!

We all have examples from our lives in which risk did not work in our favour and hopefully, we learned and continued to take risks, perhaps with a bit more of a focus on what we have learned from previous risk. For instance, when I moved to Calgary to pursue my PhD, I was going through a divorce, I was leaving my home, and I had essentially no money. I was never at risk for being homeless or anything like that—my family was able to support me, but I was (am) rather stubborn and wanted to do things my own way. In any case, I had, in my haste to get away from my troubles in the East, fallen victim to the geographical cure, the idea that relocating will somehow make our difficulties all go away. Of course, the geographical cure is rarely effective, and, in my case, I made some decisions along the way that were, in retrospect, not particularly intelligent. For instance, I arrived in Calgary with no place to stay and not enough money to get a hotel. I was driving my Dodge Shadow, stuffed with clothes and books, and with nowhere to stay, I spent my first few nights sleeping bolt upright in the driver seat (the car was stuffed so the seat wouldn't recline) in the parking lot at the university's football stadium while I tried to secure a place in residence. After a few days, I had a place to stay but still, no money. I hadn't really thought about the fact that student loans would only pay for tuition, books, and accommodation (and even accommodation would only be reimbursed, not paid outright, so my credit card was maxed out). I was now in residence, but still had no money for food. Having Crohn's Disease has its weird little advantages, and I can easily go for a few days without food, so that was okay, for the moment.

A few days after arriving in Calgary, and the day after I moved into res, I went to a new graduate student orientation. While grazing at the small banquet table, stuffing myself with mini-sandwiches and cheese & crackers, I met a professor who was in search of a teaching assistant. I jumped. I almost always jump at these sorts of things, still do, in fact, often to my own chagrin. But this was a great opportunity and, most importantly, a source of income for the next few months. I did not have a scholarship because I did not apply for one. As this was the mid-1990s, the Internet was not what it is now, so scholarships were still mostly paper-and-pen documents that you had to get from actual universities by actual mail. I had not done this rather critical step and as such, missed out on a number of opportunities. But I now had a place to live and money for food. Not too bad!

I have since learned that a bit of planning can go a long way to easing anxiety and stress. This example of poor planning and the opportunities arising from pure change and luck is my own story. One of many. You, of course, have your own stories as well. Personal examples guide personal experience, but can we move past the personal into more societal perspectives in regard to risk-taking?

From a more societal perspective, reconciliation is an important example of risk orientation. In South Africa, under the systematic racist agenda-cum-policy of apartheid, many atrocities were committed under the thinly veiled advancement of the "master race." Under Nelson Mandela, the concept of reconciliation became the new policy, given the understanding that any hope for a future for the country relied on being able to acknowledge the past while also having a spirit of hope for the future. What a risky move! Each side was deeply distrustful of the other, fear was manifest. Yet, it worked—perhaps not perfectly, but it did work. In Canada, reconciliation focuses on the acknowledgement of centuries of harm caused to the First Nations people by settlers and our governments. For the federal government to apologize and admit past and current wrong-doings, regardless of who is in office, is a dangerous and highly risky admission. To do so opens up the door to liability. But more importantly, reconciliation also has the optential to open doors to responsibility, communication, and can allow all parties to acknowldege the pain caused and—critically—what has been learned and how things will be done differently in the future. Reconciliation is again a risky move that is focused not only on the past, but on hope for the future. It is a process with no specific endgame, except for enhanced understanding and compassion. Again, there is no fate but what we make.

Learning to Push Boundaries: Ice Caking and Other Misadventures

People who are risk oriented tend to push at limits and boundaries. Their goal, in many situations, is to improve their lives by taking risk. However, one of the core components of risk is that sometimes, there is no clearly correct choice. *Auribus teneo lupum* (holding a wolf by its ears) is a Latin phrase (seriously, these Latins—exactly what kinds of lifestyles did they live to acquire so many sayings?) that applies to risk in which any decision comes with potential challenges. If we hold on to the wolf's ears, we risk being really, really close to an agitated predator with carnivorous teeth. On the other hand, if we let it go, then we run the risk of being chased by an agitated predator with carnivorous teeth. So, do we hold on and try to control, or do we release and hope to escape? Risk on all sides.

For many, taking the risk itself is enough. As we grow through our adolescence, many of us experience a shift toward risky behaviour that had been uncommon in our earlier years. In fact, risk-taking could be seen as a hallmark of development from childhood to adulthood and is well placed in the adolescent years. Adolescents are known to be experimenters, guided to some extent by "What if" thinking. In our childhood years, we tend to acquiesce to authority, especially once the stakes become higher. All kids push boundaries, and well they should. This is how we learn to differentiate ourselves from our parents and become our own unique people. But in childhood, there are arbitrators of boundaries, usually parents and teachers. There is a hard "No" that inevitably comes to all children who engage in risk-taking.

In adolescence, however, these arbitrators of boundaries and rules are no longer seen as having absolute authority. Teens question the authority of their parents and teachers, much to the chagrin of these mostly good-hearted people who now feel like their adorable kids have been claimed by shape-shifting poltergeists and have become into sarcastic, demeaning know-it-alls who can roll their eyes with such force as to actually cause heads to explode. You too were one of these little monsters (and if you were not, if you were a strict rule follower who never took risks, even imaginary ones, then there is a concern that you have not yet—and perhaps will continue to struggle with—approaching your true value as a human being). It's the compliant teens I worry about in my practice sometimes. Not while they are teens, but for when they become adults and have no sense of what it is to take a risk and live with the consequences, both good and bad.

As such, we hope to see risk-taking emerge in teens. However, while risk-taking may imply growth, it must be accompanied by a learning orientation, which is the ability to learn from one's own success and mistakes (and those of others as well). I was a moderate risk-taker as a teen. I was not into substances at all, nor risky sexual behaviour, nor traditional juvenile delinquency. I was, however, drawn to risk, like many of have been in our teen years. I lived, as noted, on PEI and our house was directly on Charlottetown Harbour, which froze over every winter (One year, we had a freeze-thaw-freeze pattern that made the ice, for a short time, smooth as glass and we could skate almost across the entire harbour itself, a mile-wide radius of outdoor rink ice). In the spring, when the ice broke up, my friends and I would go "ice-caking." Every spring, we would challenge each other to walk, and eventually, jump from one ice cake to the next to see who could get the farthest out into the harbour. I'm confident that you can see the flaw inherent in this particular game—the "winner" would invariably be stuck on a 1-metre diameter slab of ice (much, much smaller than the *Titanic's* 'berg, and far less stable), floating slowly out into the middle of the icy harbour water. A combination of hockey sticks and a series of small, pathetic little slabs of ice to create a sort-of path back toward shore would be used to collect the winner, who would in any case be soaked through with ice water before going home and figuring out how to explain his popsicle-like condition to his suspicious parents.

While ice-caking was indeed a high-risk activity, our learning capacity had not yet caught up, our frontal lobes where logic and reason reside largely being smooth and undeveloped at that point. So, we would do it day after day until the ice cleared the harbour. In the meantime, our dry land behaviours were really not significantly any wiser or free from risk. A couple of friends and I loved to drive around town in our old GMC pickup, Dodge quarter-ton, and Jeep Wagoneer, respectively (my Jeep was a brown 1979 monstrosity with a cracked frame that acted not unlike an accordion bus—the back half of the Jeep moved independently of the front; the only thing holding it together was the driveshaft and a welded-shut back door). We—as often happens with collectives of mid-teen males—made less intelligent choices as a group than any one of us would have independently. So, it struck us one evening as we were barrelling around a mall parking lot that "Hey . . . it's icy! And there are huge snowbanks piled up all over the place by snowplows." And, most distressingly, "We all have four-wheel drives!" Naturally, we decided it would be wise and intelligent to see who could get their vehicle to the highest part of one of the icy snowbanks. In fact, it would be inconsiderate to our vehicles to NOT try this experiment. We would be denying out 4×4s of their *raison d'etre*! Naturally, I went first, followed by each of my friends.

I should mention that this was not just one night—this went on for weeks. One night—our last mountaineering expedition—we were at a local mall with some friends, some of whom were girls that, well, we just HAD to impress. And nothing impresses a teenage girl quite like driving up a pile of dirty ice and gravel. (I was single through almost all of my teen years—go figure!). So, I went first, but due to the imbalance of the Jeep's structural integrity, I went up backward to prevent the Wagoneer from splitting right in two behind the driver's seat. My buddy followed suit, his little quarter-ton truck being the lightest having certain advantages (he would get up higher; getting down on the other hand was more of a challenge!). Then our remaining mountaineer, full-frontal, took a run at the largest and steepest of the hills. Instead of the wheels engaging and propelling him up the hill, the heavier truck slammed straight into the rock-solid wall of ice, immediately destroying his front grill and driving the engine down and backward. His airbags didn't deploy and he was not hurt physically. But the gorge of a hole in the front to his truck and the engine hanging in at a 15-degree angle would take some explaining when he got home. We eventually arrived at a plan to pull over on the way to his house, kick in a random snowbank, and blame the damage on icy roads which he skidded into on the way home. If his father questioned us, we could show him the kicked-in snowbank (we even left a few shards of headlight glass in the snowbank to "prove" our case). Our ploy, poorly thought out and executed with no finesse whatsoever, worked in the sense that his father was impressed with the lengths to which we would go to construct such an obvious lie.

In Ice Caking and Ice Mountaineering, our risk-taking again outpaced our capacity to learn from mistakes, a situation common in teens and some adults. Over time, though, we learn to temper our risk-taking. Most adults have the capacity to evaluate and weigh risk. Should I invest or save? Buy the house, or continue to rent? Continue practicing birth control, or are we ready for kids? And usually, these risks are not simply "either-or" situations; they carry a great degree of complexity. In social psychology, we refer to conflicting choices as approach-approach (having to choose between two positive options—I have two people I'd like to date, how do I choose which one to pursue? Do I have the chocolate cake or the cheesecake?), avoidance-avoidance (having to choose between two adverse options—I don't want to go to the dentist, but I don't like the pain this toothache is causing either!), and approach-avoidance (having to choose between two options that have both positive and negative characteristics—I want to invest in Apple, but I don't like their monopoly-style approach to business and more importantly, I would have to spend money now and risk not having anything to show for it in the future). Multiple approach-avoidance conflict occurs when there are varying levels of complexity—not only are there positive and negative characteristics to a choice, but there are different levels of possible outcomes, from low to high positive and negative. In many cases, we become overwhelmed and decide to not decide. We choose to not take a risk.

There are few aspects of our lives in which we do not encounter risk. It happens in school, the moment we enter a classroom. Hopefully, we have people around us, teachers and peers in this case, who are supportive and who offer praise and encouragement that encourages us to take further risks, enhancing our confidence and willingness to take on further risk. Risk happens at work, it happens in relationships. It happens, almost literally, all the time. Decisions around risk-taking can be overwhelming not only because of the complexity required, but also because of the frequency. A question for you: **What was the last significant risk you took?** How did you find yourself in a position that required you to take that risk? What would have happened if you did not take the risk? What happened, both positive and negative, once you took the risk? Have there been any long-term consequences? Ultimately, was taking the risk an *easy* choice?

Risk in Relationships: Moving Beyond Basic Strategies

Relational risk is perhaps one of the most powerful drivers of human interaction. Relational risk speaks to decisions and actions we take in our interpersonal relationships and communication. We are deeply connected to one another as human beings; even those of us who identify as being "introverted" (in the truest sense of the concept, which implies that we often appreciate alone time more so than our extraverted friends) require deep connections to others. But connection implies risk, because a true connection requires trust. And many of us have learned that trust is a very dangerous thing to offer or accept. I often suggest to my student clinicians that true quality therapy is built on trust, not technique. A good therapist has both the capacity to build trust and to use effective psychotherapeutic techniques, but many emerging psychologists become enamoured with technique, often at the expense of trust. The over-reliance on technique is often seen in neophyte therapists through their reliance on something new that they have learned. They are eager to try something new and unfortunately, we end up in situations in which many newer therapists perceive every therapeutic problem as a metaphorical nail to be beaten down with their new therapeutic hammer. Trust reduces the need for reliance on tools, which is not to say that we don't continue to use effective approaches in therapy. We are, after all, trained in the "scientist-practitioner-advocate" model, which suggests that in therapy, as practitioners, we should rely upon evidence-based approaches that have been shown to be effective, while avoiding trendy techniques.

A great example of the emphasis that even the most well-intentioned individuals place on technique over trust, and there are many, is the use of facilitated communication, a trend that emerged in the 1990s among professionals who worked with children and adults with Autism. Facilitated communication involved the practice of lifting the client's hand above a keyboard and gently letting it drop, allowing the client's fingers to tap at the keyboard. What emerged from their keyboarding was often surprising—coherent, self-aware thoughts and desires that were thought to be coming from the mind of the nonverbal, noncommunicative people with severe Autism.

Pretty impressive. Except, it was a sham. Some pretty basic studies were done in which the facilitator could not see the person or the keyboard (they were hidden behind a simple cardboard divider) engaged in the same "lift/drop" approach and the resulting communication was gibberish. To apply Occam's Razor to the idea of facilitated communication, was it more likely that people with Autism had somehow simply not figured out the lift/drop approach on their own to engage in meaningful communication through a computer or perhaps was the easier explanation—that the facilitator was unwittingly but hopefully and with the best of intentions—implying meaning where there was none? We have learned a lot about Autism in the intervening years and it is possible that we may not have developed some of our more contemporary and progressive thinking about Autism had we not taken the risk of questioning spurious evidence.

The nature of risk-taking in relationships is predicated on trust, to be sure. Getting away from the surface allows us to delve deeper into relationships, where the really meaningful stuff is. But digging deep is hard work, and highly risky because we may not know what lies beneath. To quote Gandalf from *The Lord of the Rings*, in reference to this history of the dwarfs who mined for treasure and in doing so, awakened an unexpected danger, "they delved too greedily and too deep, and disturbed that from which they fled." Relationships are indeed treasures and need to be treated carefully. Taking too much risk can have dangerous consequences.

What Does Your Headvoice Say? How a Noncommittal Grunt Can Start a Fight?

We all have a "headvoice." Our headvoice allows us to think things that are far too risky to say out loud. We all have it, but to varying degrees. Some people have a very strict headvoice that does not allow them to say anything to anyone, regardless of the situation, because the perceived risk is too high. They will not voice their dissatisfaction with their boss; they will not complain about a rude concert-goer who drunkenly trips over them while the band plays; they will not disagree when their partner says cruel and heartless things. The risk of saying anything makes them almost perfect subjects of abuse. To be clear, this is not blaming them in any way, as abuse is always in the hands of the abuser, not those victimized by the abuse itself. There is, however, a tendency (from my experience) for bullies and abusers to pick people with overwhelmingly intimidated headvoices who are risk-avoidant because, quite simply, they feel that they can get away with whatever they want because the risk avoidant person will not take the risk to do or say anything to defend themselves. The target may not like how they are being treated, but they are unlikely to actually say or do anything about it because their headvoice thinks of the risks of doing so and essentially say "It's not worth it." This kind of thinking can become hopeless in its nature, resulting in ongoing victimization that—to be clear—is not the fault of the target, but is magnified by their abuse, which consistently tells them that they are powerless to stop it, so why bother even try. Think back to Seligman's dogs— they learned to be helpless not because of some inherent flaw, but because of the power of the situation.

On the other hand, there are those with headvoices that are less averse to risk. Again, with all things related to mental toughness, sometimes too much of a specific orientation is not particularly helpful. Those who score high on measures of risk orientation are, interestingly, at risk themselves for pushing too hard and saying too much. If an employee wanted to push a boss for a raise, for instance, their headvoice is best advised to remain logical and therefor present a value-based argument; the higher risk option may be to tell the boss exactly what you think of them. This could have rather poor consequences. In an intimate relationship, telling your partner how you feel about their outfit may be a situation in which you live with your headvoice; telling them that those pants do make them look fat, or that they are indeed going bald and look like a stubby version of Benny Hill on a bender carries significant—and rather useless—risk. What's the point? Honesty? "I'm just saying like it is" is a problematic statement and is never true. One could honestly say "I'm just saying it like *I* see it" is more accurate and true. At least it accounts for perspective and the fact that you could be wrong. And such accountability helps us to calculate risk. Risk is based in part on consequence; high risk typically is associated with high consequence (both positive and negative) while low risk carries little weight in regard to outcome. So, feel free to tell your partner exactly what your headvoice says, but be prepared for the consequences.

What of those consequences, though? If risk implies consequence, do we actively learn to moderate our consequence tolerance? Again, in the case of relational risk-taking, if the consequences are too low or are imperceivable, what is the benefit of risk? Or harm, for that matter? I have not practiced couple's therapy (a few unpleasant sessions with high-conflict couples with kids have taught me that I have little patience for parents who cannot pull it together as adults and act in the best interests of their children). But couple dynamics are a larger part of my clinical work, especially when working with well-intentioned parents who may differ somewhat in their parenting styles. In many of these situations, the ongoing challenges of raising kids, work, household obligations, and time itself have all had a hand in taking the vibrancy out of the partnered relationships. A couple once deeply engaged with one another, in tune, finding even the smallest detail about their partner to be *absolutely fascinating*, are now barely attending to one another. Behavioural psychology has a concept referred to as *habituation*, in which we learn to ignore nonthreatening stimuli (for instance, ignoring a barking dog over time, or a monotone lecturer at university). Couples experience habituation as well, and sometimes, re-introducing risk into the relationship can be advantageous, if uncomfortable.

For instance, a couple have just entered the serious phase of their relationship. They are dating one another exclusively, they talk to their friends gushingly about their new partner, they plan weeks ahead, maybe even an extra toothbrush has appeared in one of their bathrooms. Observing them at dinner, one would see them gazing deeply into each other's eyes, taking small bites of food offered by the other. In tune, connected.

Let's visit this couple 5 years down the road. They sit at the kitchen island, slurping soup, scanning their devices for any sort of distraction for the mundane act of eating. One stops for a moment and says something. The other mumbles a noncommittal grunt of "MmmHmmm . . . "

A few moments of silence pass. The first partner says, "Did you hear what I said?" Risk enters the conversation. The "listener," no longer habituated to the other's voice, panics and says "Uhm . . . yeah, of course."

Of course, it's too late. You know what the first partner says. I don't even have to write it out, but will for the sake of narrative completion. "Okay. What did I say, then?" Risk now overpowers the couple, who are now deeply intent in their focus on one another. Habituation has left the room. Fear and anger have entered. The consequence of habituation is conflict. Consequences may be moderate, but consequential thinking may not always guide our risk-taking.

Jumping out of perfectly fine airplane is a risk, one that many actively seek out and pay a lot of money for. Jumping out of an airplane with failing engines carries a different contextual risk. A large part of risk-taking, both for those who see out risk and those who are more risk avoidant, is context. It depends on the situation. The context ties into our areas of strength and challenges. As an individual, I dislike small-talk situations. Engaging with other humans who I barely know, or only have some tangential connection to, and I am immediately going to start looking for a dog or a cat to spend my time with. Going to a social hour at a professional convention fills me with anxiety; worse still, neighborhood parties in which the only commonality I may feel with those in attendance is the fact that we all live where we can see each other's houses. So, to develop my risk-taking, I need to consider where I need to grow. I don't need growth in ice-caking—I've learned what I need to about those risks; I need growth in my small-talk skillset. Understanding what areas we need to enhance (or decrease) our risk-taking, and the ability to learn from those experiences, is a function of the learning orientation.

Learning Orientation

"I never lose: I win or I learn"

—either Nelson Mandela or Tupac Shakur, according to the Internet

The challenge of risk-taking is coupled with learning; to have one without the other makes little sense. We cannot learn without taking at least some risk, and we cannot take effective risk unless we engage in learning as a result. Absent learning, those who may be risk oriented would bounce from mistake to mistake, hurting themselves and those around them with impunity. Learning precludes repeating mistakes associated with risk-taking. Most of us learn quite effectively from our mistakes; others are condemned to repeat their mistakes over and over, with increasingly frustrating results, not only for the individual but particularly for those around them. Watching an alcoholic friend stumble drunkenly behind the wheel of their car is uncomfortable and requires a positive, engaged response. "Hey, let me call you a cab—driving right now might be a mistake." Doing this for a friend once is actually a pretty positive experience. Twice is still positive, but perhaps a little concerning. A dozen times is frustrating and alarming. What is your friend learning? Their ability to evaluate risk is impaired in the moment—but what about before they start drinking. Of course, we know that when dealing with addictions, there are a lot more complexities that make useless a response such as "Have you tried . . . not drinking?"

Regardless, such situations frustrate us because the other person does not seem to learn. Naturally, we all struggle with learning sometimes. And this can be frustrating not only to ourselves, but others as well. The learning orientation focuses on our interest in and capacity for learning. Of course, all humans are capable of and are, to varying extents, interested in learning. From birth forward, we are exposed to countless daily opportunities to learn. Our capacity to learn is enormous, perhaps unlimited, but we do have some cognitive structures that place some degree of capacity on our learning. For instance, we can get overwhelmed with data input. Too much information presented too quickly overloads our cognitive capacity, resulting in some degree of shutdown. There is a well-known concept taught in thousands of introductory psychology classes, including the ones I have taught at Mount Royal University in Calgary, Alberta, that refers to a "magic number." The magic number ($7 +/- 2$) refers to the number of "chunks" of information we can retain in our short-term working memory. With minimal effort, we can recall a list of seven items with little difficulty. More than nine becomes problematic unless we shift more cognitive energy to the task. Beyond that, interference and other factors become complicating factors and we risk remembering almost nothing. For instance, a traditional phone number in North America is usually considered to be three distinct "chunks" of information (three-digit area code, three-digit prefix, four-digit identifier). Most of us have heard television and radio jingles that make remembering these chunks of information even easier. Everyone of a certain vintage knows a few phone numbers, even if they don't know their own office number or would be adrift when calling their spouse without their cell phone. Jenny's number (867-5309, of course) is a good example. Try to remember it without the tune.

We are all infantile when recalling our letters as well . . . who doesn't count "LMNOP" as a single "chunk" of information in the alphabet song? We find shortcuts, known as heuristics, that simplify basic learning, to great effect, although sometimes, heuristics can cause us all sorts of problems.

The Short Path: Heuristics in Learning

Our ability to learn incorporates the use of heuristics to help us make logical sense of the world without having to face every situation anew. Once we experience something, we have the opportunity to develop a heuristic to guide our future behaviour. Perhaps our most effective heuristic is trial and error. We try something new and if we have success, we are likely to replicate that behaviour. If we do not have success, we learn and, ideally, adapt and try again. Heuristics underlie the learning orientation in a fundamental manner. They also prevent us from becoming overwhelmed with cognitive overload. When we learn a new task, driving for instance, we draw upon previous experience, even if we have never sat behind the wheel of a car before. We draw on our experience of observing others drive, we draw upon similar experiences that have common behaviours associated with them (for instance, riding a bike; looking around to assess location and estimate speed and direction, etc.). If we started to drive without drawing upon heuristics, we would quickly become overloaded.

Heuristics can be problematic if the thinking and behaviours arising from them are not healthy, helpful, or positive. For instance, heuristics could be seen as underlying all manner of dangerous and harmful thinking. Racist thinking, for instance, could be based on heuristics. If one's experience with people of a certain racial background is not universally positive, there may be a tendency to overemphasize the negative experiences and minimize the positive. As a result, a confirmation bias starts to emerge. Racist thinking is both highly complex and amazingly simplistic. It is complex in that it is a compilation of history, culture, language, economics, and other highly complex factors. It is, however, also deeply simplistic in that it requires the use of basic heuristics. If I have a negative experience or interaction with one person of a certain race about who I already have a stereotyped way of thinking, that interaction will take on more weight and power, becoming the case that proves the point. I would argue, however, that this simplistic use of heuristic is learning in only the basest form. True learning goes beyond heuristics, especially simple ones, into more complex interactions between our intellect and the world around us, incorporating not only our own past history but that of those around us.

The learning orientation presumes that the individual enjoys learning and has the tendency to view learning as a positive experience both in terms of process and outcome. Those high in learning orientation see both the good and the bad (and, invariably, the range between) when it comes to learning outcomes. There is also a tendency to want to see learning applied. While learning is aspirational, it is also action oriented. Some people who have a high degree of learning orientation are satisfied with learning for learning's sake, but I would argue that these folks are in the minority. Those interested in learning are often also interested in *doing*, in experimenting to see how their learning has real-world application. It is the difference between a biblical scholar who reads the scriptures but acts in no way that would seem to indicate any real learning from their research and the individual who, upon reading the same scripture, sees within it the need to act in a way to help and show true compassion for those around them. It is the musician who can read notes and musical notation but cannot play, and the musician who plays with passion, using the musical sheet as a guide, not a script.

Being Open to Learning

The learning orientation speaks to our openness to learning, and our abilities to learn well and once. It is, after all, it's okay to repeat mistakes, just not the exact same mistakes all the time! I admit that my own learning orientation, as assessed through the MTQ Plus, was somewhat low, which I found to be odd given my passion for learning and education. Upon deeper analysis and reflection, though, it became clear to me that I am actually pretty high in the learning orientation—provided that I am learning about something in which I am interested. If I am interested, I consume knowledge and try to learn everything I can about that topic. If the topic does not interest me—for instance, cricket—I know nothing and care not to change that condition. I'm either on or off. Many people who are higher in learning orientation are omnivorous learners, wanting to learn a lot of things deeply. Others wish to learn a bit about everything, while yet others want to learn a few things well. Those who have a lower learning orientation may have limited interest in learning new things and those things they do show an interest in may not be particularly varied nor deep.

People who experience lower levels of learning orientation are not unintelligent people, nor are they lacking in motivation or are they particularly "lazy." They solely may not see any particular real and applied value in learning specific things. What works, works. Of course, so long as life does not become too complex, this approach may be relatively adaptive, though I would suggest that human beings are designed for learning. Our brains are never at full capacity. The old myth of "we only use 10% of our brains" is absolute rubbish, but there are few times when our brains are operating at full capacity. Those with lower learning orientations may not specifically need to use their learning to its capacity because their worlds are relative basic and the nature of their daily challenges are limited. Again, though, I would expect that many of those folks would also experience a certain degree of existential emptiness. It's like owing a Ferrari that sits unused in a dusty garage. It runs, but it is only every used to run occasional chores. It is a great vehicle, but its potential remains unfulfilled.

Occasionally, or even often, we are faced with challenging situations that require us to learn even if we would prefer not to. The loss of a loved one through death or through abandonment, the loss of work and subsequent loss of capacity to care for self and others financially, loss of health. All of these situations require that we learn new ways of being and in the moment, or even for lengthy periods afterward, even lifespans, can be spent trying to figure out what it is we are supposed to learn from such difficult situations. How do we recover from the death of a parent we love, or the termination of a marriage that, despite its conflict, was a source of identity and a means of relating with others? Those with a higher degree of learning orientation tend to be more open to learning and moving forward in such situations because they perceive learning as a natural, though difficult, part of living. They adapt because they know that they *must* adapt.

Those lower in learning orientation may feel that they are dragged, kicking and screaming, into learning. Adaptation is difficult, even when they know at an intuitive level that things cannot continue as they are. In this sense, those with a lower learning orientation mirror those—and may even *be* those—with lower risk orientations. Their hesitancy to take risk is intertwined in their unwillingness to learn from difficult situations, which goes a long way to helping us understand why people with lower risk orientations are also those with lower learning orientations. It is possible that an individual can be low in risk orientation but high in learning orientation, which suggests that the inverse could also be true. However, my clinical experience suggests that such dynamics are uncommon. A low risk/high learning orientation profile would suggest that individuals are reluctant to take risks, but are effective at learning from day-to-day situations and challenges and perhaps, are effective at observational/vicarious learning, while those high in risk orientation but low in learning orientation may be fated to take significant, uncalculated risk without really learning from the consequences, resulting in repeated mistakes.

Learning Through Observation and Experience: The Peanut Butter Sandwich of Frustration

True learning—that which carries ongoing weight and tends to be more permanent, although not necessarily rigid—is enhanced by experiencing (or witnessing) mistakes and identifying alternative approaches to similar problems that could be applied in similar circumstances. A child learns how to make a sandwich for lunch by observing a parent do the same, but they find that once they start spreading peanut butter on a warm piece of bread, that the bread tears and they end up with a ball of bread, peanut butter, and whatever detritus they picked up from the kitchen counter because they did not observe their parent wipe the counter before making their sandwich. The same child can become frustrated, throwing their peanut butter and bread ball on floor (creating even more of a mess). They may just give up, crying in frustration—why does it seem so easy for mom and dad and so hard for me? They took a (admittedly small) risk based on observational information and did not meet with immediate success. The mentally tough child will think "Ah well, THAT didn't work" and will look to what they may have done incorrectly or ask for guidance. More commonly, because children do not always have such excellent emotional regulation abilities, they will do as we saw in this example—they will flood with emotion (anger, frustration) and quit. It is critical that children be provided with a safe and trusting environment in which experimentation, within limits, is encouraged in order for mental toughness to develop. Judgement is not helpful, nor is taking over the sandwich-making duties, which only serves to reinforce the child's inherent belief that they are not capable and if they make a mistake, mom or dad will fix it for them, removing any sense of personal agency. As always, back to Goldilocks—a moderate amount of correction is necessary, as is some support. Too much or too little of either is likely to result in frustration and a lack of independence.

Napster and Moral Risk-Taking

Another factor involved both with risk-taking, but especially with the learning orientation, is related to our moral sense. Are we capable of learning independently in morally ambiguous situations? For instance, we learn in childhood that stealing from someone else is wrong and that we should not take what is not ours without asking for and getting permission. This is a pretty basic moral tenant—every religion has honesty as a core value and theft is addressed in most religious texts. Going beyond religious beliefs and structures, our society is built upon a common belief that we need to trust others not to take what is not theirs and a good portion of common law deals with theft. So, it's safe to say that taking that which is not yours without permission is essentially a universal expectation.

But, what of downloading music, for instance? In the late 1990s, Napster and other peer-to-peer data sharing networks made possible the ability to share music freely online. If you didn't want to buy the whole *Nsync album, for example, you could just download "Bye Bye Bye" online for free. Free! Not even the $3.49 it would cost for a CD single from your local Best Buy. A generation since has largely learned that music is a free commodity that can be obtained freely (if illegally, but there are few folks who have been fined or provided any consequences for downloading music online) or purchased for a negligible fee through Apple Music or Spotify. What of the artists—remember them? The folks who write, arrange, produce, and perform the music itself? They make fractions of pennies on the dollar per song streamed. The only income they earn is from touring and merchandising. Yet again, a generation (Hi, Millennials!) have been conditioned and subsequently learned that music is free, that stealing is sort-of okay, and that the consequences for doing so are nonexistent. So, what is the role of morality in learning? Can a high degree of learning orientation lead us to the conclusion that our behaviour is acceptable and even behaviour lacking in morality is justifiable provided we don't get caught?

There is a well-known saying, attributed to UCLA basketball coach John Wooden, that goes something like "character is who you are when no one is looking." If we have a high learning orientation, we learn for learnings sake. Learning itself is not necessarily a moral task—it is how we act *upon* learning that incorporates morality. Some would argue that morality does not enter this discussion at all, but as noted previously, it is important that we have a governor for mental toughness. Absent morality, those with high degrees of mental toughness can become manipulative and controlling. While it would seem that being mentally tough should remove, or at least limit, the need to control others, there are certain aspects of learning (and risk-taking) that could become problematic. What of the rare individual who is high in both risk-taking and learning orientations who uses their willingness to take risks to control and manipulate others, even to the point of abuse? Morality is not directly addressed in most of the research on mental toughness, but the entire concept of mental toughness is infused with a sense of morality in the sense that it is targeted toward behaving in the best interests not only of ourselves, but of those around us and our communities.

Of course, the learning orientation can also be used in a proactive manner. Those with high learning orientations, for instance, may be more resilient to challenges related to substance abuse, for instance. While there is no direct evidence of such a link, there is a parsimonious connection that would suggest that when one drinks too much (a), the result is a hangover (b). The simplest line to draw is between points a and b. As such, a person with a high degree of learning orientation would draw out this line and reach the simple conclusion "Drinking made me feel horrible; therefore, I will not overdrink again." We know that this example is a vast oversimplification of a highly complex interrelationship between substance use/abuse and any number of underlying psychological, social, physical, and other determinants. So, in this case, the learning orientation is only one single factor, but it is a powerful factor. The learning orientation facilitates new behaviours and allows us to make decisions far more easily than if we are lower in the learning orientation. So, while a high learning orientation may not be a "cure" in any sense for issues such as substance abuse, it is an explanatory factor that potentially could make behaviour change more efficient and durable over time.

Learning Orientation and Identity

Another consideration related to the learning orientation is the concept of choice. Ideally, we should have the freedom to decide for ourselves what we wish to learn about (again, taking into consideration the governor of morality and community-mindedness; we should not seek out learning that is potentially harmful to ourselves, others, our communities, or our environment). This freedom of choice carries with it enormous weight. Even on an individual basis, our learning orientation can lead us into some critically important areas. What kind of job do I want? How can I get better at my job? What do I want my relationships to be like? How do I make the best of my current relationship? These are all aspects of living in which learning is clearly implied. If we have a high learning orientation, we can explore these options openly and with optimism. If, on the other hand, our learning orientation is low, we may not explore these areas at all, becoming foreclosed on these and other related ideas.

In Chapter 4, we discussed James Marcia's four "identity statuses" that individuals could be identified as being associated with based on the degree of exploration and commitment to different areas of potential exploration (vocation, religion, sexuality, political affiliation, and so on). While Marcia's work has since been rightly criticized as being too simplistic to account for the complexity of human identity development, his model does have some components that align nicely with mental toughness in general, and the challenge component in particular. Specifically, the risk orientation would be comparable with Marcia's idea of exploration—the willingness to explore life options, while the learning orientation would compare to commitment, or the desire to learn about each of these areas and make decisions as to where we, as individuals, "fit" in each area. A high degree of learning orientation, therefore, leads to a higher degree of commitment based on a high degree of exploration. Marcia would refer to such individuals, those who have explored options and committed to different areas based on those explorations and what they have learned, as having "achieved" a sense of identity. Those who are in the active enjoyment associated with exploration (risk orientation without learning) would be in moratorium. Those who commit without exploration (in mental toughness language, those who have high learning orientation but low risk orientation) are said to be in identity foreclosure. Perhaps the best examples of foreclosure are individuals who engage in specific careers because that is what is expected of them (taking over the family business; becoming a dentist because dad was a dentist, etc.) or taking on religious beliefs because of family tradition without any significant personal exploration. Identity diffusion, finally, is a result of engaging in neither exploration nor commitment. These are individuals who have not engaged in any real exploration and who have not made any subsequent commitments. They have neither taken risks nor have they learned. Diffusion is a dangerous status as a lack of exploration/risk and commitment/learning can be seen as being a precursor to (or perhaps even a result of) depressive thinking.

The core of the learning orientation lies in our beliefs, hopes, and expectations of becoming *better*. Learning is a fundamental component of human advancement and we are all, to varying extents, learning machines. The wet computer we call a brain thrives on learning. Our social and professional relationships also thrive on learning. Absent learning, we risk dulling the tools we have been provided with to become more effective humans. Our enjoyment of even mundane tasks is enhanced by learning. Have you ever been bored? Of course, you have, we all have! But a higher learning orientation is the best defense against boredom, in much the same way that boredom can be a tremendous fuel source for learning. Bored? Try learning something new, through reading a book or an online article about something you've never learned about before—I enjoy going in Wikipedia's home page when I am bored—lots of featured articles and a "Did you know . . .?" section that is full of interesting facts, taking on a musical

instrument you've not played before (or trying to master one you are familiar with); build some IKEA furniture (if you dare!); even just try something
basic but new to you—hem some pants, drive somewhere you've never
driven before. NOW you're learning! Bored while making dinner? Make it
into a Gordon Ramsay-esque trial by setting a timer (play Rimsky-
Korsakov's "Flight of the Bumblebee" to make it a real challenge!). Again,
learning! Bored in traffic? Name as many different makes and models of
cars you can see, perhaps choose the one would most like to trade up to and
the one you hope you would not have to trade down to. Learning. Remember
when you were a child and you said, "I'm bored." In my home, and many
others, that was huge mistake. Before you could say "But . . .!" or "I
didn't mean it!" there would be a list of chores pages long just waiting to be
completed. Lots of learning!

Boredom is the crucible in which learning can be purified, yet we often
find ourselves so busy that there is little time for boredom. Our contemporary world seems intent upon keeping us from being bored and our senses
are under constant bombardment that prevents us from being even remotely
bored. No one would argue that a possible advantage of contemporary living
is the sheer amount of learning available to us. However, is it possible that
the volume of learning and sheer information overload may actually prevent
us from engaging in true learning, making us consumer of information, not
reasoned learning? One way to enhance our learning orientation is to allow
boredom to exist in our daily lives. As an educator, I have witnessed what I
think may be a downward trend in the value placed on boredom at school.
Kids want (and to be clear, this is a *want*, not a need) to be entertained.
Should we indulge this want? Likely not. Yet at the same time, teachers are
in the conundrum of feeling that they are in competition with the variety and
immediacy available through highly entertaining online world. How can a
teacher compete with the reinforcement offered by online gaming? Perhaps
one consideration is that educators need not compete—we can incorporate
the online world into the classroom and many excellent teachers do exactly
that, with outstanding results. Additionally, teachers have one significant
advantage over technology that will almost always exceed anything technology can offer—quality, depth relationships.

Relational Learning

In order to develop meaningful relationships which capitalize on the learning orientation, teachers and adults who interact with children and adolescents need time. Of course, one of the most significant challenges faced by

contemporary educators is not only class size (which by nature reduces the amount of time they have to spend with each student), but also increasing demands on the time available, along with the multi-faceted roles that teachers are expected to fulfill. A teacher with a class of 25 students has not only 25 teacher—student relationships to enrich, but also 25 unique learning profiles to adapt to, 25 sets of parents (or perhaps many more), 25 pieces of documentation due at multiple points of the year (report cards, individualized learning plans, among many others), along with various other documentation demands (professional growth plans, unit plans, lesson plans, communication logs, behavioural logs, reading logs, and so on). This is a very short list that is, in reality, much longer. And they have approximately 6 hours per day with their students, less if one takes away specialist time in PE, music, art, and so on. At some point, the relationships cannot flourish and our best teaching tool becomes dull. While the relationship may be less helpful, it does not become less valuable, though. When faced with any significant learning or behaviour/social/emotional concern, the relationship will almost always be the single most effective tool that will support the student and will make the longest-lasting impression.

Those with a higher learning orientation tend to see the value in the student–teacher relationships which, in turn, along with the parent–child relationship, establishes how we relate to others as we age. We can see the benefits of positive relationships and see the outcomes as being worth seeking out, which in turn creates a desire to replicate those relationships. Of course, the opposite also holds true—poor relationships teach us as much, if not more, than quality relationships. We understand from the research literature from John Bowlby, the British psychologist who investigated the nature of attachment in infants and those who followed up on and challenged his work, including Canadian researcher Mary Ainsworth, that attachments formed in infancy and early childhood became the templates for the relationships we have as adults. Positive, securely attached relationships in which trust is at the core allows for securely attached relationships as adults. While not a complete linear relationship, the ability to form a positive and secure attachment as a child made it easier (though not guaranteeing) a similar relationship as adults. The same researchers found, perhaps not surprisingly, that the opposite also tended to be the case. Poor quality attachments, those associated with mistrust and inconsistent care, tended to result in poor quality relationships in adults. There are a lot of challenges with the research in this field, as there is in any area of psychological research, but the logic appears to be consistent with clinical experience. Many of my adult clients report poor or strained relationships with their parents, often coloured with themes of inconsistency, fear and, most dominantly, judgement.

If our relationships are, to a large extent, learned, and if we have a learning orientation that makes us either more or less likely to take advantage of learning opportunities, can we essentially "unlearn" unhealthy habits? There is an entire industry of self-help that makes billions of dollars annually hoping that this is indeed the case! Of course, I am well aware that even a book like this could—and perhaps should—be considered to have a self-care orientation. But I would also suggest that an interesting and engaging novel, a good graphic novel, a physics text, and even a car operating manual could be construed as being self-help in that they lead us to discover new ways of thinking and support us in our problem-solving. However, "self-help" is often conceptualized in pop literature as being associated with books, podcasts, videos, programs, workshops, and other media designed to create healthier ways of being and to that extent, I will agree that this is indeed a self-help book. However, I would also suggest that there are many tomes of "self-help" that are little more than advertisements for products that make one feel better temporarily. Mental toughness does not need a "sales pitch," per se. To quote a character in Michael Mann's classic heist film *Heat*, "This kind of sh*t here sells itself." The learning orientation itself, in particular, is a fantastic example of how mental toughness can be, and has almost always has been, a critical part of self-enrichment.

Taking advantage of our learning orientation to learn new, more healthy and adaptive behaviours and relationships is perhaps one of the single most valuable applications of the mental toughness model. If we are motivated to make changes, and the learning orientation itself presupposes some degree of motivation, then our opportunities are almost limitless. We must be careful, though, not to overstate the case.

Mental toughness in general and the learning orientation in particular cannot, in themselves, facilitate significant growth on their own. Larger social systems, similar to those proposed by American psychologist Urie Bronfenbrenner in 1974, are usually at play. Bronfenbrenner proposed an Ecological Systems Approach to human development, with each level having a significant but diminishing impact upon the individual's development, starting with the microsystem (including immediate family, school religious organization, neighborhood, and peers), extending to the mesosystem (a mediating barrier between the microsystem and the subsequent ecosystem). The ecosystem incorporates extended family, parent's economic situation, mass media, health care, social systems, government agencies, school boards and districts, while the macrosystem includes attitudes and beliefs of the larger society. All of these systems are suffused with the chronosystem (environmental changes that occur over the life span). Each of these systems are important, but the ones closer to the microsystem are those that have more direct impact upon the individual.

Assuming that Bronfenbrenner's system is accurate, then we see a range of opportunities for learning, but those that focus on the individual are the ones that will make the most immediate and lasting change. Changing a society (the macrosystem) is hard work, as we all know. It is almost incomprehensible to think about the impact one person can have on a macrosystem, although we have many examples from history in which individuals have done exactly that—people like Rosa Parks, Mahatma Ghandi, Bill Gates, Steve Jobs, Marie Currie, Albert Einstein, Charles Darwin—the list is extensive and provides numerous counterarguments to the comment "I'm just one person—what can I do to make a difference?" Things can and do change over time. Can we use a model of learning, based on a high learning orientation, to make ourselves better people using resources from our larger systems? Mental toughness, as a model, fits in anywhere in this ecological system and as such, is a significant generator of potential change.

Okay, time for an example. You are a truck driver. You want to be better with managing your money and you also want to work fewer hours. A conundrum—how is this even do-able? The risk orientation would lead you to perhaps taking on different routes or perhaps even purchasing your own rig and operating as an independent. The risk is high, but the opportunity to work better hours for potentially more income is appealing. On the other hand, you have done some work on the business case and found that what time you would not be spending on the road would be consumed with accounting, finding the next gig, servicing your truck and the associated costs of running a business. So, while you are willing to take the risk, you have reasonable fears. But you take the risk. And it works out—for a while. But eventually, of course, things start to happen. You blow a head gasket. Your transmission gets dodgy. Fuel rates go up due to a change in the markets. What do you do?

You learn.

You adapt and change based on your own learning and, perhaps better yet, the learning of a mentor. You need a truck-driving Yoda. Or even a small-business Yoda, a Yoda who may have never driven a truck (I mean, how would he reach the pedals, anyway—oh, right . . . the Force!), but who is a guru of small business operation. You can read, you can watch videos, you can learn! Trial-and-error may not be your best approach when it comes to your financial well-being and security, but your high degree of risk-taking has led you to make a rather impulsive decision in purchasing your own rig in the first place, so now you have to work backward a bit. However, your high learning orientation has allowed you to be willing to learn in reverse, so to speak. You are willing to admit an error and are also willing to learn from your mistakes and move forward.

More intimate challenges also benefit from having a high learning orientation. Let's say you are in a romantic relationship that seems to be going nowhere. You do not feel connected to your partner in any real sense, intellectually, physically, emotionally, spiritually. Do you pull the plug? Maybe. But maybe take the risk and see if there is some learning that could be done. Have the hard conversation with your partner. It may well be that having that difficult conversation may reveal that the other person feels the same. Or perhaps not. It's a risk, but there is a great deal of learning that could be done. However, if I might offer some unsolicited advice—try not to have that conversation on Valentine's Day. As I did. With two different people on two separate and unrelated occasions. Your honesty and desire to learn will not likely be appreciated and please, don't ask me how I know. Just trust me!

When Being "Gifted" Isn't: Learning Orientation and Self-Awareness

A significant portion of my clinical clientele are children, adolescents, and adults with "gifted" profiles. These folks have a great deal of intellectual capacity in one or more areas of cognitive functioning, but their "gift" is often misunderstood as being a universal positive. I put the word "gifted" in quotation marks because many of my clients do not view their intellect as being a gift at all. In fact, they find that their intellect sets them apart in often uncomfortable ways from their peers, resulting in challenges with relationships. This is a significant challenge regardless of the developmental level of the individual. They often tell me that they would, after some consideration, trade in their "gift" just to feel socially normal. As we work together, often they come to learn that there is no need for such a compromise. They can maintain their impressive intellectual abilities and have social success without sacrificing their integrity, nor feeling like they need to "dumb down" their social interactions. This adaption is, however, learned. My experience is that individuals with gifted profiles may not have a great deal of learning orientation. This is an interesting paradox. They are very intelligent and have a great deal of curiosity about certain things, but self-awareness is often not one of their strengths. They will learn about financial investment, physics, aerodynamics, philosophy, religion, history, music, but when it comes to learning about themselves and their interactions with peers, teachers, employers, and employees, they can be almost frustratingly inhibited in their ability to learn about others or from their own mistakes. I recall one client, a gifted individual to be sure, who could not climb the corporate ladder as efficiently as those around him, resulting in a situation that all of his superiors were people who he viewed as being his intellectual inferior (and statistically speaking, he was probably correct, given that only about 2% of the population would be considered to be "gifted"). His frustration was magnified by the fact that he was aware of why they were passing by him on the climb toward the top of the organization chart. They had better social skills. They could read a room as effectively as he could read a financial spreadsheet. But what mattered was people skills, an area that my client recognized (after some time) was an area in which he was not particularly gifted. So we worked on developing relationships, which started with having him develop a sense of learning orientation that made sense to him. Initially, he wanted to learn soft skills in the same way he learned about accounting, by reading. Ever see someone try to implement a new social skill that they obviously have not practiced but perhaps have read about somewhere? It's like watching Arnold Schwarzenegger in the *Terminator* films try to smile. Or they will try to engage in small talk in a manner similar to Ralph Wiggum on *The Simpsons*: "So . . . do you like . . . stuff?"

However, this particular client persevered and once he got past reading about how to socially interact with success, we tried out a few practice strategies and he worked on some homework tasks. He would ask a clerk how their day was going. He would ask someone what they did over the weekend (someone specific—this guy would be quite literal and if asked to inquire about someone's weekend, he would ask pretty much anyone—like, for instance, a random stranger on the street while waiting for a "walk" signal). From there, we discussed other avenues of social enjoyment, perhaps in an area of interest. He went to some live stand-up comedy nights to learn how to get a laugh (though under the advisement that he was NOT a stand-up comedian, nor should he try to be one—just look for ways of using timing, engagement, and self-deprecation in a positive and eventually comfortable manner). While he never do climb the professional hierarchy the way he had hoped, he did create some new friendships and even developed an intimate relationship with a fellow "gifted" woman who eventually agreed to marry him. I'm deadly curious about their offspring!

Competition and the Learning Orientation

One of the dichotomies of the learning orientation is that those with a high learning orientation tend to be quite competitive. They are individuals who wish to learn a lot about a lot of things and, as such, can be at risk for coming off as "know-it-alls." Tempering a high degree of learning orientation with positive interpersonal confidence is important in that by doing so, the individual appears knowledgeable yet approachable and humble. However, it is an unfortunate side effect of learning that on one hand, the more we learn, the less we *actually* know (since we become increasingly aware of our deficits of knowledge) and at the same time, the more we learn, the more we *feel* we know. This is best described as being a part of the Dunning—Kruger Effect, a well-known psychological phenomena that has become more prevalent in our increasingly fragmented and polarized society. The Dunning—Kruger Effect suggests that those of low ability tend to overestimate their actual knowledge. This is an illusion that becomes increasingly clear upon examination of an individual's perception of "fact." For instance, a person with little to no medical training may overestimate their ability to diagnose a medical condition. "What you have there is monohypogalucinosia. I read about it on Facebook." Not an uncommon statement that litters the online world, where everyone is an expert while at the same time, no one knows anything.

As I write this, the global COVID-19 pandemic is well underway and the online world has recently become overwhelmed with amateur epidemiologists, virologists, pathologists, and other experts in the initiation, spread, and means of controlling and eliminating the virus (presuming, of course, that it actually exists—many online crusaders believe that the virus itself is a hoax . . . future readers, I kid you not!). The Dunning–Kruger Effect is evident in all corners of the Internet. The competitive nature of the learning orientation is perhaps a contributing factor, but awareness of this competitive approach in itself is a preventative measure. The more we are aware of our weaknesses and biases, the more we can counteract them, which is, in itself, a demonstration of a strong learning orientation.

It is probable that a low learning orientation makes the Dunning–Kruger Effect even more powerful given that those with a lower learning orientation also have lower expectations of achievement and set low minimum standards. Their lack of interest in learning results in low thresholds for standards, making the questioning of facts that do not fit nicely with their mindset problematic. It is easier to accept a "that's what they say" mentality than it is to do independent research or to ask truly challenging questions with an open and honest intent to learn from those questions. It is frustrating to hear otherwise intelligent people say things like "I am only asking questions" when it is apparent that their mind is made up already and that their "questioning" is simply a means to distract and make it possible to say that they are genuinely asking questions when in fact, they have little to no interest in the response if that response does not fit with their preconceived notions of reality.

Those who have lower learning orientations also have difficulties with accepting failure, since they view failure not as a learning opportunity but as some sort of statement on their intellect or ability. I can empathize with this mindset to an extent. When learning to ride a bike as a child, I immediately faced failure. My father took me out one Friday evening to teach me how to ride. We never went in for training wheels, so it was rather a do-or-die situation. Unfortunately, it was a beautiful evening with a fantastic sunset only found in coastal areas, so all of the neighbours were out strolling and chatting . . . and watching me learn to ride a bike. Holding on to the bike, my dad ran alongside me and then eventually behind me and I gained some wobbly control of the bike to the point where he let go. I sensed his presence fading behind me and steered directly into the ditch. Falling over, I rammed into the metal culvert, not enough to draw blood, but enough to hurt. I tried my best, but I could not restrain the tears. I started bawling. Dad came up and whispered to me "It's all okay, you can try again, no one cares that you fell, they only care that you may have hurt yourself." I wasn't having it. I kicked the bike and stormed off, snuffling and muttering about the "stupid bike and the stupid ditch and the stupid neighbours and the stupid culvert and the stupid day and my stupid life . . ." and so on (no one mutters like an embarrassed 6-year-old with an "owie"). I'm not proud to admit it, but that was the last time I tried to ride a bike for a long time. I still remember running beside my bike-riding friends, gasping that my bike was broken and that's why I was running instead of biking. My honour was at stake, but it was a losing battle. Eventually, I recognized that I could continue to lie and avoid and live a life of shame or I could just learn to ride the bike. So, we borrowed a training wheel (just one—I can't remember why, but we continued to test the biking waters with a lopsided approach on one training wheel and my father's ongoing support). Eventually, I got it. I learned. But wow, did I take the hard way. As adults, many of us take the hard way unnecessarily, and often repetitively. Developing a strong sense of learning orientation results in far better results than simply reacting to poor outcomes with a sense of fatality and finality.

Wrapping Up

The challenge component of the mental toughness model incorporates risk and learning. Risk requires some degree of confidence and ideally results in learning. Learning absent risk is minimal while a moderate to high degree of calculated risk can lead to a great deal of learning. The learning orientation focuses on the capacity and interesting learning new ways of being and has a significant impact upon performance and relationships. Moderate to high learning orientation is encouraged as it allows us to learn from not only our mistakes but also the mistakes of others while also helping us avoid some of the more significant pitfalls associated with overconfidence or fear of learning new things that can bring us a great deal of opportunity.

Characteristics of the components of challenge in relation to mental toughness are perhaps best summarized as follows:

Risk Orientation	
High	**Low**
• Enjoy challenge • Actively seek out challenges • Enjoy and practice effective problem-solving approaches • Enjoy taking on new tasks and responsibilities • Interested in making positive changes for self/others/community • Enjoy healthy competition • May take unnecessary risks • May not think through potential consequences • Can be impulsive • May be overconfident	• Dislike change, especially sudden change • Enjoy familiarity and routine • Fear actions that could lead to failure • Overemphasize failure over learning/opportunities • May not put in a strong effort on challenging tasks • Avoid risk • May lack confidence • Focus on how they are perceived by others • Not motivated by new opportunities • May follow routine to a fault, neglecting alternative approaches to challenging situations • Are predictable and can be comforting in their focus on routine • Good at maintaining stability in organizations

Learning Orientation	
High	**Low**
• See the opportunities in challenging situations • Enjoy learning • Consume new ideas and approaches with enthusiasm • Apply learning effectively • Can be creative and engaging to work with • Actively look for the positives in new situations • Enjoy making mistakes from which they can learn • View learning as opportunities • View failures as opportunities to learn • Actively seek out new ways to do traditional things • Actively engaged in enhancing their performance and doing better each time • Have an evolutionary approach—adapt and change according to circumstances • Can be perceived as being "know-it-alls" • Can be unpleasantly competitive • Can have a drive to be "right"	• Can be satisfied with meeting minimal standards • Avoid and fear learning • Dislike conflict in competition • View failure as fatal, not as an opportunity to learn • Easily dissuaded from learning upon experiencing barriers to success • Find learning to be stressful and prefer doing things the "usual" way • Hyperfocus on failure and underemphasize success • May take things out of proper perspective • Have difficulties applying new learning to new or unique situations • Tend to stick with the "known," avoiding creative or innovative approaches • Can be highly stable and predictable • Provide a sense of routine and familiarity to those around them • Can be effective in focusing on standard procedures and approaches • Can be falsely "overconfident" when anxious about their knowledge • May not examine all relevant factors when making decisions or in discussions about topics they are not knowledgeable about • Not particularly competitive

Chapter 6

Confidence

"I've Got This"

—Literally billions of people, just before they didn't

A long time ago, in a galaxy far away, Han Solo once quipped "Sometimes, I amaze even myself." This single line, perhaps more than other, captured the confidence of the brash captain of the *Millennium Falcon* (itself a "hunk of junk" piloted by Solo, who was referred to by others as being a "scoundrel," "pirate," and a "scruffy looking nerf-herder"). One is amazed indeed that a person so described would feel so amazed by himself. One thing Captain Solo did not lack was confidence. I believe it safe to say we all know a Han Solo character in our lives, or perhaps *you* are that character. Confident to a fault, unaware of any significant failings. Or perhaps we are quite the opposite, uncertain of what to do, never knowing if we are making a tragic mistake at any moment. It's like ordering from a Denny's menu—the choices are overwhelming and once the server returns to our table to take the order, we feel knotted up in doubt. We place our order but the moment the server leaves, we wonder "I *know* I should have gone with the Moons over My Hammie . . . what was I thinking?" I mean, it's *Denny's*, for crying out loud, but the uncertainty lingers. Our confidence in our ability to make a simple choice has been eroded.

Confidence is the extent to which we have belief in our abilities to see through to a conclusion difficult tasks, especially in the face of setbacks. Confidence is a very tricky concept. On one hand, too much becomes arrogance, too little becomes insecurity. There is a middle ground that is razor sharp in which our confidence can lie without being too much or too little.

As a concept, confidence speaks to our capacity to believe in our own abilities. In psychology, we have studied various angles of confidence using different concepts and terminology (self-efficacy or the belief in one's own capacities; self-confidence, or confidence in one' own self, not just one's abilities; self-esteem, which is the resulting feeling associated with positive confidence, and so on). None of these concepts individually can be said, nor would they claim, to encapsulate the breadth of the concept of confidence. For our purposes, confidence will refer to the self-belief in our own abilities to see through to a conclusion for which we have worked hard and overcome obstacles.

Confidence in Balance

Finding a balance between too confident and not confident enough is a rather challenging tightrope to walk. Confidence lies in a highly complex network of life experience, inborn traits, physical and mental characteristics, social and cultural factors, among others. We all know that we can have confidence in certain areas yet be crippled by self-doubt in others. Confidence tends to arise most genuinely from positive and authentically earned experiences. Through the late 1970s to the 1990s, there was a considerable amount of energy and effort in education placed on enhancing self-confidence in children. I am a product of this interesting time in educational practice. We were taught, both implicitly and explicitly, that our very existence implied worth. All people are worthy of love and affection and success. While certainly true and something even the most cynical among us would agree upon—human life is intrinsically valuable and deserving of respect, the slippery slope starts with how we define "success." As humans, we often cannot even secure the most basic degree of respect warranted us by our existence as sentient beings, and if even this fundamental, basic exception cannot be met, how can we expect to have everyone experience the "same" opportunities for success, happiness, and so on? However, I get the intent. We are a species that aspires. So, why not start young?

I can recall going into my elementary classrooms and the thrum of excitement tinged with anticipation and a touch of giddy hope that something would go wrong when our teacher hauled out the large, limited box with a bright blue dolphin on its lid. It was time for DUSO, people!

For those not in the know, DUSO was a curriculum package used across North American in the 1970s to 1980s with the intent to develop understanding of self and others. DUSO, get it? The blue dolphin, unsurprisingly named Duso, was a puppet brought to varying degrees of animation by teachers who also voiced the enthusiastic stuffed sea mammal. Of course, the degree to which Duso was animated and enthusiastic varied wildly based on the mood and temperament of the symbiotic host teacher. One of our teachers was a highly enthusiastic and energetic individual who perhaps missed her calling as a cruise ship entertainer and in her hands, Duso was a trip. One of our other teachers, a rather by-the-book dictatorial type, made

Duso a somewhat aloof and superior parental figure, analogous to Sam the Eagle from *The Muppets*. As such, Duso became a functionary not only of the prescribed self-esteem curriculum, but also of the whim of the teacher manipulating the puppet (and even time of day—morning Duso was generally higher energy and more enthusiastic than the more despondent and dismissive afternoon Duso).

Duso would tell us that we were all important and valuable people. We are all unique and our uniqueness made all special. So, in a nutshell, Duso had us believing in the myth that simply existing was worthy of celebration. Now, without being too cynical, I agree that all life is worth celebrating and by its very diversity, all life is essentially unique. However, the overarching message was that this worthiness was perhaps all that was needed. There was no real need for work or effort or energy expenditures. Just *being* made us worthwhile. Of course, Duso never said it THAT way, but the message was implied fairly plainly.

DUSO, the program, not the dolphin, was designed to enhance the self-esteem of elementary school-aged children across North America. The thinking was to develop a program that would make kids feel good about themselves because kids who felt good about themselves learned better, didn't get into fights, and were more compliant because they were happy in their current state. Of course, it didn't work, nor did numerous other similar programmes offered across North American and the rest of the world. Self-esteem, it would seem, could not really be taught. Rather, self-esteem seemed to arise from genuine success on things that were challenging. Genuine feelings of self-esteem cannot be simply created—they must be earned.

The self-esteem movement got its start in the heyday of the *I'm Okay, You're Okay* era of the 1970s, when educators were looking at increasing dropout rates, academic underperformance, and other school and community-based challenges that had actually started to emerge a decade earlier. One of the most significant contributors to this movement arose from the surprisingly powerful California Task Force to Promote Self-Esteem and Social Responsibility, which defined self-esteem as the ability to appreciate one's own self-worth and importance and to have the character to be accountable to oneself and act responsibly toward others. The concept itself is appealing and simple, though perhaps wrong-headed in the sense that leans heavily on one's innate importance, perhaps overlooking the value of humility. However, the intent was to suggest that if we presume that people who do not feel good about themselves do not perform well, then we need to make people feel good about themselves. Of course, the more arduous path, in which we focus on performance to enhance our positive feelings about ourselves, was not given serious weight, because some people struggle with performance due to a wide range of highly challenging factors that are complex and require real work to overcome, if they can be overcome at all.

Additionally, the measurement of performance can be problematic in that it is often competition based and often follows a rank-order approach. We all remember the *Lord of the Flies* scenarios into which we were thrust in elementary school physical education classes. Team captains, often the best athletes in the class, would select, one-by-one, the classmates they wanted on their team. Given that the goal was to win at whatever activity it was (dodgeball—it was *always* dodgeball!), the best odds for success was to pick the best athletes. One at a time. In front of everyone. Logic dictates that the last player would be the least athletic. This, by the way, is not an artifact of educational practices from 30 years ago. It still happens. Self-esteem education approaches often worked on the same principles.

The thinking was that those who had low self-esteem needed to be taught that they were good people and therefore, worthwhile to others. Confidence would be imparted upon students not unlike a gift from above. Teachers were encouraged to praise students *just because*. Ideally, the use of positive praise and the absence of positive punishment (consequences) would enhance the self-esteem of children, leading them to enhanced performance. Millions of Gen-X and Millennials experienced this approach to mental wellness, with questionable results.

First, true confidence arises from a sense of success for having tried. The result of effort on challenging tasks is a feeling of positive self-regard. By putting self-esteem at the front of the train, we are placing the engine of realistic and positive feelings about oneself behind the caboose. Self-esteem is earned. We need to be aware of the implications of teaching self-esteem as existing within a vacuum. Just telling someone that they are good, worthwhile, and worthy of success does not make any of those things essentially true. But if that message is repeated over and over, we may start to believe it. However, the feeling of self-esteem is not connected to any real action outside of simply existing. From an existential perspective, there is no meaning attached to these prescribed positive feelings and as such, we remain lost despite feeling good. It could be said that teaching self-esteem in absence of meaning is not unlike substance use. The individual may feel euphoria and other pleasant emotions, including a numbness to any problems they may be having, but both the euphoria and numbness is short-lived and contingent upon an external agent.

What happens, though, when we try and do not experience success? The fear that this question elicits can lead us to an unhealthy pattern of avoidance. Avoidance is a fantastic approach to challenge because it works. If we feel that something is going to cause us anxiety, one of the most basic instinctual drives we have is to avoid. And if we avoid well, as many of us do, we can have the dubious pleasure of not having to confront unpleasant realities. Of course, I am being somewhat facetious here. Avoidance works because it gives the individual a temporary free pass. But the challenging situation has not gone anywhere. In fact, often our avoidance simply feeds the beast. We all have had moments when we see a call coming in that we don't want to take. We have received big, fat envelopes from our credit card companies and know that we do NOT want to open it and look inside. We don't do our homework; we watch Netflix instead of doing the laundry. Or maybe that's just me?

There is a bit of a myth of laziness that arises from avoidance. Laziness, I would argue, is far less common than we think. Human beings are not designed to be lazy—if we were, we would have ceased to exist as a species a long time ago. Humans are designed to do. Look at your hands for a moment. They are highly dexterous, capable of a million different tasks. They are the Swiss Army Knife of our bodies. Did they evolve just so we can use our highly advanced opposable thumbs to text or flip a channel using a remote? Laziness is often misunderstood and arguably has it's roots more embedded in fear and avoidance than a lack of motivation.

When we avoid, we are basically feeding fear. Such an approach can work temporarily, but over time, fear simply becomes more powerful. As fear becomes more powerful, the less power *we* feel, leading to more avoidance. It's a very unhealthy dance. However, we can escape this cycle by making even moderate efforts to engage, not avoid. By engaging, we develop our confidence, even if we "fail." Failure only exists in the sense that we perceive it as *being* failure. It is likely that reconceptualizing failure as a learning opportunity would have significant benefits to our confidence. No longer would we see ourselves as lacking capacity or ability, but more realistically as being individuals with certain strengths and gifts in some areas, and challenges in others. If we can avoid avoiding, we can enhance our confidence. People who have higher levels of confidence also tend to be more optimistic and be somewhat more extraverted in nature. Again, the casual relationship here is not clear, but it does seem that it would be logical that there is a positive relationship between confidence and optimism and extraversion, though perhaps not a causal relationship. Again, mental toughness implies self-knowledge and understanding and knowing where our confidence lies is a critical component of being self-aware.

There are also those who find a different path, and avoidance is simply not a part of their mindset. They can experience any number of challenges, barriers, roadblocks, and yet they persevere. Tommy Wiseau, director of what has been referred to as "the worst movie ever," 2003's *The Room*, is a man who—as best one can tell—has confidence that far, almost comically, exceeds his talent. Watch the movie (which was also written by and stars Wiseau), you'll wonder how this man secured any funding—even the paltry amount he did—for the charming assault on the senses that *The Room* is. Wiseau could be said to have a considerable wealth of confidence in his abilities and perhaps even interpersonal confidence, but his example is one that shows that confidence *in* abilities does not always equate with *actual* abilities. But, no one could ever say that he was a man who avoided or quit easily. He persevered to get his vision on screen and, in a Hollowood-esque turn of events, eventually became famous for doing something astoundingly inept. Confidence, then, can lead us down certain paths that we may not anticipate, but as always, we must be aware of our own sense of self, our abilities, and our comfort in taking risks to really see where those paths lead.

Second, self-esteem education can result in oversatiation. Think of a food you particularly like. I'm thinking of a nice, tasty donair, spiced well, fresh onions and tomatoes, sweet cream sauce, lightly grilled—tasty! I could eat one right now. But, as I write this, it's 10 a.m. on a Saturday morning. Not prime donair time. Your particular favourite food may differ from mine (and likely does). But most of us recognize that there is a time and a place. And we also recognize that we can overdo it. Too much of a good thing is simply too much. It actually can make us sick. Self-esteem education, the construction of confidence from the top down, is not dissimilar in the sense that after a while, being told we are good, valuable people irrespective of actual behaviours that would warrant such statements can become disingenuous at best and harmful at worst.

In training teachers, I often discuss classroom management strategies. What do we do when we enter a classroom as the teacher for the first time and a student challenges us? Many newer teachers indicate that their greatest fear lies not in being unable to deliver a solid education to their students, or being incapable of developing and implementing effective lesson plans. Their greatest fear is confrontation with students. What happens when you ask a student to do something and they say "No"? Contemporary teacher training programs tend to focus on developing genuine, positive relationships with students to prevent this kind of defiance in the first place and, in general, such approaches can be highly effective. But the challenge to the confidence of the neophyte teacher remains because kids are kids and kids can be unpredictable. Additionally, some students have significant difficulties with managing their behaviours and can become very defiant. In many classrooms, when a student defies a teacher, the rest of the class goes quiet and looks to the teacher to see how they will respond. In general, if a teacher can pull together a calm, confident, and gentle response, the conflict can be reduced (of course, there is more to it than that, but this approach is a general truism in classroom management). However, sometimes teachers become frustrated. They are, after all, human beings and their authority is being questioned. So, they raise their voice. My question is always this—where do we go from a raised voice?

This is a valid question not only of teachers trying to manage inappropriate student behaviours, but it is also true of all of us in many different circumstances. Have you ever heard a couple get into a voices-raised fight? Typically, the voices get louder and louder and the tone becomes more aggressive and eventually, spite enters the fight. There is a tendency for the arguing couple to enter into a devolved phase of development—they yell, they name-call, they make hurtful comments based on past experiences that have long-since passed but obviously, still hurt. I recall one couple I was working with—well, I was working with their son Jack, but this highly combative pair of adults who had long-since separated were the ones who really needed some help, as their son was actually doing quite well, all things considered. This couple was in a school meeting that I was facilitating, along with the school principal, some of the boy's teachers, and some of the resource and counselling staff who were working with the boy on some of his academic challenges. Within minutes, the meeting had to be discontinued, aggressively. I am not, by nature, a yelling or even aggressive person. I try to be as diplomatic as possible, but this couple were seeming not terribly interested in anything currently happening with their son. The meeting started with me saying "So we are all here because we are on Team Jack and we are hoping to help him find success with his reading. We all have the same goal and we are all here to find some strategies that can help him feel more confident as a learner." Teachers, administrators, all nodding. Mom, sitting quietly with her head down, did not move a muscle. Dad, sitting across the room, arms crossed, said "Okay, that's all fine, but I think you should all know that *she*" gesturing to his ex-wife "*never* does anything to help Jack and lets him do whatever he wants whenever he wants and if she doesn't change then there is no purpose to this meeting."

Mom's head raised, fury in her eyes and venomously said, "I don't want to get off track here, but since HE brought it up, maybe I let Jack away with things at my house because his *father*" (and I have never heard that word used with such sarcasm and contempt before) "expects him to be perfect because HE thinks HE's perfect and that's why he sleeps around, to puff up his ego."

It was like the school staff and I had disappeared within seconds, leaving only this really angry couple behind. Dad's face flushed with anger and he flexed his chest, saying "Well, if SHE didn't let herself turn into a hag, then maybe . . ."

"GUYS!" I yelled, amazing even myself. He stopped and looked at me. She stopped and looked at me. The staff took an interest in their notepads. "This stops. NOW. We are here to talk about Jack's education. If we can do that, we will continue. If not, we will have to find another time and approach." Even recalling this situation makes me feel uncomfortable. The silence that followed lasted a moment at which time Jack's father said "I'm happy to stay, but only if SHE . . ."

"Okay, we're done here." I folded up my laptop. "We will reschedule by email." I was shaking a bit. What if they kept fighting? What if I had made the wrong call? What were the staff members thinking? Their school psychologist had just blown a gasket. The principal and teachers stood up to leave, mom made a beeline for the door to get out of the room, dad sat sullenly, arms still crossed. Eventually, he got up and left, uttering "So, you'll email, then?"

In this situation, I was actively surprised by my confidence, despite my initial nervous response. I had taken a risk that only could have happened if I had confidence in the possible success. However, it was certainly a risk. Again, what if they kept yelling at each other or, worse, me! I had yelled. In a professional context. Where would I go from there? Yell . . . more? Louder? Toss in some colourful vocabulary?

So again, where do we go from yelling? Screaming, I suppose. Not a great approach to classroom management or relationship enhancement. But we all find ourselves there on occasion. Developing a sense of confidence reduces the need to escalate because we do not feel personally challenged and therefore, a need to be defensive. These parents were both highly defensive and in retrospect, I hear the fear and anxiety in their interactions. Neither wanted to be called out as being a less effective parent than the other. They both seemed to be deeply insecure and lacking in confidence in their own parenting. And years of conflict had resulted in a heighted awareness of how to really hurt the other. Had one or even both of them felt more confident in their parenting approaches, then there would be a diminished need to try to hurt other parent and, at the same time, less defensiveness when the other was trying to hurt them. Confidence acts as a sort of forcefield that can deflect hurtful comments, while not ignoring the possibility that there can, on occasion, be some truth to what others say to us. Of course, being open to hearing criticism also takes a considerable amount of confidence.

Third, self-esteem is a process, not a product. One of the most interesting things about self-esteem education, particularly through the 1980s, was the fact that while well-intended, it was approached with little criticism, despite one significant and logical consideration that you have likely already drawn. Is it possible that self-esteem is not something that should be taught, but rather is more likely to be the *result of success*? Varied research found a positive correlation between self-esteem and success, in which success was poorly defined but generally associated with academic success, income, and other highly suspect measures of relative success. Was it not possible that those who did well academically had higher self-esteem because they did well academically? Those who had success in the workforce had high self-esteem because they were competent or better at their jobs, resulting in higher self-esteem?

Confidence within the 4C model could be seen as being similar in this sense. Confidence is earned through risk-taking and the process of striving toward success. No one can give you confidence any more than anyone can give you motivation, happiness, or anything else that is truly yours to earn. You can be given encouragement, however. Confidence is earned through effort and hard work, through a process of making attempts at things that are challenging. Self-esteem, it would seem, has very similar characteristics. There is nothing intrinsically wrong with having confidence that has been earned, nor is there anything wrong with having a high degree of self-esteem that one has worked for. The challenge is what happens when confidence is present in absence of effort or capacity. How do we manage those who have confidence in abilities when the abilities themselves may be lacking? This was the challenge faced by educators in the 1990s and 2000s who now had to work through the post-self-esteem hangover that now existed in which students had developed feelings, to some extent, of entitlement. They had high self-esteem because they were told that that were intrinsically worthwhile and as such, did they not also deserve success (perhaps even absent the work required to achieve true success)?

Again, to be clear—yes, we are all intrinsically worthwhile and yes, we all deserve the right to experience success. The argument is that by not attaching that sense of being worthwhile to anything of meaning creates an existential crisis, even in kids. If we attach meaning to intrinsic worth, then we can truly feel that our accomplishments are valuable, even if only to ourselves. To be clear, the focus here is on intrinsic worth and value. Extrinsic worth and value—positive feedback from those we respect, income, prestige, and so on—are also significant factors in motivation for many, but they are not prerequisites for feelings of worth. Any number of examples exist of people with all sorts of material wealth, the respect of their peers, all of the extrinsic measures of worth seem to be in place, but they remain fundamentally unhappy. Others have no significant worldly successes, per se, but are very content with their sense of confidence.

We can see that within the construct of mental toughness, there is a significant opportunity to reconceptualize our approach to enhancing self-esteem. Rather than top-down educational programming, focusing on genuine relationships at school and work is where true growth in confidence and self-esteem is strongly encouraged. If we have trust in those around us, we are more likely to take risks and if we take risks and learn, then we become more confident in our abilities and in our relationships. Developing confidence is possible and should be encouraged, but in doing so, we must be mindful of the lessons learned through DUSO!

Confidence in Abilities

Confidence in abilities is best described as being the extent to which an individual feels worthwhile and content in their own abilities. It is similar, though not synonymous, with self-efficacy, which refers to the belief in one's capabilities to achieve success in certain situations. Poker provides an excellent analogy. When playing poker, the player with the best hand wins. Mostly. Sometimes, and this is what makes poker really interesting, the player with the best hand may fold, allowing a player with an inferior hand to win. This occurs when a player purposely bets on a potentially losing hand with the intent to mislead their opponents into thinking that they actually have a strong hand. It's bluffing, and it makes poker a lot of fun!

Confidence in abilities does not presume bluffing, but there is a sort of internalized bluffing that can occur. It might even be that confidence in abilities is a primary factor in what makes for a "successful" individual, or perhaps more accurately, what makes for people to feel a sense of success. People with higher confidence in abilities may be more willing to take on risk, resulting in a mathematically higher probability that they can experience success. Certainly, this can also have the contradictory effect in that more experiences also increase the probability of "failure." However, if we take calculated risks that align with our abilities, the probability of success would seem likely to be higher. Of course, if we take an unnecessary risk in an area that is not at least generally within our wheelhouse, the probability of a lack of success is higher. For instance, I am a barely competent bass player, so I could likely take on a challenge to learn a new song and maybe even perform in front of others. I may do horribly, but there is a chance I will do enough to at least get by. If all else fails, I can just return to the root note. On the other hand, I will not be signing up for any rap battles soon (does one "sign up" for rap battles?). I can talk quickly, but my voice has no sense of rhyme. A sea shanty, sure. A rap? Not on your life!

Confidence in Abilities and the Self-Fulfilling Prophecy

There is a danger, though, related to confidence in abilities that lies with others. For many people, there has been a negative attitude that has permeated their lives through dismissive and demeaning voices telling them that they are not worthwhile, that they are not capable, that whatever their abilities are, they are not enough. This can become embodied in how they approach new situations. The concept of the self-fulfilling prophecy can come into play in such situations.

The self-fulfilling prophecy is a well-researched area of social psychology that essentially suggests that we live up or down to our own expectations. The future we anticipate is largely created by our predictions and we engage in behaviours and ways of thinking that lead us to confirm the expectation. Simply put, if you believe that you will fail, you will find a way to do so. If you anticipate success, you will be more likely to experience success. The Pygmalion effect is similar in that it is "other-imposed" self-fulfilling prophecy—the effect that other people's beliefs about you have a direct effect upon your behaviour.

A good example is a classroom teacher receiving a list of students at the start of the school year. This list has the names of each student in one column and a seemingly random number next to each name. Student A is 106, Student M is 112, Student R is 85, and so on. The teacher, in absence of any other evidence, assumes that, based on the range of numbers, that perhaps these numbers are the student's IQ scores. So, the teacher goes about differentiating their lesson planning to accommodate for the range of intellect present in the students. The students with scores in the low 80s get extra support and remedial lessons, somewhat lower than their actual grade level, while those in the 110 to 120 range get the standard curriculum and, in some cases, are even given enhanced learning opportunities. Months go by and the report cards start to go out. The 80 to 90 students have comments like "not meeting potential" and "experiences difficulties with reading despite support." The 110 to 120 students get comments such as "actively engages in discussions" and "provides good evidence of learning." The Pygmalion effect is at play and may be having a self-fulfilling prophecy effect on the students. Until one day in November, the principal comes to visit the teacher and asks to see the list with the student names and associated numbers.

"I've been looking all over for this list of locker numbers . . . we have a bunch of empty lockers and it seems no one in your class was given their locker number at the start of the year."

So, our thoughts and beliefs about our own abilities and the abilities of others need to reflect reality as much as possible so that we don't make a similar mistake, placing restrictions on ourselves and others where none are necessary.

Confidence in Abilities and Social Success

As noted earlier, confidence in abilities has been found to have a positive relationship with extraversion, which, in itself, is a wildly misunderstood term. Extraversion as a personality trait has been misused in a number of contexts. It would seem that the common understanding of extraversion is the most basic definition of the term which implies an outgoing personality. Of course, it is far more complex than that, and there are any number of factors related to extraversion that suggest that to be an "extravert" does not simply imply being outgoing. Extraversion does suggest that one finds energy from being around others, they tend to be talkative and socially engaged, they tend to enjoy the company of others, and they tend to be rather gregarious in nature. However, like most things, there are likely few dichotomous/binary "true" extraverts. Most people could be said to fall along a continuum of extraversion/introversion, having perhaps a preference for being with others, but not always and not under all circumstances. Introversion, on the other hand, suggests that the individual derives energy and strength from time alone. Most people are a complex combination of both. There is some evidence, though, that would suggest that those higher in confidence in abilities may also tend to lean into extraversion. This, of course, is not particularly surprising. If one feels that they are good at something, there may be more willingness, even eagerness, to share that ability with others.

The willingness to share one's abilities with others speaks more to confidence in abilities than extraversion or introversion. There are many artists, for instance, who feel a strong desire to share their talents with others but are simultaneously deeply introverted. In such cases, there is often a stage persona that develops to help the artist communicate their work with others while hiding in plain sight. Kurt Cobain was famously introverted, as is Kate Bush and Bruce Springsteen. Nelson Mandela, Michael Jordan, Larry Bird, Sydney Crosby, Mia Hamm, Bill Gates, Steven Spielberg. All have introverted personas. Of course, human beings are incredibly complex and few would argue that Cobain, Bush, or Springsteen, among a multitude of others, are "100% introverted." But all have reported a preference to be alone and some degree of discomfort with public life. Yet a commonality among these and other talented individuals is a confidence in abilities. Not arrogance, not overconfidence. A confidence that they have the capacity to overcome challenges.

For many, one of the areas of struggle is social interaction in itself. Having confidence in abilities but no means to share these abilities is a very frustrating experience. The capacity to share with others lies in confidence in social interactions. Again, we all know people who have a great deal of confidence in their abilities, including their social abilities, but who may lack the substance to support their confidence. In the political realm, we often see leaders who have a great deal of confidence, almost to the point of hubris, but who lack the capacity to back their confidence with actual performance. In politics, the confidence in abilities often supersedes the actual abilities, but this if forgiven in many cases as no one is expected to be an expert in all things. Effective leaders have a strong sense of confidence in abilities and also have the capacity to select advisors who can be their experts in their respective fields. One would not expect the leader of a corporation to know details about how mail is handled in the office, but they would be expected to have people who develop and implement effective policies and procedures around mail handling. Principals would not be expected to be exceptional grade 1 teachers (unless that was their training background)—they are expected to hire and coach exceptional grade 1 teachers. And in the same way, we would not expect a president or prime minister to understand the intricacies of global banking—but we do expect them to have knowledgeable and wise advisors.

In our daily lives, our own confidence in abilities is something we wish to enhance. Developing a sense of confidence in abilities again lies in risk-taking. Developing confidence means that we have to do certain things outside of our comfort zones. Those who may be lacking in confidence in their own abilities experience failure much more acutely, in part because of their own self-imposed self-fulfilling prophecy ("I tried something and it didn't work out—what did I *expect* to happen?"). A single, limited failure is generalized to a broader context, resulting in a diminished sense of confidence in abilities and, not surprisingly, a reluctance to take further risks. The reluctance to take risks is the hallmark of the hopelessness that often underlies depressive thinking. By engaging in challenging one's sense of confidence in abilities and encouraging individuals to rethink and reconceptualize their capacities and strengths, we can start to awaken a sense of confidence that may have been dormant or perhaps even eroded over time.

Perhaps the best venue to witness such change is in the social arena. It is probable that those with a lower sense of confidence in abilities may be less comfortable in social situations as they may feel that they have little to contribute or that their contributions would be minimal compared to those of others. Again, avoidance becomes part of the profile. Perhaps one of the most common fears cited by my undergraduate and graduate students, echoed by friends and colleagues, is a fear of public speaking. I share—or used to—this fear and here's why.

In grade 7, we had to do a book report in front of all of the other grade 7s in our section of the school. I was in "House B" (creative naming!), so there were 4 classes of grade 7 students, with approximately 30 students per class. I knew most of the kids in my class fairy well, but the other 90 were largely unknown faces. I was never a huge fan of public speaking, but I made it through elementary school by doing the bare minimum. Now, I was being asked to do a 5-minute presentation in front of my entire social world. So, I did what came very naturally to me at the time. I avoided. I avoided reading the book. I avoided even thinking about the presentation. I avoided thinking about the due date. However, the due date did not care. The due date crept closer and closer, a bobcat stalking its prey. Then, the day came. We herded into the school's theatre and the teachers started calling out the names of the students who would be presenting that day. I was confident that I would be okay. They were going in alphabetical order, the teacher had told us, and as an "M," I figured that I was safe. My teacher went up first.

"Aaron?"

"Aaron?" Alphabetically by *first* name? I'm a *B*! Aaron got up, but I was in no way paying attention. I was scrabbling to read the back jacket of the book I'd selected (Clive Cussler's *Raise the Titanic*, a spy adventure featuring Cussler's Bond-like hero, the unlikely named Dirk Pitt), looking for any sense of what the book was about. I mean, it was obviously about raising the *Titanic*. But why would anyone do that? And, perhaps more importantly, how? Nothing in the picture on the cover nor on the back cover gave much of a hint. I was hooped. Sweat started running down my back, a cold flop sweat that only served to make me aware of the fact that I was sweating.

"Brent?"

Turning what I am confident was an interesting shade of scarlet, I went to the front of the theatre. One hundred twenty sets of eyes looking back at me. Book in hand, I tried to clear my throat. Of course, I started to choke, resulting in a 10-second-long moment in which I was gasping, choking, and my eyes started to water. Also, still sweating. I had brought a piece of paper up with me, some notes from another class so that it at least looked like I was prepared. I held up the book and looked at my notes.

Then I looked at the book I was holding—it was shaking. My notes were shaking. *I* was shaking. I looked past the book and into the audience and made eye contact with a girl sitting near the front. A girl upon who I had been nursing a significant crush. I looked at her. She looked at me. My eyes, still watering, lost focus. I was sweating, tearing up, had turned a bright glowy red, and started to speak.

A high-pitched squawk left my mouth. It was at that very moment that my voice decided to change. I squeaked out "This book is about the *Titanic* and the author, Dirk Pitt, he, uhm, didn't write it, he's actually the guy in it and he was . . . a . . . spy . . . who. Wanted. To, erm, raise it. The *Titanic*." I paused. My teacher, finally sensing my crushing humiliation, said quietly, "Brent, want to try this another day?" I nodded quietly and slunk back to my seat, where my buddies were simply killing themselves laughing. "Good job, Captain Titanic."

Thus ended my public speaking career for the next 8 years. The next time I spoke in front of a group was in my third year of university, when I had avoided as long as possible any courses that had a public speaking requirement. I snuck through high school and my first 2 years on university by taking classes that did not have any public speaking requirement. But in third year in a social developmental psychology class, my time had run out. But something was different.

I now had confidence because psychology had truly turned my head. It was something I was interested in, something I had read about and by the time I was in this class, something I felt sufficiently conversant in. Over time, my confidence increased, occasionally bordering on arrogance, to be sure—to be teaching introductory psychology at the university level to students only a few years younger or, in some cases, even older, made me feel very confident indeed. But occasionally, my confidence would be balanced out by humility when I did not know how to answer a question or when I was proven incorrect in a statement, which happened from time to time. I learned to appreciate those corrections, as they kept me honest and kept my confidence in abilities from becoming too strong, which is interesting in that initially, my grade 7 experience had taught me to have very little confidence in my abilities. Again, mental toughness was something that I learned over time, through trial and error, through success and a willingness to learn.

"No Really, I've Got This"

Having a high degree of confidence in abilities serves to enhance performance in many ways. It can make an individual more willing to take a risk, more comfortable in taking criticism, and less susceptible to needs for external validation. The student who thinks "I can do this—I've written dozens of tests, and I am well prepared for this one" is more likely to do well on the test itself and even if they do not do as well as they would like, they are also capable of using that experience in order to enhance their performance on future assessments. The athlete who believes in their capacity to be a valued and contributing member of their team is more likely to engage at a higher level than one who does not have confidence in their abilities. The partner who believes in their capacity to make meaningful contributions to their relationship is more likely to make those contributions and, when not provided with external affirmations, continue to make those contributions simply because they have confidence in the value of their contributions.

However, while these can all be benefits of a high degree of confidence in abilities, there can also be a downside in relation to *over*confidence and a reluctance to seek out support when necessary. The concept of "I've got this" can serve a valuable and positive purpose, but ultimately, no one individual can say that they've "got this" when whatever "this" may be is not something that one person can manage independently.

In terms of criticism, having a high degree of confidence in abilities suggests that one would be open to criticism, but not dominated by it. Lower confidence in abilities would make one more susceptible to feelings of worthlessness and shame when criticized, no matter how valid the criticism. **If you are an individual who identifies as having lower confidence in abilities, think for a moment about how you respond to criticism. Do you take it as being a valid observation and perhaps even as a suggestion for improvement? Or is it perceived as a character judgement, as being a personal assassination attempt, designed to undermine your performance?** In either case, we can learn from our reactions to criticism, along with learning from the criticism itself. How we react may give us clues as to what our actual confidence in abilities really is. And it is certainly possible that a high degree of confidence in abilities could be seen as being a defense against criticism.

Additionally, even the most competent person, regardless of their confidence in their abilities, needs support. We rely on resources beyond ourselves. Our society is built upon a mutual sharing of resources and skills. People with a high degree of confidence in abilities may tend to overlook their own need for resources, over relying on their own skill sets. This is not only unwise, but also potentially harmful to the individual and those around them. I would prefer that my doctor has a high degree of confidence in his abilities, but I want a nurse to start my IV because odds are, the nurse has more experience with that task than does the doctor. I don't want a physician who is a "true" general practitioner. A good GP is a physician who knows when to refer!

People with a high degree of confidence in abilities often look to role models to enhance their performance. They look to those who have had success in whatever field may be of interest and then try to emulate their behaviour and mindset. Often, this selection of a positive role model may be successful and, depending on who the person sees as being a positive role model, can elicit positive behaviours and ways of thinking. On the other hand, we need to recognize that all of our role models are fallible, and so are we. There is a risk of dilution when we look to role models and expect perfection, because neither they nor you nor I are perfect. *The Office*'s Michael Scott, when asked who his role models were, cited "Bob Hope, uhm, Abraham Lincoln, definitely Bono . . . uh probably and God." That's an interesting selection, but Michael's an interesting guy. And I would cite Michael Scott as being an individual surfeit in his confidence in abilities, but lacking in actual abilities to support his confidence.

Continuing with the example of Michael Scott, but broadening to a larger population of people with high confidence in abilities, is the ability to manage feedback. As noted earlier, people with lower confidence in their abilities may view criticism as being judgemental of character. Those with a higher sense of confidence in abilities tend to see criticism and being valid feedback that can fuel growth and improvement. Michael is a character who simply cannot handle even the slightest of criticism, suggesting that his confidence in his abilities is built upon a very fragile foundation. True confidence in abilities presumes a certain degree of competence in the first place.

Confidence in Abilities: Challenges

As noted, those who have a high degree of confidence in abilities can experience considerable success in academics, career, relationships, and other domains. There are, however, certain challenges that can accompany this aspect of mental toughness. Some of these (overconfidence, arrogance, a lack of actual abilities) have already been addressed.

Those with a high degree of confidence in abilities can overestimate their abilities and as a result, take on too much. "No" is rarely part of their vocabulary. For them to say "No" is to admit a lack of capacity rather than a lack of resources; also, very often these people feel a sense of being overwhelmed, often simply because they do not protect their own boundaries. They are the team member who everyone else goes when something needs to be done because (a) they will agree to do it and (b) they will fight hard to get it done, even at their own expense. I have worked with a lot of teachers who have this particular challenge. They do way too much "for the kids," who, ultimately, would be fine without some of the extras that these teachers do. But even reading that might make some readers uncomfortable. How could a caring and engaged teacher say "No" to doing something *for the kids*? My argument, and I have had this conversation with many teachers, is that if we keep doing things for the kids, our own resources will be overextended and our long-term ability to help when we are really needed will be foreclosed on. When we spend our finite energy on others, we are left with little to no energy or, worse, a sense of resentment toward our colleagues and, more concerningly, toward the kids themselves. Of course, this difficulty in saying "No" because one's strong confidence in their own abilities infiltrates all aspects of that person's life, not just work. It happens at home, in couple relationships, in parenting. It is worth reflecting on our rationale for saying "Okay, I can do that" when we know at some level, we cannot. Who are we trying to impress?

The analogy often used to clarify this point is the airplane mask analogy. You know this one. When you are on a plane, the flight attendants do their safety demonstrations at the start of the flight. Part of the demonstration encourages travellers to don their own masks before assisting someone else with their masks should there be a sudden change in cabin pressure. The lesson here is that we need to engage in protecting our own safety so that we are in a position to help others. The part of the message that gets lost on many, though, is the emergency nature of the situation. How about we plan our flight and design our planes in such a way that the probability of a need for the masks to drop in the first place is limited? For those in helping professions, how about we examine systemic issues that underly anxiety, fear, depression, and other such conditions as opposed to focusing our resources on symptom management?

Another challenge for those with higher degrees of confidence in abilities is how they represent that confidence to others. Even in the most good-willed person, an intense confidence in one's abilities can project a certain arrogance. As such, others can feel intimidated and overwhelmed, even by those who use their confidence in abilities in an optimistic and positive manner. We have all spent time in the presence of the overwhelmingly positive optimist. It's *exhausting*! Imagine working with a real-life Tigger! In fact, most Disney movies have at least one such character (Dory, Olaf, Baloo, Timon, and Pumbaa, etc.). These characters are most decidedly NOT the heroes of their stories—they are comic relief at best, and occasionally serve the need for a sense of pathos. It's a shorthand to use a comic character to show the comparative suffering of the hero. But their overly enthusiastic optimism is never far away. Could you work with a Dory? Could you live with an Olaf? Have any expectations of a relationship with Timon or Pumbaa? Unlikely. Balance again is the key, maintaining a positive yet humble sense of confidence in abilities.

One of perhaps most concerning characteristics of those with high confidence in abilities is the tendency to be intolerant of the perspectives of others. Because they have confidence in their own abilities, and may discount the relative contributions of others, they can see others as being less capable and their viewpoints as lacking in merit. Such tendencies can be held well in check through the application of humility and in many situations, those who are high in confidence in abilities may actively seek out those who can challenge them to prevent them from becoming overwhelming to others. Left unchecked, patterns of bullying can emerge. In a compassionate society, bullying has little room for growth and should be actively discouraged. We can ask those who act in bullying ways why it is that they do what they do and when we do this, we discover a great deal of complexity that goes beyond conventional wisdom, which suggests that bullies are largely people who have been hurt and therefore hurt others in a grasp for some sense of control. In fact, in many situations, bullies do what they do simply because it has worked for them in the past. They have learned that to get what they want—which really could be a sense of control, but could be anything—they can manipulate and control others. Of course, this approach is ultimately self-defeating and is rightfully discouraged in contemporary society. Bullying exists, without question, but if we can understand the patterns of behaviour through the lens of mental toughness in general, and confidence in abilities in particular, we can actively understand and discourage such behaviours. We can also empower those who have been targeted by bullies to become not only more resilient but also more active advocates for themselves and others. Bullying cannot be tolerated, but the next step following simple intolerance of bullying is the movement toward its eradication.

Confidence in Abilities: Balance

By now, you know that my appreciation of the *Star Wars* films goes beyond appreciating them as simple films. The *Star Wars* universe is rich in metaphor and has been studied in numerous academic environments over the past 40 years. In the context of this current discussion, perhaps one of the best examples comes to us in the person of Luke Skywalker, a simple moisture farmer from a backwoods outpost who dreams of more. When we first meet Luke, he is a whiny, dissatisfied teen who does his chores only reluctantly, while finding any excuse to wander off and spend time with his friends in town. This sounds familiar!

In time, Luke meets Obi-Wan Kenobi, a man who will become his mentor in the ways of the Force. You know the story from here—Luke and Obi-Wan, along with their droids, the aforementioned Han Solo and his co-pilot, Chewbacca head off to save Princess Leia from the clutches of the evil Empire, personified by Grand Moff Tarkin and the cybernetic Darth Vader. The first film ends with the good guys, led by Luke, blowing up the Empire's ultimate weapon (for now). The second film starts with a far more confident Luke, now a hero who finds himself under the tutelage of Jedi Master Yoda. Despite an accelerated training program, Yoda and Obi-Wan warn Luke that he is not yet ready to confront Vader, yet despite their strong advice, Luke bundles up his growing confidence and heads off to confront the bad guy. Things do not turn out well. By the end of the film, he has lost a hand, is battered from his duel with Vader, and he is emotionally devastated by some newly learned information (spoiler alert for a film released in 1980—Darth Vader is Luke's father! If this IS a spoiler, maybe get out once in a while☺).

Luke's journey neatly encapsulates the idea of confidence in abilities. He starts off unsure, but eager. His confidence in his abilities is quite low. He wants to leave his uncle's farm in search of adventure, but uncertainty and fear overwhelm him until he is forced to make a choice. Low confidence in abilities is, in itself, not an unhealthy thing. In many ways, people with low confidence in abilities act as societal stabilizers, keeping everyone else in check. They can be regulators and governors, providing stability and familiarity. They can maintain our cultural rituals and are often sought after as purveyors of our societal norms. Luke, before he meets Obi-Wan, was on track to be a potential force of stability and longevity on the farm. Nothing wrong with that at all, his uncle had done so for decades, providing a valuable service to his family and community.

By the mid-point of the second film, however, Luke's confidence had superseded his actual abilities. He could manipulate the Force, but he was no match for Vader. Yet, his confidence led him into a premature conflict for which he was ill-prepared, costing him, well, not an arm and a leg (that's what his father lost a few movies earlier), but a hand and a great deal of confidence. By the third film in the original trilogy, Luke's confidence had been soundly balanced with humility. He knew that he had to confront his father, but he was not sure that he could win. But, he had to try. The balance he found was in the effort to try, not to win, not to be right, nor to avoid or escape. Our own confidence in abilities is often at its best when it is balanced. This sense of balance also applies to the other aspect of the 4C component of confidence, interpersonal confidence.

Interpersonal Confidence

Interpersonal confidence refers to the extent to which we are prepared and willing to assert ourselves and our preparedness to deal with challenges/ridicule, and also our ability to have an impact upon the emotions of others. Interpersonal confidence speaks to social skills, social effectiveness, social comfort, and social interaction. It is our capacity to use our social communication skills effectively and to be able to some extent express empathy and an understanding of the emotions of those around us. The ability to read and work a room, so to speak.

Interpersonal confidence, like all of the other components of the 4C model, requires a sense of balance. We have all spent time with the glad-handing, overwhelming, overbearing, unpleasantly confident social creature. These are folks who believe that any party only gets better with their presence, that any meeting only gets better when they are making comments, that any relationship is enhanced by talk (and little else). They can be just a *lot* to deal with. They are the reason the expression "a little goes a long way" exists. Unlike their compatriots who have high confidence in abilities but who lack the actual abilities to support that confidence and who, in turn, become overly optimistic and enthusiastic, those with high interpersonal confidence can have a great deal of confidence in abilities and the authority to back it up, but they tend to actively use that confidence to enhance their interpersonal relations. Unfortunately, they can come off a little strong, so some seasoning is often required to settle them down. We have all seen infomercials and their equivalents online. Often, these advertisements feature innovators or thinkers who have a great deal of enthusiasm and charm. They sound good, they sound confident, they sound knowledgeable. They sound convincing. In real life, this persona often continues. There are entire platoons of Tony Robbins protegees seeking to build their empires on charisma and *perhaps* some sort of idea, but largely, they may be bereft of any actual new idea or approach to wellness. There are those who succeed with the approach, and there always have been those who can work a room. I'd bet that the Snake in the Garden, Loki of Norse mythology, Iago from Shakespeare's *Othello*, the Man in Black from Stephen King's *Dark Tower* series, and many other villainous characters would all be considered to be high in interpersonal confidence. That said, for the most part, it would seem that to be high in interpersonal confidence, one would have a vested interest in the common good. Being positively engaged with others presumes, at least in part, an active engagement in the well-being of others. So, with the darker side of interpersonal confidence identified, what of the benefits?

Interpersonal Confidence and Empathy

Interpersonal confidence requires the capacity to effectively empathize with others. In most cases, this sense of empathy builds the confidence of those in a group, leading to a group cohesion that can be very productive and positive in nature. As previously noted, there is always a need for a governor of morality to prevent group cohesion from drifting into exclusionary thinking, which can be the source of all sorts of societal problems. Provided that the intent is positive and there are no particular Machiavellian mechanisms at play, those with high interpersonal confidence can enhance group performance and can themselves experience considerable success both in terms of their own confidence and also in enhancing the confidence of others.

Interpersonal Confidence and Persuasive Communication

Empathy itself is a valuable characteristic which, along with a strong moral sense, can temper some of the less positive aspects of interpersonal confidence. That said, an important component of interpersonal confidence is the ability to effectively communicate with others. Persuasive communication in particular would seem to be a common characteristic of those with higher interpersonal confidence. Interpersonal confidence, you will recall, encompasses both the ability to read and work a room, so to speak. Empathy helps one *read* a room. Persuasive communication helps one *work* the room. It is a tool that allows for individuals to convince others in situations in which convincing is advantageous for both parties.

Like all tools, persuasive communication, when used by an effective craftsperson, can be very positive and can result in some wonderful things. But tools can also be used bluntly and ineffectively, typically resulting in destruction. We have seen persuasive communication used effectively by some of the most skilled orators in history and also used clumsily by advertisers and marketing departments who desire to sell you through persuasion. Those who are higher in interpersonal confidence tend to be more skilled at persuasive communication through a variety of applications of skills and attributes. Social psychology teaches us that in many cases, people are persuaded most effectively by arguments that appeal to a combination of logic and emotion. Logically, data and trustworthy information delivered with authority from a position of knowledge and wisdom is more persuasive than questionable information coming from sources that lack authority. However, the direct route of persuasion, which focuses on logic, reason, and intellect, is often overshadowed by arguments based on fear or other strong emotions which follows the peripheral route of persuasion. Why do we allow ourselves to be persuaded by emotional arguments when we like to think of ourselves as being beyond such intellectually immature approaches?

Our minds are really super-complex structures that we are only starting to understand. The brain itself is incredibly complex, but sometimes, it is also frustratingly simple. The brain seems to work, in a *very* general sense, on the heuristic of the path of least resistance. We take mental shortcuts where possible. And a basic heuristic is the assumption that if someone is *loud*, they are more likely to be right. Why would someone who is wrong be loud? On a very basic level, we perceive the confidence of a speaker as conveying more accurate information than someone who is soft-spoken or hesitant in their speech, despite our awareness that many of the most intelligent arguments are made by people who may lack interpersonal confidence. As a psychologist (certainly *not* a neurologist), I have found that this phenomena exists in all sorts of situations. In therapy, clients often have difficulty exiting their logical and rational minds to enter into a world of emotion because they do not feel comfortable with the uncertainty that emotion elicits. At the same time, many clients have a difficult time explaining their heightened emotional reactions in a logical or rational manner. They know that their emotions are out of proportion to the situations they find themselves in, yet they cannot explain in any rational way why this happens.

Similarly, in social situations, those who have high interpersonal confidence can often outargue others largely through a charm offensive. They *sound* right, so they must be right. We have all been in discussions with people with whom we disagree (unfortunately, this kind of communication has become increasingly problematic because it is occurring online, where nuance goes to die). In these discussions, facts initially matter, but as the disagreement heats up, the facts become less important than the emotion driving the need to convince the other person that you are right and that they are wrong. However, those with positive interpersonal confidence are again good at reading the room and know when to resist the urge to compel an argument further, focusing rather on maintaining the relationship.

In the workplace, those who have strong interpersonal confidence tend to be very effective in staff meetings and can communicate their points in a highly persuasive manner. If you are a person with high interpersonal confidence, however, it might be worthwhile experimenting with your role a bit. For instance, in staff meetings, there are those who may not have a high degree of interpersonal confidence but who do have some excellent ideas. They are simply not confident in their abilities to have the interpersonal skills to share their ideas or to persuade others. If those with higher interpersonal confidence become cheerleaders for those who have lower interpersonal confidence, and allow them room to share rather than leaning into their own tendency to dominate social situations, then some really powerful ideas can emerge that otherwise would not be shared.

Interpersonal Confidence and Social Engagement

When I completed my first MTQ+ questionnaire, one of my "lowest" areas was on interpersonal confidence. As an acknowledged introvert, this was not particularly surprising in that I rarely share in staff meetings (part of the reason I entered private practice was to get *away* from staff meetings!) and I find many social situations to be uncomfortable and awkward. If I have a presentation, a structure, something to teach, I can be very confident. Absent that structure, however, I am useless. I am *that guy* at parties, the guy who can talk weather and local sports, but that's about it. I duck out early when possible. I am a master of the Irish Goodbye, which is a challenge given that my wife feels that the party only starts when we have our boots and jackets on to leave. The long goodbyes and chit chat that occurs when leaving a party is, to me, interminable, but to my wife, is when the fun gets started. I believe that her interpersonal confidence surely supersedes mine.

On the other hand, my training and experience as a psychologist has led me to ask the deep questions. That is an admirable trait in the therapy room. It is perhaps not so much in social gatherings. In social engagements that are intended to be light and fun, I can tend to go *way* too deep. I have asked people about their sense of identity being challenged simply because their favourite hockey team didn't make the playoffs. I have asked people I have just met if they are in love. I have, to my own horror, had an almost out-of-body experience in which I watched myself ask a person I'd met 2 minutes earlier if perhaps he was unhappy with his career choices. So, I need to work a bit on my interpersonal confidence. And the best way I have found to do this has been to take risks in social situations, but with the support of my wife, who helps me monitor my conversational gambits.

Of course, in our contemporary world, many relationships are now a hybrid of in real life (IRL, as the kids say) and online interactions. While the global nature of the Internet allows us to be exposed to a far broader range of perspectives than at any time in history, we are also in a time in which positions have become increasingly polarized and dichotomous. Like most people, I maintain a social media presence and I try to balance those who I interact with online between those whose positions I tend to agree with those whose positions may be antithetical to my own in an attempt to maintain some sense of balance and prevent the echo chamber from becoming overwhelming. Interpersonal confidence online has not, to my knowledge, been an area of research at this time, but I am curious to see the data when it emerges. Is it possible to have high interpersonal confidence online but not IRL? My suspicion is yes, but until there is compelling research, it remains an area of interest for exploration.

Interpersonal Confidence at School and Work

Many people who have strong interpersonal confidence do very well in school and work largely because of their interpersonal confidence, but as with confidence in abilities, it is best when the confidence is backed by actual skill sets. For instance, in hiring teachers and psychologists and administrative assistants and others in my various roles through the years, I have seen any number of people who provided exceptional interviews. Their interpersonal confidence, I would argue, was high and they could both read and work the room. Occasionally, we would hire people based more on their strong interview skills than on their CVs. And occasionally, this had unfortunate consequences. They did not have the skills to support their interpersonal confidence, and this lack of skills would quickly become evident in the workplace. By the same token, some of the best employees I have had the opportunity to hire have a degree of humility in their interviews and there is a good degree of consistency between their interview presentation and their CVs.

Perhaps my most successful job interview was for a job I really didn't want. It was a position as a psychologist in a private school and my bias was that while there was nothing wrong in principle with private schools, I bought into the myth of the private school kid—spoiled, obnoxiously rich, Mercedes-driving bullies who looked down upon anyone who did not conform. Obviously, there is a shadow of truth in most stereotypes, but such thinking is ignorant and wrong-headed. However at the time, that was my perspective and I really didn't want to work with that kind of population. I was of the opinion that these kinds of kids would not need psychological support— how bad could their lives be compared to some of the more at-risk kids I had worked with in the past? But, I needed a job and even the interview experience would be helpful. So, I submitted my CV and was contacted for an interview.

I entered the school and was led into the boardroom, which featured a stereotypically huge conference table and a number of imposing leather chairs stationed around it. I was introduced to the superintendent, the head of the school, the principal (how many administrators did one school need, anyway?), and a member of the parent council. Remember, I did not want this job, so I was very relaxed indeed. I took a seat at the end of the boardroom table, opposite the superintendent, a silver-haired gentleman who had a very genteel persona. As I sat, I noticed that the swivel chair also reclined a bit . . . so, as I introduced myself, I leaned back and, well, being so very comfortable, placed my foot on the table for a quick moment. This action drew a look from the headmaster, who narrowed his eyes and tightened his lips. I casually answered the questions and used my own charm offensive in a relaxed manner, not showing any anxiety because honestly, I didn't really want the job and as such, the level of threat was very low.

At the end of the interview, the panel thanked me for my time and the principal brought me around for a tour of the school. This is where things changed. While a private school, the population of this particular program was constituted of students with a wide range of learning challenges— learning disabilities, ADHD, Autism, behavioural disorders, and combinations of all of these. As I met the students and chatted with staff, I became rather charmed with the school and its faculty and students. I left now wanting the job and kicking myself for not taking the interview seriously, certain that my overconfidence had cost me the position.

Fortunately, my behaviour did not cost me the job—in fact, I believe that it helped me find success because had I really wanted it, I would have been far more anxious and my performance in the interview itself would have been less natural and more forced. My interpersonal confidence was actually enhanced by a lack of anxiety, which is not particularly surprising, but leads to an excellent strategy for those who struggle with interpersonal confidence. Approach situations in which you may feel anxious with a "Let's experiment with *not* being anxious" mindset.

In school, many students, especially those in their early to mid-teens, experiment with their own concept of interpersonal confidence. By their teen years, they have been exposed to a variety of social situations and their relative successes and failures in these situations have started to develop beliefs about their own interpersonal confidence. These perceptions become intertwined with the exploration of personal identity and depending on how they negotiated social situations in the past, they can become more comfortable with social interactions or they can become increasingly withdrawn. In my clinical experience, the exploration of interpersonal confidence is a very valuable experience, though like most things of value, is not easily earned. It takes risk and hard work to become more interpersonally confident, especially in adolescence, when we feel that the eyes of everyone around us are laser-focused on us. Of course, this perception of being constantly under scrutiny in adolescence (known as the "invisible audience") is both common and deeply familiar to many of us. We can well recall feeling that we are being judged for what we are wearing, our hair, the way we talk, who we spend time with, our musical tastes, our relative interest in sport, and so on. Ultimately, we learn that in fact, almost no one cares and those who do care not nearly as much as we *think* they do. As we emerge from adolescence, our interpersonal confidence can become enhanced when we learn to be more confident in our skin, as we become increasingly self-aware.

Wrapping Up

Confidence is essentially all about how we face difficult situations. Do we have the self-belief that we can meet with success, or do we tend to avoid challenges because we lack confidence in our ability to overcome? Confidence in abilities suggests not actual abilities, but rather our confidence in those abilities. If we lack abilities, we can still have confidence in what we do have, but we end up bluffing our way through life. Alternatively, we may indeed have the ability to overcome specific challenges, but we lack confidence in those abilities, leading us to avoid potentially positive outcomes. The goal to which we aspire is a balance of confidence and actual abilities.

Interpersonal confidence speaks to our ability to read and work a room. Do we feel comfortable in our interpersonal relationships and our ability to persuade people? Do we lack the interpersonal confidence necessary to engage effectively with others, leading us to feel somewhat isolated and withdrawn? Again, balance is essential—too much interpersonal confidence can be perceived as being overbearing, while too little leads others to perceive us as being easily manipulated and controlled.

Characteristics of confidence in relation to mental toughness are perhaps best characterized as follows:

Confidence in Abilities	
High	**Low**
• Believe they are right (even if they are not) • Capable of internal validation, requiring little external validation • Happy to ask questions and learn • Enjoy contributing to group communications • Provide detailed responses • Enjoy communicating their ideas	• Low self-belief • Uncertain in their own capabilities, even if they have the capabilities • May produce limited responses for fear of being judged as being wrong • Reluctant to speak out in group situations • Reluctant to ask questions for fear of being judged as being "stupid" • Avoid public speaking/ presentations

Interpersonal Confidence	
High	**Low**
• Stand their ground happily • Challenge criticisms • Enjoy participating in staff meetings/group projects • Effective debaters • Enjoy social situations • Can read and work a room • Rely on social skills (occasionally at the expense of knowledge) • Persuasive • Well-liked by others • Can be overbearing • Can manage uncomfortable situations and defuse conflict effectively • Good self-advocates—will ask for help when necessary • Not easily embarrassed	• Easily intimidated • Reluctant to engage in staff meetings/group work • Provide minimal details in discussions • May avoid social situations, particularly those lacking in structure • Take criticism personally • Tend not to "fight back" when treated unfairly/poorly • Back down when challenged • Allow others to dominate debate, even if they know more than others • Find assertive people to be unpleasant • May not ask for help when needed • Reluctant to self-advocate • Easily embarrassed

Chapter 7

Making Mental Toughness Work

W hen I do professional development workshops with educators and other professionals, one of the most common requests is to provide them with strategies that they can use, effective *immediately.* They may appreciate theory and the deeper work associated with an enhanced understanding of a topic, but by the end of any session, their request is simple: "This is all good, but what can I *do* about it?" This is, of course, a valid question and a healthy expectation of professional development. However, I am always cautious with front-loading strategies as I fear that there may be a tendency to simply take the strategies and apply them without a measured understanding of why they are doing what they are doing. It's like working out using different weight training techniques without understanding human physiology on at least a basic level or following a recipe without understanding what the final product could taste like with minor personal touches to enhance flavour. Strategies without context is like operating on someone following a textbook without understanding how blood pressure works. You could do it and might even accomplish the task, but you are far more likely to have better results if you truly understand the *why* of what you are doing, not just the *how.*

Through the preceding chapters, we have come to understand the concept of mental toughness, what it is and what is it not. We understand the nuances of the 4Cs and the orientations associated with each. We know that there is value in the model and that mental toughness can be a valuable asset in our journey to be better human beings. And there have been a lot of strategies for enhancing mental toughness embedded within the discussions of mental toughness. This current chapter will provide further specific frameworks which will include strategies to enhance mental toughness while at the same time providing you with approaches that can be used in developing approaches to mental toughness that could be applied to your own situation. We will focus on pathways for developing mental toughness to enhance our performance in professional and educational environments, in relationships, and in our own well-being.

Back to Basics

Before we start examining frameworks to develop effective strategies, let's take a quick moment to refresh ourselves on the mental toughness concept. Mental toughness is, at its core, a path to self-knowledge that helps us understand how we effectively approach and deal effectively with challenging situations, stressors, and pressures. It focuses not only on how we are resilient to stress, but also how and why we seek out challenging situations in the first place. It also helps us understand why some people may avoid challenging situations while others take risks to actively seek out challenges.

The 4C model incorporates Control, Commitment, Challenge, and Confidence. Each of these components have two intertwined orientations that help us understand our reactions to external situations and also help us to conceptualize our inner experiences.

Control, or the sense of one's self-worth and their ability to control both themselves and the world around them, is comprised of life control and emotional control. **Life control** describes our sense of control over ourselves and how we interact with our environments (including other people). **Emotional control** refers to our ability to control our own emotions and, to some extent, have an influence on the emotional responses of others.

Commitment describes our ability to set and make progress toward goals. The **goal orientation** focuses on the ability to set reasonable and achievable goals while the **achievement orientation** examines our abilities to have the wherewithal to actually take action to achieve our goals. Together, control and commitment are often construed as being the core features of resilience.

Challenge refers to our capacity to push our boundaries and move forward. The **risk orientation** describes the extent to which we feel comfortable taking on risk, while the **learning orientation** is associated with our ability to learn from our mistakes (and the mistakes of others) and to learn effectively without having to repeat mistakes.

Confidence refers to our self-belief in our abilities and our abilities to engage in proactive behaviour in interpersonal relationships with a focus on becoming more effective as individuals and teams. **Confidence in abilities** is best characterized as being our ability to believe in our own abilities, even if, on occasion, our abilities themselves may be somewhat lacking.

It is the ability to believe in oneself and one's abilities to the extent necessary to perform at a high level. **Interpersonal confidence** speaks to our abilities to engage effectively in social situations and other interpersonal relationships in which we can have an influence on others in a positive way.

While not part of the 4C model, we have also discussed the idea that there is a need for a governor for mental toughness to prevent some of these characteristics from becoming overpowering or from being used in manipulative ways. Moral reasoning and ethical decision-making have been proposed as sources of such governance. I would consider this moral governor to be essentially the "5th C" of mental toughness: Conscience.

Basics of Developing Mental Toughness

Developing mental toughness, then, would seem to be a valid approach to enhancing our well-being in relation to work, education, and relationships, among other areas. We also understand that mental toughness is a teachable trait; more specifically, we can coach people to develop mentally tough approaches which build on theory, practice, and life experience. In terms of developing mental toughness, a coaching approach is encouraged as coaching emphasizes not only a learning component, but also an experiential component that builds on pre-existing skill sets that can be focused and enhanced, while at the same time eliminating unhelpful approaches that may detract from performance.

Building on pre-existing skill sets presumes that very few people would have universally low levels of mental toughness. Statistically, presuming a normal distribution, most people would be expected to have at least average levels of mental toughness across all eight domains. There would be outliers, those who are exceptionally sensitive or exceptionally, perhaps even rigidly "tough," but the greatest number of those who would benefit from mental toughness coaching would be in the average range.

In developing mental toughness, we can look to our own experiences (as I have frequently through this book) to see where we may be relatively tough, relatively sensitive, and relatively flexible. It is important to reflect on our own experiences in order to best develop an understanding of our capacities and to identify those areas most clearly we may need to work on. It is through reflection that we can learn more about our own mental toughness. It is often valuable to reflect in a structured, goal-oriented manner. Once we have identified areas in which we could stand to benefit from working on engaging our mental toughness, we can work on setting goals that we can work toward. Of course, if we are more sensitive in relation to goal orientation, this step will be complicated, but this is where having someone support us as an accountability partner can be beneficial. Having someone else be aware of our journey toward enhance our mental toughness can help us be more accurate in our perceptions of our own mental toughness and, at the same time, can provide us with an external support that can keep us focused. Of course, we need to be cautious in selecting the person with whom we wish to share. If they have a tendency toward being judgemental or unnecessarily critical, they may not be a great accomplice in developing your mental toughness. A teacher, a coach, a therapist, any individual from whom you can maintain some degree of emotional distance might be more beneficial as they are less likely to be judgemental and therefore less likely to inadvertently impair your progress toward enhanced mental toughness.

Another factor critical to the enhancement of mental toughness is also based in effective coaching. Purposeful practice takes thought and intent and transforms the abstract into reality. It is rarely enough to simply try to "will" enhanced mental toughness into reality. **We must take action**. Small steps can be helpful here. Think of developing any skill set. Rarely do we start at the end. Instead, we take on the smaller component tasks first, easing gradually into more advanced skills. Riding a bike is rarely a spontaneous occurrence. It is an advanced skill that requires dozens of smaller steps, starting with the ability to manage even the most basic ability to balance oneself without falling over, even when crawling. Crawling itself requires dozens of microskills. The ability to lift your head and move it from looking right to looking left is an initial skill that forms the basis for the ability to look around, to examine one's environment, to create a desire to explore, to get us to prop ourselves up on our arms, to lift our bellies, and eventually to wiggle ourselves into a rudimentary crawl. From there, we learn to gasp, to pull ourselves up, to stand independently, to walk upright, to run without falling over, and eventually, we have sufficient skills to ride a bike. It takes years of development and dozens, if not hundreds of failures. And in doing so, we take numerous risks. It seems like almost all adults have a "coffee table scar" somewhere, a result of a fall when we were first learning to walk. My coffee table scar is on the left side of my chin, suggesting that at some point, I fell into something hard when I was trying to walk. Perhaps I even bit my tongue or lip in the fall . . . who knows? But here I am, walking around. My early failure didn't stop my progress for long. You likely had a similar experience, or have seen it happen to a child in your family. We all recover. If we can recover from minor incidents and wear-and-tear in our childhood, think of what we can survive as mentally tough adults!

Developing mental toughness follows a similar pathway, from rudiments of confidence to more advanced risk-taking and enhanced capacity to seek out and recover from challenging situations. This basic model, starting with a curiosity and desire to become more than we currently are to engaging in risk-taking behaviours, to practicing skills which, in turn, encourage us to be more confident, is that path to developing mental toughness in children and adults.

The goal of enhancing mental toughness does not necessitate a final, summative end point. As we discussed at length in regard to the goal orientation component of commitment, once we achieve a previously set goal, our tendency is to set a new goal. Therefore, when our goal is to enhance our mental toughness, we are actually embarking on a journey with no clear destination, since the destination will likely be a constantly moving target. This does not invalidate the need to set goals; rather, we need to refocus on the journey itself as one of goal striving, not simply goal setting. Goal striving suggests that we are aware of the need to be in a constant state of development and evolution. To remain stagnantly focused on a single goal is limiting and is ultimately an exercise in frustration.

To effectively engage in a positive coaching approach to developing mental toughness, goal striving needs to be a central feature. Even in elite sport, the goal may be to win a championship, to set a record, to place on the medal podium, but if that is the only goal, then the likelihood of success is limited. A greater opportunity lies in the work toward that goal. The process, not the product, is the point of emphasis. Good coaching, like good teaching and good management, relies on understanding that goal striving is, in itself, a worthwhile goal.

Coaching, Teaching, Managing, and Leading: Variations on a Theme

Many of the best coaches in sport have had limited success in their own athletic careers. Some of the best teachers of teachers are not particularly good teachers themselves. There are any number of excellent sales managers who could not close a sale on their own. Why is it that many of the best leaders may not be the most successful in their own fields, while in many cases, those who are the best in their performance may not make the best leaders? Wayne Gretzky (NHL), Isaiah Thomas (NBA), Diego Maradona (World Cup Argentina), and numerous others provide excellent examples of players who dominated their sport—as players. As coaches and managers, however, their records ranged from poor to abysmal. While I am not aware of any research into this phenomena, one could speculate that it is likely difficult for these elite performers to communicate the nuances of their skills to those who invariably do not have their innate abilities.

Strength-based coaching, in which coaches knowledgeable about a specific area of development (in our case, mental toughness) builds upon pre-existing skill sets and uses positive psychology approaches to support individuals in achieving their goals. Typically, such approaches incorporate emotional (**affective**), **b**ehavioural, and **c**ognitive components (ABCs). In incorporating all three components, we can facilitate goal striving and attainment, enhancing our performance at school, work, and in relationships (among other areas, including athletic and artistic performance). The ABC approach, in which all three areas are involved in developing mental toughness, leads to an enhanced sense of cognitive hardiness, a greater sense of hope and optimism that things can and will change for the better.

An example of application of the ABC approach related to school, for instance (although ideally, the ABC model could be seen as having implications in any number of environments and relationships), could involve test-taking. Let's take a student who feels that they do not perform well on tests. Perhaps there is even evidence that supports this belief. For a student who may lack mental toughness, they may perceive their challenges as being immutable and end up blaming themselves for their own lack of ability or others for creating unfair testing situations. In any case, they abdicate their personal responsibility and come to fear all tests, regardless of the weighting of the test or their competence to do well on it. If we apply the ABC model, we examine their emotions regarding test performance. How do they feel about tests? By extension, how do they feel about evaluation and assessment in general? Do they feel judged? Do they feel "less than" their peers? Do they feel that their performance is somehow disappointing to others, perhaps their teachers, perhaps their parents? Do they feel stupid? Do they feel that their peers are superior to them? There are a lot of emotions to work through and an effective teacher could take a moment to check in with the student to see how they feel about their test performance. Sometimes, a positive relationship with a trusted adult can result in surprisingly honest self-disclosures.

Further to the ABC model, what behaviours are associated with their approaches to studying and test preparation? DO they prepare well ahead of time, or do they cram the morning of the test? And finally, what are their thoughts about their testing practices? Do they think "I can do this!" "I'm prepared to do well!" Or do they catastrophize? "I am not prepared, and I'm not smart and this test will prove that and if I fail this test, I will fail the course, meaning that I will fail the grade, and I'll not get my diploma, and not get into university—not even a crappy one—and I'll not get meaningful employment so I won't be able to attract a spouse, and I won't be able to afford a house, and I'll end up lonely and poor!" This may seem extreme, but I have heard high school students say almost those exact words—and they *believe* them! These negative cognitions can be changed and replaced with more positive self-talk, but coaching may be necessary to help the individual make effective changes to their "ABCs."

Mental Toughness at School

Teachers and students are ideally placed to learn about and enact mental toughness approaches. One of the concerns, however, raised by many teachers with whom I have worked has focused on the use of the phrase "mental toughness" itself. There is a misconception that in teaching students to be mentally tough, we are encouraging macho ideas of competition, a win-at-all-costs mentality that runs the risk of developing little power-hungry self-focused, nonempathetic control freaks. Of course, mental toughness implies none of these characteristics; quite the opposite. As has been discussed at length, mental toughness is a path to self-knowledge and empathy. More than the self-esteem movement of the previous decades, though, it is also based on genuine action, not just meaningless platitudes. If we need to rephrase mental toughness into something more palatable to enhance the comfort of educators, administrators, and parents, then we can do so, provided that we keep in mind that the research on mental toughness uses common phrasing. So, for instance, if a school wishes to implement mental toughness into its curriculum, phrasing such as "Strategies for Success" or "Self-Knowledge Skills" may be appropriate, though again, it should be clear to program developers that mental toughness is the nomenclature under which any such program should be constructed.

Mental toughness has a number of practical benefits that would suggest that it has a potentially central role in enhancing student performance. Mental toughness, for instance, is not associated with socioeconomic status, race, parental prestige or income, or other factors that are typically well outside of the student's sphere of control. As such, pretty much anyone can benefit from developing mental toughness. It can help those who may be coming from a less privileged background to become more capable of working through their daily stressors. It can help those who have suffered trauma to re-examine their experiences and re-frame them in a manner that will advance their mental wellness. It helps students and teachers to become more resilient in the face of challenges, even those outside of their control.

Clough and Strycharczyk (2012) have found that "up to 25% of the variation in a young individual's test performance can be explained by mental toughness" (p. 169). While test performance should only be one small part of a more fulsome assessment of student performance and success, it is promising to know that mental toughness can be a potentially significant factor that can be taught to enhance performance across subject area domains. Students who are more successful and attribute their success to intrinsic factors are also more likely to have better attendance, perceive feedback as being positive, and have enhanced social relationships. This latter point is critically important in our evolving society in which there are increasing calls for social justice. A socially engaged student who has strong interpersonal confidence and who can engage effectively with others is more likely to take a socially responsible stance because of their sense of empathy which extends beyond their immediate peer group to a larger social understanding.

Mental toughness could also be seen as an effective construct in approaching transitions. As students transition from grade to grade, and from developmental stage to developmental stage (keeping in mind that some transitions are far more clear than others—graduation is a clear transition while the transition for childhood to adolescence is far more nuanced), mental toughness is an approach rich with possibilities to make positive and effective transitions. Developing a sense of confidence and looking at transitions as being positive challenges serve to enhance mental toughness which, in turn, leads to more openness to make further transitions. The cumulative effect of successful transitions lies in enhanced mental toughness.

On a daily basis, teachers could implement mental toughness to increase prosocial behaviour and reduce disruptive behaviour in class. Students who engage in maladaptive behaviours do so for myriad reasons, far more that could be encapsulated here. Through the introduction of mental toughness, many students can start to understand the reasons for their behaviours and the consequences that may exist if they continue. The engagement of a learning orientation can potentially be quite valuable in reducing problematic behaviours. Additionally, it is possible that many maladaptive behaviours could be conceptualized as arising from a lack of life control, so helping the student to develop a positive sense of life control may be effective in reducing inappropriate classroom behaviours.

I wish to be clear that no one approach to problematic behaviour is perfect. Theoretically, a purely behavioural approach, in which inappropriate behaviour is followed by unpleasant consequences, could be seen as being the most effective means of controlling behaviour, yet we know that this approach, while effective in certain specific situations, is not completely effective. A more cognitive-behavioural approach, in which the student is encouraged to think about their behaviours and alter them appropriately is also effective, sometimes. Mental toughness work alone is also unlikely to provide a panacea. However, some strategies, detailed later in this chapter, are drawn from a wide variety of theoretical orientations and models that collectively may be effective in the development of mental toughness.

Mental Toughness at Work

Implementing mental toughness approaches in the workplace has a high potential return on investment, not only in terms of an enhanced bottom line, but also in terms of human capital. As people learn to understand their mental toughness profile, they become better equipped to do their job more effectively and to work on teams in a more collaborative manner. There are some other tangible benefits associated with mental toughness in the workplace that are immediately apparent. Those higher in risk orientation may apply for more jobs and if they also have high confidence in abilities and interpersonal confidence, may be more likely to actually get the jobs for which they are applying. If one has a strong sense of life control, then they are more likely to have a strong sense of job satisfaction. Additionally, with a strong sense of life control and job satisfaction comes a reduced risk for depressive thinking (though to be sure, the presence of mental toughness does not preclude depression; rather, life control can help create a more positive mindset that may help the individual be more capable of seeking out support). The individual who has a heightened sense of emotional control may approach challenging situations with less anxiety, but just enough anxiety to enhance performance. If you are new to a job, but you have a well-developed sense of risk orientation, then you will be likely to make ongoing and frequent attempts to improve your performance, which over time, may result in more openness to new ways to engage in unfamiliar tasks.

It is probable that those who identify as being mentally tough may also experience better physical health since that are likely open to the connection between their self-chosen behaviour and their health-based decision-making. Their sense of life control allows them to make decisions about sleep, nutrition, and exercise that are rooted in enhancing their functioning, not simply doing so because they have been told to.

In developing mental toughness in the workplace, we take a proactive stance. Rather than reacting to challenging situations (which is certainly one aspect of mental toughness), we can become future-oriented, building upon previous learning, both from our own experiences and from the experiences of others. Most corporations, for instance, have extended health-care benefit plans for their employees. Dental care, for instance, is not considered to be "basic" health care, so employers have extended health-care plans that provide coverage for most dental work, including preventative work. It is so far less expensive, and far healthier, to engage in regular dental hygiene than it is to have cavities filled and other restorative work done. Proactive approaches are, by and large, significantly more cost effective than reactive work. Mental wellness is area in which employers can and should invest if they wish to see a high return on investment. Good mental wellness plans implemented across different industries have had overwhelmingly positive effects on employee health, workplace culture, and ultimately, on the bottom line due to enhanced employee effectiveness and decreased loss due to absenteeism and work cessation due to mental health challenges.

While proving a negative is difficult (how do we prove the nonexistence of something?), we know that preventative measures can be highly effective, even if any data that might be present is often speculative. It is challenging to prove that a specific educational approach, for instance, will result in less of a burden to the legal system, but there are statistical models that do suggest that this is indeed the case, that enhanced educational opportunities effectively result in fewer legal issues for individuals. Other potential negative outcomes that might be avoided through the application of mental toughness in the workplace (or in schools, for that matter) include:

- Poverty/debt
- Lower education
- Under/unemployment
- Poor mental health
- Poor physical health, challenges in relationships
- Social isolation
- Higher stress
- Depressed mood
- Low life satisfaction
- Physical fatigue
- Burnout

- Cognitive exhaustion
- Emotional exhaustion

At the same time, the following are positive outcomes that may be associated with mental toughness at work and school:

- Enhanced attendance
- Better self-esteem
- More optimistic perspective
- Increased performance
- Higher life satisfaction
- Less conflict
- Better communication
- Enhanced social skills
- Less anxiety
- Increased sense of hope
- Increased exercise participation

Mental Toughness in Leadership

There have been innumerable texts written on effective leadership and there seems to be an overarching factor consistent across these perspectives. It would appear that ultimately, there is no one common characteristic of effective leadership. So, the only certainty is uncertainty. There is evidence that suggests that mentally tough individuals find themselves in leadership roles more frequently than those with lower mental toughness scores, although this phenomenon does not imply a causal relationship. It is logical to assume that those with higher mental toughness scores would be more likely to find themselves in leadership roles, on one hand because of their goal orientation and their desire to better themselves, and on the other hand, because of their interpersonal confidence and confidence in their abilities. Strong communication skills associated with interpersonal confidence and emotional control, along with approachability, focus on goals, determination, consistency, risk-taking, the ability to see not only the big picture but also the details, and many other characteristics associated with mental toughness are also commonly associated with effective leadership. There does seem to be some degree of commonality across each of these and other associated characteristics, and that commonality often lies in the quality of relationships and the ability to exhibit mental toughness.

It seems that there is also some degree of commonality between effective leadership and effective counselling that we see practiced by skilled therapists. Therapeutic counselling, as opposed to leadership in its traditional sense, requires a strong sense of empathy, effective active listening skills, a sense of genuineness with the client, honesty, a collaborative nature, the ability to reflect, and a sense of purposeful communication. It would seem that these traits are consistent in effective leaders, for the most part. In some situations, leaders do not practice most or any of these effective counselling skills, resulting in a more dictatorial style. While a dictatorial style can be effective, it is likely not optimal for true growth in an organization and certainly not in personal relationships.

Developing Mental Toughness: A Counselling Approach

Some of the best teachers I have had the opportunity to work with often exhibit characteristics of effective leaders, manifested in strong counselling skills, which are often more intuitively constructed than directly taught. They can develop a relationship with even the most challenging students and they do this by focusing on active listening and displaying genuine empathy. They are *present*.

In developing mental toughness, then, one would be well advised to utilize effective counselling skills into their daily lives. In doing so, you can become a far more effective learner and leader. The skill sets you may want to focus on include the following:

1. **Active listening.** Active listening implies full-contact listening; being observant of all forms of communication, including not just the words the other person may be using. We benefit from listening to tine and cadence, from body language and facial expressions. Proximity also matters. The "Close Talker" from *Seinfeld* is not the model we are hoping to emulate. Think more Oprah instead. Oprah, regardless of your thoughts on her and her empire, is renowned almost universally as an extremely effective interviewer and communicator. She demonstrates active listening, appears to be genuinely interested in those with whom she interacts, and uses both verbal and nonverbal cues to guide her approach to questioning in which she appears to really want to get to know her subjects.

2. **Congruence.** Congruence refers to the state that exists between the inner and outer world of the individual and the relationship. The less distance between one's inner experience and their outward display of emotion and interest, the more congruent the relationship is. The congruent individual is usually a genuine individual, one who others innately trust and feel safe around. Everyone benefits from congruence, from the business leader and the teacher to the employee and the student. We feel comfortable to take risks when in the presence of a congruent individual because we can trust that they are who they say they are and their outward expression is a genuine representation of who they are. Mentally tough people are often congruent because they see little benefit in putting on a persona.

3. **Openness.** Openness is a characteristic that allows the individual to be truly open to who other people are. Openness largely eschews judgement in favour of being willing to wait for the other person to really be themselves. Openness allows for a more genuine and positive interaction, which again builds trust and enhances positive communication. In being open, we must attempt to put aside preconceived notions of the other person. While a completely unbiased perspective on others might be impossible to achieve (we are all biased in some way or another), awareness of our own biases and expectations can enhance our sense of openness.

4. **Unconditional Positive Regard.** Carl Rogers, often identified as the father of humanistic psychology, coined the phrase "unconditional positive regard." Three small words with a great deal of complexity. Unconditional means "without conditions." Humanistic psychologists refer to conditions as being those expectations we place on others, often expressed as a relational "if/then." "If you are positive when you talk with me, then I will respect you." Rogers proposed that "if" conditions placed unhealthy boundaries on communication and, ultimately, forced relationships into awkward compartments. Positive regard suggests that we look at others as being valuable human beings, worthy of respect and consideration. Unconditional positive regard does not imply that we happily accept all human behaviour. There are consequences to poor behaviour, but the goal in many cases is to find out what factors lead to such potentially harmful behaviours. If your supervisor is constantly rude and dismissive, you have a choice to continue to accept their negative communications, even if it

causes you considerable stress and anxiety. But we need to be mindful of our own boundaries as a way of exhibiting our own self-worth. So, we can challenge their negative comments from an unconditional positive regard perspective. In doing so, we enhance our own mental toughness by developing our confidence in our abilities through the practice of interpersonal confidence.

5. **Empathy.** Empathy is perhaps the cornerstone of a positive and healthy relationship, be it at work, school, or home. Empathy is the capacity to genuinely share in an emotional experience, even if we ourselves may not be having the same emotional experience. We have all experienced empathy. The times when we have experienced difficult emotional experiences, we have hopefully had someone with us who has been there to lean on. They may not have had the same experience, but they "get it." True empathy is difficult to prescribe in the sense that it cannot truly be taught. It's a "I know it when I see/ experience it" sort of thing. In terms of mental toughness development, empathy is perhaps best associated with emotional control and interpersonal confidence. Developing a sense of empathy makes it more likely that you will be sought out when others *need* you, not just because you are there.

6. **Collaboration.** In developing our mental toughness, we need to be cognizant of the reality that we do not do so in isolation. We are social creatures and the development of mental toughness, while in part an interior job, is largely dynamic in nature, requiring the presence of others. It is worthwhile to engage others in our journey to enhance our mental toughness, in part because we can learn from them, but also so that we can effectively collaborate in an interactive manner.

   Business leaders and managers who collaborate with their teams tend to have far better bottom lines than those who dictate agendas. A collaborative leader is one who encourages novel approaches to problem-solving and may veer away from standard practices that are traditionally implemented because "that's the way we've always done it." A collaborative manager delegates effectively and, not surprisingly, learns to earn the trust of the team by trusting them to do what it is they have been hired to do. A collaborative leader is a mentally tough leader, one who will see far better results and more innovation than a more *lassie-faire* or dictatorial leader.

   A teacher who is working on their own mental toughness can collaborate not only with peers, but also their students. Developing a common awareness of mental toughness in the classroom (at developmentally appropriate levels, of course) allows both the teacher and the students to support one another in their development not only of mental toughness itself, but some of the beneficial "side effects," including enhanced social interaction, less bullying, increased motivation to achieve academic goals, less absenteeism, and so on.

7. **Purpose.** In any effective counselling relationship, a sense of purpose is critical to the effectiveness of therapy. At the end of each therapy session, the therapist often collaborates with the client to establish goals for the next session, often returning to goals previously established as being the "purpose" of therapy. In the work world, we tend to work better when we have a sense of purpose, which could be viewed as being a broader sense of the goal achievement orientation. Goals are usually fairy specific, which is great because that is what goals should be. However, a sense of purpose is more of an existential issue. Goal striving is essentially useless unless there is a broader sense of purpose attached. Purpose answers the "why" questions, those larger questions around our sense of identity. In most workplaces and relationships, a sense of purpose is important. When faced with challenging situations, many people ask, "Why do we need to do this?" A valid question, one that we should always have an answer for. And "Because it is important" without saying *why* the task is important is the equivalent of "Because I said so," a nonresponse that actually damages trust and reduces the ability to collaborate because it is incongruent (how can an educator or any other leader claim to be congruent, yet say "because I said so" and expect anything but antipathy as a result?) and does not reflect genuineness, trust, compassion, or empathy.

8. **Reflection.** As we have learned, mental toughness really only develops when we learn from our past behaviours and those of others. We can also learn from our emotional responses. We learn from risks taken and from our successes and "failures." Reflection is another skill that requires practice and time. We often feel a need to immediately react, to fill the conversational void because of our own discomfort with silence. In many relationships, the opportunity for reflection is limited by our strong desire to move on to the next thing. Taking a moment—or more—to reflect upon our experiences is an undervalued skill that we can develop. Much has been made of mindful meditation as an approach to developing the capacity to reflect, and rightfully so.

There are any number of similar strategies that allow us to develop our reflection abilities, including deep breathing/"box breathing," self-guided imagery, progressive deep muscle relaxation, journalling, going for a walk, listening to music, creating art, exercising, the list goes on and can be as unique as the individual who seeks to become more reflective. Personally, my best reflection occurs when listening to music while driving—my brain is occupied by the tasks of driving on one level, listening to the music on another, allowing for a deeper processing of emotions and experiences. Reflection is a skill set that helps us amalgamate our experiences into something meaningful, driving us back to a sense of purpose.

The intent here is not to imply that to develop mental toughness, you need to become a therapist. Instead, the goals is to take effective skills that have long been associated with personal change and apply them to the development of mental toughness. Ideally, in our journey to enhance our own mental toughness, we can become models to others in terms of how they can also develop a more effective sense of mental toughness. Additionally, it would be rather foolish to suggest that only those highly trained in the theory and practice of mental toughness are qualified to help people enhance their mental toughness. In providing these approaches, the hope is that individuals and groups can develop their own capacity to find effective approaches to enhance mental toughness both as individuals and as teams.

Process for Developing Mental Toughness

As we work to develop our mental toughness and, perhaps, the mental toughness of those around us, we benefit from following structured approaches that enhance the likelihood of success. Following a standard model in the development of mental toughness, such as that proposed by Peter Clough (2012), is encouraged. Clough's model is as follows, with the implementation phase (#5) added here to provide enhanced opportunities for practice of skills:

1. Introduce the concept of mental toughness
2. Assess mental toughness (ideally using a psychometrically strong measure, such as the Mental Toughness Questionnaire MTQ48 or MTQ+)
3. Review the results, ideally 1:1 with someone experienced in the field of mental toughness

4. Identify opportunities of growth and development (individually or in a team environment, including a classroom)
5. Implement opportunities for practice of skills
6. Reassess to evaluate areas of potential growth and evaluate progress to date
7. Discussion of learning (again, 1:1 or in groups)
8. Celebration of positive outcomes

Clough's approach implies a scientifically consistent means to evaluate the effectiveness of mental toughness education, allowing for more consistent applications of the concept across individuals and environments.

General Strategies for Developing Mental Toughness

CONTROL	
• Take a positive self-perspective • Focus on what you can control • Reduce focus on what is outside of your control • See setbacks as being normal and healthy • Remember—what you do matters • Find support to reduce anxiety/nervousness • Be self-compassionate and extend compassion to others • Develop realistic multitasking skills, but try to focus on one thing at a time • Recognize and honour the need to recharge	• Identify specific areas in which you have achieved success (recently; in the past) • Use reflection to identify possible areas to enact change • Use positive visualization to "see" yourself having success • Use positive self-talk • Challenge negative self-talks (evidence should supersede opinion) • Delegate where possible • Accept your areas of difficulty, but avoid using them as excuses • Find reasons, not excuses • Acknowledge realistic limitations (i.e., time constraints, financial limitations, etc.)

COMMITMENT	
• Try to persevere—don't give up too early • Think optimistically • Find motivation even in small tasks • Identify your sources of motivation • Break tasks down into achievable components • Take the time to plan your activities • Learn how to say "No"	• Reflect on setbacks—What have you learned? What will you do differently next tie? • Get support from others to enhance motivation • SWOT analysis (Strengths, Weaknesses, Opportunities, Threats) • Engage a positive mindset • Set short—and long-term goals and try to stick with them • Find motivation in small accomplishments
CHALLENGE	
• See challenge as opportunity • Change is a constant • Look for the upside • Learn about your capacity for change • Break tasks into smaller components • Enhance the structure of your work • Expand on your ways to relax and reflect	• List benefits to a new challenge • Seek out variety • Focus on positives; acknowledge challenges • Make subtle changes to your routine to keep things interesting and new • Group similar tasks together • Plan your day and stick with that plan • Work on establishing effective priorities • Find what works best for you to relax

CONFIDENCE	
• Focus on feelings of self-worth • Ask questions and in doing so, do not presume that you are "stupid" for asking • Offer suggestions with confidence • Work on being more assertive • Understand that while you may be wrong, you also may be right! • Monitor self-talk, and focus on positive self-talk and challenge negative self-talk • Focus on successes • Limit focus on setbacks • Keep things in perspective	• Identify positive characteristics about yourself • Increase your involvement in challenging tasks • Set clear targets for engagement (i.e., make one comment in a staff meeting; ask one question in class) • Engage in unstructured social activities • Avoid generalizing—one setback is one setback • Learn how to say "Yes" • Understand that success is not final, and failure is not fatal

Wrapping Up

Mental toughness is a powerful construct that can be used to enhance performance and well-being in a number of ways. It is a concept that, while rooted in sport and business performance, has applications for everyone. A well-developed understanding of mental toughness can lead to the development of effective personalized strategies that can be used to enhance one's own mental toughness.

Call to Action—Your Journey with Mental Toughness

Our journeys with mental toughness are ongoing. We hopefully will never be "done" with developing our mental toughness. There will be times when our mental toughness will be challenged. For instance, the COVID-19 pandemic has brought many of us into direct confrontation with our sense of control, particularly life control. But we do not need a pandemic to teach us that we need to have some degree of flexibility in relation to control in order to adapt effectively to the changing circumstances of the world around us. Similarly, our sense of confidence may be challenged by unanticipated changes in relationships, work, health, or any number of possible situations that lead us to ask "Can I manage this?" The answer, of course, is "Yes"—we can manage more than we sometimes give ourselves credit for!

As a reminder, mental toughness is not a new concept, nor is it particularly unique, given its historical roots in philosophy, psychology, and more contemporary concepts such as positive growth mindset, resilience, and so on. However, what makes mental toughness stand out from some of the more contemporary models of mental wellness is its comprehensiveness and the fact that it can be accurately and validly be assessed. Intervention strategies can also be developed to enhance mental toughness. So, knowing that mental toughness is a "real" thing, what can you do to enhance your journey with mental toughness?

1. **Start where you are**! It is advisable that you start with assessing your current mental toughness status. As noted, the Mental Toughness Questionnaire suites offered through AQR International are a good starting point, but even simple reflection on each of the eight orientations would be a worthwhile starting point. The goal here would be to find out what your unique patterns of relative sensitivities and strengths may be so that you know where you are fairly solid and where you may need to do some enhancement work.

2. **Set a direction.** Once you have identified your unique pattern of mental toughness according to the eight orientations, select the one that you wish to prioritize as an area for growth. Use SMART[2] Goal Setting (see below) to set your target.

3. **Partner up!** Like going to the gym or an art class, sometimes it can be helpful to have an accountability partner who can support you in enhancing your mental toughness. This person does not have to be on the same trajectory as you in terms of mental toughness. In fact, often your accountability partner may know very little about mental toughness. They should simply be a person to whom you can, in a trusting manner, share your approach to enhancing your mental toughness and having them provide feedback on your goals. Essentially, this is simply someone you can check in with on an ongoing basis. If there is no one you trust to share your journey with, you can simply set up reminders in your calendar to do a personal check-in and in doing so, become your own accountability partner.

4. **Select a strategy.** It will be important to operationalize your efforts by being specific in the approach you take to enhancing your mental toughness. At the end of each chapter, there are a number of descriptors presented relative to a specific mental toughness component (Control, Commitment, Challenge, Confidence) with specific strategies in Chapter 7.

   For instance, do you want to enhance your risk orientation? One of the approaches you could try, coming from Chapter 5, would be to "enjoy challenge." So, a strategy you could employ would be identifying something that is a challenge for you—let's say reading a book a month. Find a book that you think you might actually enjoy (there are a LOT of on-line resources to help you find books aligned with your personal interests) and set a goal to read a set number of pages per week. Write down the page range for each week somewhere where you will see it. You will end up actually completing the activity and, more importantly, enjoying the process and, ideally, the book itself!

5. **Be precise.** You do not need to be so specific as to say, "I plan on enhancing my emotional control by 25% over the next 6 months." That would be a bit nuts! But you do need to be *somewhat* precise in defining what it is you are hoping to achieve and the actions required to get you there. So, something like "I will work on enhancing my emotional control every day by purposely exposing

myself to something moderately frustrating and then engaging in calming techniques until I feel closer to a sense of mastery of those techniques." For instance, I find reading the comments sections of different news stories to be interesting, but occasionally quite irritating and frustrating. So, I habituate myself to them (remember habituation—getting used to uncomfortable stimuli?) by reading them and then using a calming strategy—in my case, taking a moment to close my eyes, take a deep breath and repeat to myself "Everyone has a different path that leads them to their opinions and I do not have to agree with those opinions or even respect the path." (Actually, my real reaction is "Good lord, other people's children" and then I mentally roll my eyes). I have practiced this strategy enough that I can now read comments sections with almost no emotional reactivity at all. It works remarkably well!

6. **Expect changes!** There will be setbacks. I make no guarantees at all, except the usual certainties ("death & taxes"). However, I would add setbacks as a certainty we all face as human beings. "This too shall pass" is an expression based on an old Persian folk story in which a wealtlhy king set his wise men off to find a universal truth. One retuned with the expression "This too shall pass." Initially, this made the king very happy, because it let him know that all of his challenges and strife would eventually cease; however, he immediately became sad when he realized that the saying also referred to his family, his riches, and his legacy. In terms of our journey to enhance our mental toughness, we need to anticipate that there will be barriers to our growth, there will also be times in which our growth will be exponential. Both the achievements and the challenges will eventually pass. The reality is that we all constantly be in a state of flux, but the intent is to keep moving forward!

7. **Evaluate honestly.** If you find yourself developing your mental toughness in a positive way, great! Keep going and change your goals accordingly. If not, be honest with yourself. Many of us have a tendency—perhaps unwittingly—to lie to ourselves when we feel that we have fallen short of a goal. This is no time for such egotistic dishonesty. In lying to ourselves, we are actively causing ourselves pain. And I don't know about you, but I am not a big fan of self-inflicted pain. So, while honesty may hurt, it will not hurt as much as the results of lying to yourself.

SMART2 Goals

A very familiar and perhaps even overused approach to goal setting is using the SMART acronym, as follows:

- **Specific**—the goal should be specific and neither too narrow nor too broad
- **Measurable**—the goal should be observable and measurable
- **Achievable**—the goal should be something you can actually achieve
- **Realistic**—the goal should be realistic and something that the individual is capable of given the resources available
- **Time-sensitive**—the goal should have a start and end date

While his model is highly practical and presents an easy approach to setting and achieving goals, it may feel a bit incomplete, so I propose a SMART^2 model that builds on SMART goals by adding more motivational/ intrinsically driven factors:

- **Self-Directed**—YOU should set the goal, based on your assessment of what you need to work on
- **Meaningful**—the goal should have personal meaning, which enhances its intrinsic value and as such, make the goal far more achievable
- **Adaptable**—the goal should have flexibility built-in so that it does not become a rigid taskmaster that removes all joy from the process
- **Rational**—the goal needs to make sense in your own personal and professional context
- **Thoughtful**—the goal should reflect a mindful and thoughtful approach, focusing on the *why* of the goal more so that the *what* or the *how to* components.

Wrapping Up

The journey to enhancing our mental toughness is never finished. It is ongoing and ideally, highly rewarding. As individuals, our mental toughness can make us feel much more confident. It enhances our self-awareness and ultimately makes us feel like better people, even for having *tried* to improve.

Your journey is yours, but not yours alone. We are social creatures and I encourage you to share what you have learned about mental toughness with others. However, even if you choose to keep what you have learned personal and private, you hopefully have become more aware of your personal strengths and how best to use those to continue your journey forward. And in your journey, I wish you all the very best!

References

Bahmani, D. S., Gerber, M., Kalak, N., Lemola, S., Clough P. J., Calabrese, P., . . . Brand, S. (2016). Mental toughness, sleep disturbances, and physical activity in patients with multiple sclerosis (MS) compared to healthy adolescents and young adults. *Neuropsychiatric Disease and Treatment, 12,* 1571–1579.

Bahmani, D. S., Hatzinger, M., Gerber, M., Lemola, S., Clough, P. J., Perren, S,. . . Brand, S. (2016). The origins of mental toughness— prosocial behavior and low internalizing and externalizing problems at age 5 predict higher mental toughness scores at age 14. *Frontiers in Psychology, 7,* 1221.

Bandura, A. (1977). Self-efficacy: Towards a unifying theory of behavioural change. *Psychological Review, 84,* 191–215.

Bandura, A. (1997). *Self-efficacy: The exercise of control.* New York: Freeman.

Bandura, A. (1997). *Self-efficacy in changing societies.* Cambridge: Cambridge University Press.

Bédard-Thom, C., & Guay, F. (2018). Mental toughness among high school students: A test of its multidimensionality and nomological validity with academic achievement and preference for difficult tasks. *Social Psychology of Education, 21*(4), 827–848.

Birch, P. D. J., Crampton, S., Greenlees, I. A., Lowry, R. G., & Coffee, P. (2017). The mental toughness questionnaire-48: A re-examination of factorial validity. *International Journal of Sport Psychology, 48*(3), 331–335.

Bowers, E. P., Johnson, S. K., Buckingham, M. H., Gasca, S., Warren, D. J., Lerner, J. V., & Lerner, R. M. (2014). Important non-parental adults and positive youth development across mid- to late-adolescence: The moderating effect of parenting profiles. *Journal of Youth and Adolescence, 43*(6), 897–918.

Brand, S., Gerber, M., Kalak, N., Kirov, R., Lemola, S., Clough, P.J., . . . Holsboer-Trachsler, E. (2014). Adolescents with greater mental toughness show higher sleep efficiency, more deep sleep and fewer awakenings after sleep onset. *Journal of Adolescent Health, 54*(1), 109–113.

Brand, S., Gerber, M., Kalak, N., Kirov, R., Lemola, S., Clough, P.J., . . . Holsboer-Trachsler, E. (2014). "Sleep well, our tough heroes!"—In adolescence, greater mental toughness is related to better sleep schedules. *Behavioral Sleep Medicine, 12*(6), 444–454.

Brand, S., Kalak, N., Gerber, M., Clough, P. J., Lemola, S., Pühse, U., & Holsboer-Trachsler, E. (2014). During early and mid-adolescence, greater mental toughness is related to increased sleep quality and quality of life. *Journal of Health Psychology, 21*(6), 905–915.

Brand, S., Kalak, N., Gerber, M., Clough, P.J., Lemola, S., Sadeghi Bahmani, D., . . . Holsboer-Trachsler, E. (2016). During early to mid adolescence, moderate to vigorous physical activity is associated with restoring sleep, psychological functioning, mental toughness and male gender. *Journal of Sport Sciences, 35*(5), 426–434.

Brand, S., Kalak, N., Gerber, M., Pühse, U., & Holsboer-Trachsler, E. (2013). During early to mid adolescence, greater mental toughness is related to better sleep and vigorous physical activity. *Pharmacopsychiatry, 46*(6).

Brand, S., Ratzinger, M., Stadler, C., Bolten, M., von Wyl, Al, Perren, So., . . . Holsboer-Trachsler, E. (2015). Does objectively assessed sleep at five years predict sleep and psychological functioning at 14 years?—Hmm, yes and no! *Journal of Psychiatric Research, 60,* 148–155.

Clough, P. J., Earle, F., Earle, K., Perry, J., & Strycharczyk, D. (2014). Mental toughness – what is it and why is it so important? In Dr. Strycharczyk & C. Elvin (Eds.), *Developing resilient organizations.* London: Kogan Page.

Clough, P. J., Earle, K., & Sewell, D. (2002). Mental toughness: The concept and its measurement. In I. Cockerill (Ed.), *Solutions in sport psychology* (pp. 32–43). London: Thomson.

Clough, P. J., Houge Mackenzie, S., Mallabon, E., & Brymer, E., (2016). Adventurous physical activity environments: A mainstream intervention for mental health. *Sport Medicine, 46*(7), 963–968.

Clough, P. J., & Sewell, D. F. (2000). Exercising the mind: An investigation of the psychological benefits of non-physical recreation. *Journal of Sports Sciences, 18*(1), 46–47.

Clough, P. J., & Strycharczyk, D. (2008). Developing resilience through coaching. In J. Passmore (Ed.), *Psychometrics in coaching.* London: Kogan Page.

Clough, P. J., & Strycharczyk, D. (2010). Developing resilience through coaching – MTQ48. In J. Passmore (Ed.), *Psychometrics in coaching.* London: Kogan Page.

Clough, P. J., & Strycharczyk, D. (2010). Leadership coaching. In J. Passmore (Ed.), *Leadership coaching.* London: Kogan Page.

Clough, P. J., & Strycharczyk, D. (2012 & 2015). *Developing mental toughness: Improving performance, wellbeing and positive behaviour in others.* London: Kogan Page.

Clough, P. J., & Strycharczyk, D. (2012). Mental toughness and its role in the development of young people. In C. Van Nieuwerburgh (Ed.), *Coaching in education: Getting better results for students, educators and parents.* London: Karnac.

Cowden, R. G., Clough, P. J., & Anti, K. O. (In Press). Mental toughness in South African youth: Relationships with forgivingness and attitudes towards risk. *Psychological Reports.*

Crust, L. (2008). A review and conceptual re-examination of mental toughness: Implications for future researchers. *Personality and Individual Differences, 45*(7), 576–583.

Crust, L. (2009). The relationship between mental toughness and affect intensity. *Personality and Individual Differences, 47*(8), 959–963.

Crust, L., & Clough, P. J. (2005). Relationship between mental toughness and physical endurance. *Perceptual and Motor Skills, 100*(1), 192–194.

Crust, L., & Clough, P. J. (2006). The influence of rhythm and personality in the endurance response to motivational asynchronous music. *Journal of Sports Sciences, 24*(2), 187–195.

Crust, L., & Clough, P. J. (2011). Developing mental toughness: From research to practice. *Journal of Sport Psychology in Action, 2*(1), 21–32.

Crust, L., Earle, K., Perry, J., Earle, F., Clough, A., & Clough, P. J. (2014). Mental toughness in higher education: Relationships with achievement and progression in first-year university sports students. *Personality and Individual Differences, 69,* 87–91.

Crust, L., & Keegan, R. (2010). Mental toughness and attitudes to risk-taking. *Personality and Individual Differences, 49*(3), 164–168.

Crust, L., & Swann, C. (2011). Comparing two measures of mental toughness. *Personality and Individual Differences, 50*(2), 217–221.

Crust, L., & Swann, C. (2013). The relationship between mental toughness and dispositional flow. *European Journal of Sport Science, 13*(2), 215–220.

Csikszentimichalyi, M. (1990). *Flow: The psychology of optimal experience.* New York: Harper and Row.

Delaney, P. F., Goldman, J. A., King, J. S., & Nelson-Gray, R. O. (2015). Mental toughness, reinforcement sensitivity theory, and the five-factor model: Personality and directed forgetting. *Personality and Individual Differences, 83,* 180–184.

Dewhurst, S. A., Anderson, R. J., Cotter, G., Crust, L., & Clough, P. J. (2012). Identifying the cognitive basis of mental toughness: Evidence from the directed forgetting paradigm. *Personality and Individual Differences, 53*(5), 587–590.

Dienstbier, R. A. (1989). Arousal and physiological toughness: Implications for mental and physical health. *Psychological Review, 96*(1), 84–100.

Dienstbier, R. A. (1991). Behavioral correlates of sympathoadrenal reactivity: The toughness model. *Medicine and Science in Sports and Exercise, 23*(7), 846–852.

Gerber, M., Best, S., Meerstetter, F., Walter, M., Ludyga, S., Brand, S., . . . Gustafsson, H. (2018). Effects of stress and mental toughness on burnout and depressive symptoms: A prospective study with young elite athletes. *Journal of Science and Medicine in Sport, 21*(12), 1200–1205.

Gerber, M., Brand, S., Feldmeth, A. K., Lang, C., Elliot, C., Holsboer-Trachsler, E., & Pühse, U. (2013). Adolescents with high mental toughness adapt better to perceived stress: A longitudinal study with Swiss vocational students. *Personality and Individual Differences, 54*(7), 808–814.

Gerber, M., Feldmeth, A. K., Lang, C., Brand, S., Elliot, C., Holsboer-Trachsler, E., & Pühse, U. (2015). The relationship between mental toughness, stress, and burnout among adolescents: A longitudinal study with Swiss vocational students. *Psychological Reports, 117*(3), 703–723.

Gerber, M., Kalak, N., Lemola, S., Clough, P. J., Perry, J. L., Pühse, U., . . . Brand, S. (2012). Are adolescents with high mental toughness levels more resilient against stress? *Stress and Health, 29*(2), 164–171.

Gerber, M., Kalak, N., Lemola, S., Clough, P. J., Pühse, U., Elliot, C., . . . Brand, S. (2012). Adolescents' exercise and physical activity are associated with mental toughness. *Mental Health and Physical Activity, 5*(1), 35–42.

Godlewski, R., & Kline, T. (2012). A model of voluntary turnover in male Canadian Forces recruits. *Military Psychology, 24*(3), 251.

Golby, J., & Sheard, M. (2004). Mental toughness and hardiness at different levels of rugby league. *Personality and Individual Differences, 37,* 933–942.

Golby, J., & Sheard, M. (2006). The relationship between genotype and positive psychological development in national-level swimmers. *European Psychologist, 11,* 143–148.

Golby, J., Sheard, M., & Lavalee, D. (2003). A cognitive behavioural analysis of mental toughness in national rugby league football teams. *Perceptual and Motor Skills, 96*(2), 455–462.

Gucciardi, D., & Gordon, S. (2009). Development and preliminary validation of the Cricket Mental Toughness Inventory (CMTI). *Journal of Sports Sciences, 27*(12), 1293–1310.

Gucciardi, D., Gordon S., & Dimmock, J. (2008). Towards an understanding of mental toughness in Australian football. *Journal of Applied Sport Psychology, 20*(3), 261–281.

Gucciardi, D. F., Gordon, S., & Dimmock, J. A. (2009a). Evaluation of a mental toughness training program for youth-aged Australian footballers: I. A quantitative analysis. *Journal of Applied Sport Psychology, 21*(3), 307–323.

Gucciardi, D., Gordon, S., & Dimmock, J. A. (2009b). Development and preliminary validation of a mental toughness inventory for Australian football. *Psychology of Sport and Exercise, 10*(1), 201–209.

Haghighi, M., & Gerber, M. (2019). Does mental toughness buffer the relationship between perceived stress, depression, burnout, anxiety, and sleep? *International Journal of Stress Management, 6*(3), 297.

Horsburgh, V. A., Schermer, J. A., Veselka, L., & Vernon, P. A. (2009). A behavioural genetic study of mental toughness and personality. *Personality and Individual Differences, 46*(2), 100–105.

Jackman, P., Crust, L., & Swann, C. (2017). Further examining the relationship between mental toughness and dispositional flow in sport: A mediation analysis. *International Journal of Sport Psychology, 48*(3), 356–374.

Jackman, P. C., Swann, C., & Crust, L. (2016). Exploring athletes' perceptions of the relationship between mental toughness and dispositional flow in sport. *Psychology of Sport and Exercise, 27,* 56–65.

Jahangard, L., Rahmani, A. l., Haghighi, M., Ahmadpanah, M., Sadeghi Bahmani, D., Soltanian, A. R., . . . Brand, S. (2017). "Always look on the bright side of life!" – Higher hypomania scores are associated with higher mental toughness, increased physical activity, and lower symptoms of depression and lower sleep complaints. *Frontiers in Psychology, 8,* 2013.

Jones, G., Hanton, S., & Connaughton, D. (2002). What is this thing called mental toughness? An investigation of elite sport performers. *Journal of Applied Sport Psychology, 14*(3), 205–218.

Jones, G., Hanton, S., & Connaughton, D. (2007). A framework of mental toughness in the world's best performers. *The Sport Psychologist, 21*(2), 243–264.

Kaiseler, M., Polman, R., & Nicholls, A. (2009). Mental toughness, stress, stress appraisal, coping and coping effectiveness in sport. *Personality and Individual Differences, 47*(7), 728–733.

Kalek, N., Gerber, M., Brand, S., Clough, P. J., Lemola, S., Sadeghi Bahmani, D., . . . Holsboer-Trachsler, E. (2017). During early to mid adolescence, moderate to vigour physical activity is associated with restoring sleep, psychological functioning, mental toughness and male gender. *Journal of Sport Sciences, 35*(5), 426–434.

Kaplan, D. S., Liu, R. X., & Kaplan, H. B. (2005). School related stress in early adolescence and academic performance three years later: The conditional influence of self expectations. *Social Psychology of Education, 8*(1), 3–17.

Kobasa, S. C. (1979). Stressful life events, personality, and health: An inquiry into hardiness. *Journal of Personality and Social Psychology. 37*(1), 1–11.

Kobasa, S. C., Maddi, S. R., & Kahn, S. (1982). Hardiness and health: A prospective study. *Journal of Personality and Social Psychology, 42*(1), 168–177.

Kobasa, S. C., Maddi, S. R., Puccetti, M. C., & Zola, M. A. (1985). Effectiveness of hardiness, exercise, and social support as resources against illness. *Journal of Psychosomatic Research, 29*(5), 525–533.

Lang, C., Brand, S., College, F., Ludyga, S., Pühse, U., & Gerber, M. (2019). Adolescents' personal beliefs about sufficient physical activity are more closely related to sleep and psychological functioning than self-reported physical activity: A prospective study. *Journal of Sport and Health Science, 8*(3), 280–288.

Leary, M. R., Diebels, K. J., Davisson, E. K., Jongman-Sereno, K. P., Isherwood, J. C., Raimi, K. T., . . . Hoyle, R. H. (2017). Cognitive and interpersonal features of intellectual humility. *Personality and Social Psychology Bulletin, 43*(6), 793–813.

Levy, A. R., Polman, R. C. J., Clough, P. J., Marchant, D. C., & Earle, K. (2006). Mental toughness as a determinant of beliefs, pain, and adherence in sport injury rehabilitation. *Journal of Sport Rehabilitation, 15*(3), 246–254.

Loehr, J. E. (1982). *Mental toughness training for sports: Achieving athletic excellence* (pp. 58–70). Lexington, MA: Forum Publishing Company.

Loehr, J. E. (1986). *Mental toughness training for sports: Achieving athletic excellence.* Lexington, MA: Stephen Greene Press.

Loehr, J. E. (1995). *The new toughness training for sports.* New York: Plume Publishers.

Marchant, D. C., Polman, R. C. J., Clough, P. J., Jackson, J. G., Levy, A. R., & Nicholls, A. R. (2009). Mental toughness: Managerial and age differences. *Journal of Managerial Psychology, 24*(5), 428–437.

Marchant, D. C., Polman, R. C. J., Clough, P. J., Jackson, J. G., Levy, A. R., & Nicholls, A. R. (2011). Mental toughness: Managerial and age differences. *International Journal of Health Care Quality Assurance, 24*(5), 428–437.

Martin, A. J. (2013). Academic buoyancy and academic resilience: Exploring 'everyday' and 'classic' resilience in the face of academic adversity. *School Psychology International, 34*(5), 488–500.

Mattie, P., & Munroe-Chandler, K. (2012). Examining the relationship between mental toughness and imagery use. *Journal of Applied Sport Psychology, 24*(2), 144–156.

McGeown, S. P., Clair-Thompson, H. S., & Clough, P. (2015). The study of non-cognitive attributes in education: Proposing the mental toughness framework. *Educational Review, 68*(1), 96–113.

McGeown, S. S., Putwain, D. S., Clair-Thompson, H. S., & Clough, P. S. (2016). Understanding and supporting adolescents' mental toughness in an education context. *Psychology in the Schools, 54*(2), 196–209.

McGeown, S. S., Putwain, D. S., St. Clair-Thompson, H., & Clough, P. (2017). Understanding and supporting adolescents' mental toughness in an education context. *Psychology in the Schools, 54*(2), 196–209.

Montgomery, T., Ross, M., Perry, J., & Hansen, A. (2017). The mental workout: Implementing phase 1 of the Ten-Minute Toughness mental training program. *Journal of Sport Psychology in Action, 9*(2), 73–82.

Muntz., J., Clough, P. J., & Papageorgiou, K. A. (2017). Do Individual differences in emotion regulation mediate the relationship between mental toughness and symptoms of depression? *Journal of Individual Differences, 38,* 71–82.

Nicholls, A. R., Poiman, R. C. J., Levy, A. R., & Backhouse, S. H. (2008). Mental toughness, optimism, pessimism, and coping among athletes. *Personality and Individual Differences, 44*(5), 1182–1192.

Nicholls, A. R., Poiman, R. C. J., Levy, A. R., & Backhouse, S. H. (2009). Mental toughness in sport: Achievement level, gender, age, experience, and sport type differences. *Personality and Individual Differences, 47*(1), 73–75.

Onley, M., Veselka, L., Schermer, J. A., & Vernon, P. A. (2013). Survival of the scheming: A genetically informed link between the dark triad and mental toughness. *Twin Research and Human Genetics, 16*(06), 1087–1095.

Papageorgiou, K. A., Malanchini, M., Denovan, A., Clough, P. J., Shakeshaft, N., Schofield, K., & Kovas, Y. (2018). Longitudinal associations between narcissism, mental toughness, and school achievement. *Personality and Individual Differences, 131,* 105–110.

Pekrun, R., & Perry, R. P. (n.d.). Control-value theory of achievement emotions. In *International Handbook of Emotions in Education.* New York: Routledge. doi:10.4324/9780203148211.ch7

Perry, J. L., Clough, P. J., Crust, L., Earle, K., & Nicholls, A. R. (2013). Factorial validity of the Mental Toughness Questionnaire-48. *Personality and Individual Differences, 54*(5), 587–592.

Perry, J., Stamp, E., Crust, L., & Swann, C. F. (2017). Relationships between mental toughness, barriers to exercise, and exercise behaviour in undergraduate students. *International Journal of Sport Psychology, 48*(3), 262–277.

Polman, R. J., Clough, P. J., & Levy, A. (2010). Personality and coping in sport: The big five and mental toughness. In A. R. Nicholls (Ed.), *Coping in sport: theory, methods, and related constructs.* New York: Nova Science Inc.

Raufelder, D., Kittler, F., Braun, S. R., Lätsch, A., Wilkinson, R. P., & Hoferichter, F. (2013). The interplay of perceived stress, self-determination and school engagement in adolescence. *School Psychology International, 35*(4), 405–420.

Sabouri, S., Gerber, M., Bahmani, D. S., Lemola, S., Clough, P. J., Kalak, N., . . . Brand, S. (2016). Examining Dark Triad traits in relation to mental toughness and physical activity in young adults. *Neuropsychiatric Disease and Treatment, 12,* 229–235.

Seligman, M. E. P. (1969, June). For helplessness: Can we immunize the weak? *Psychology Today,* 42–45.

Seligman, M. E. P. (1972). Learned helplessness. *Annual Review of Medicine, 23,* 407–412.

Seligman, M. E. P. (1972). *Learned helplessness and depression.* Proceedings of the XVIIth International Congress of Applied Psychology. Brussels: Editest.

Seligman, M. E. P. (1973). Fall into helplessness. *Psychology Today, 7,* 43–58.

Seligman, M. E. P. (1974). Depression and learned helplessness. In R. J. Friedman & M. M. Katz (Eds.), *The psychology of depression: Contemporary theory and research.* New York: Winston-Wiley.

Seligman, M. E. P., & Beagley, G. (1975). Learned helplessness in the rat. *Journal of Comparative and Physiological Psychology, 88*(2), 534–541.

Seligman, M. E. P., & Groves, D. (1970). Non-transient learned helplessness. *Psychonomic Science, 19,* 191–192.

Seligman, M. E. P., Maier, S. F., & Solomon, R. L. (1971). Consequences of unpredictable and uncontrollable trauma. In Brush, F. R. (Ed.), *Aversive conditioning and learning.* New York: Academic Press.

Sheard, M. (2010). *Mental toughness: The mindset behind sporting achievement.* London, UK. Routledge.

Sheard, M., & Golby, J. (2006). Effect of psychological skills training program on swimming performance and positive psychological development. *International Journal of Sport and Exercise Psychology, 4*(2), 7–24.

St Clair-Thompson, H., Bugler, M., Robinson, J., Clough, P., McGeown, S. P., & Perry, J. (2015). Mental toughness in education: Exploring relationships with attainment, attendance, behaviour and peer relationships. *Educational Psychology, 35*(7), 886–907.

St Clair-Thompson, H., Giles, R., McGeown, S., P., Putwain, D., Clough, P., & Perry, J. (2017). Mental toughness and transitions to high school and to undergraduate study. *Educational Psychology, 37*(7), 792–809.

Stamp, E., Crust, L., Swann, C., Perry, J., Clough, P., & Marchant, D. (2015). Relationships between mental toughness and psychological wellbeing in undergraduate students. *Personality and Individual Differences, 75,* 170–174.

Stankov, L., Morony, S., & Lee, Y. P. (2013). Confidence: The best non-cognitive predictor of academic achievement? *Educational Psychology, 34*(1), 9–28.

Strycharczyk, D., & Bosworth, C. (OCR). (2016 in press*). Developing employability and enterprise – for the 21st century.* London: Kogan Page.

Strycharczyk, D., & Clough, P. J. (Eds.). (2014). *Developing mental toughness in young people for the 21st century.* London: Karnac.

Strycharczyk, D., & Elvin, C. (CEO for ILM). (2014). *Developing resilient organisations.* London: Kogan Page.

Veselka, L., Schermer, J. A., Margin, R. A., & Vernon, P. A. (2010). Laughter and resiliency: A behavioral genetic study of humor styles and mental toughness. *Twin Research and Human Genetics, 13*(05), 442–449.

Veselka, L., Schermer, J. A., Petrides, K., & Vernon, P. A. (2009). Evidence for a heritable general factor of personality in two studies. *Twin Research and Human Genetics, 12*(3), 254–260.

Zalewska, A. M., Krzywosz-Rynkiewicz, B., Clough, P. J., & Dagnall, N. (2019). Mental toughness development through adolescence: Effects of age group and community size. *Social Behavior and Personality: An International Journal, 47*(1), 1–8.

CPSIA information can be obtained
at www.ICGtesting.com
Printed in the USA
BVHW060028030922
646098BV00002B/2